"*The Drama of Scripture* is a model of biblical scholarship, integrating sound critical methods with a disposition of faith that is open to the revelation of the living God through his Word. This engaging book opens up for students the panoramic vision of the Bible that has been obscured by centuries of confessional battles and has been fragmented by Enlightenment rationalism. It succeeds in rendering the biblical world truly habitable, thus bridging the gap between the Bible and Christian experience."

Mary E. Healy, Notre Dame Graduate School of Christendom College

"This brief yet penetrating and riveting overview of the Bible's dramatic message of creation, fall, and redemption—from Genesis to Revelation—will become a must not merely for students beginning theological studies but for all who wish to see the biblical forest rather than merely its trees."

Max Turner, professor of New Testament studies,
London School of Theology

"The rediscovery of the significance of story is one of the most important recent insights in biblical interpretation. This masterly book is a fine introduction for the aspiring student, combining evangelical commitment to the normative authority of Scripture with a deep understanding of modern scholarship. Bartholomew and Goheen have provided a fine service to the Christian community by opening up the story of the Bible in a way that can be lived in today's world."

Trevor Cooling, University of Gloucestershire

"In *The Drama of Scripture*, Bartholomew and Goheen provide a Christian reading of the biblical story from Genesis to Revelation. They do so in a way designed to remind contemporary Christians that they too inhabit that same story and are meant to live *inside* it, continuing the works and words of Jesus in today's world. The result is a challenge to reappropriate the Scriptures as a basis not only for church and theology but also for life itself."

Raymond Van Leeuwen, professor of biblical studies, Eastern University

"Here is a book whose time has come. Bartholomew and Goheen have produced a brief, accessible presentation of the entire biblical story that highlights both the unity of Scripture and its profound cultural relevance today. For readers who think of the Bible as a succession of unrelated devotional fragments geared primarily toward individual morality and spirituality, this book will come as a salutary shock, a reminder that the Christ-centered canonical Scriptures constitute a coherent Word of God that challenges the underlying religious direction of Western civilization. Based on deep and wide scholarship, but engagingly written for a broad audience, *The Drama of Scripture* promises to be an indispensable tool for the many Christians who have been awakened to God's call for serious cultural engagement, in the name of Christ, with a post-Christian world in thrall to the idols of both modernism and postmodernism."

Albert M. Wolters, author of *Creation Regained: Biblical Basics for a Reformational Worldview*

# The Drama
# of *Scripture*

## Finding Our Place
## in the Biblical Story

Craig G. Bartholomew
and Michael W. Goheen

Baker Academic
Grand Rapids, Michigan

Published by Baker Academic
a division of Baker Publishing Group
P.O. Box 6287, Grand Rapids, MI 49516-6287
www.bakeracademic.com

Second printing, June 2005

Printed in the United States of America

Library of Congress Cataloging-in-Publication Data
Bartholomew, Craig G., 1961–
    The drama of Scripture : finding our place in the biblical story / Craig G. Bartholomew and Michael W. Goheen.
        p.    cm.
    Includes bibliographical references and index.
    ISBN 0-8010-2746-2 (pbk.)
    1. Bible—History of Biblical events. 2. Bible. N.T.—Relation to the Old Testament. I. Goheen, Michael, W., 1955– II. Title.
    BS635.3B37  2004
    230′.041—dc22                                                    2004017400

To Doug Loney, for his sacrifice and gift of writing

To Al Wolters, for his formative influence on both of us

To Gordon Wenham, for his faithful biblical scholarship
over many years

# Contents

# Figures

# Preface

This book had its beginnings in a meeting of Mike Goheen and Craig Bartholomew in Birmingham, England, in the summer of 2000. Needing a text for the biblical theology course he taught, Mike approached Craig (a biblical scholar) to write one. Craig proposed that the two of them work together on the book, to keep it sensitive to biblical scholarship (Craig's strength) as well as missiology and worldview studies (Mike's focus). It has been said that if you want to ruin a friendship, you should write a book together! We're happy to report that as we have come to the end of this project we are still good friends. In fact, the project has been mutually enriching.

*The Drama of Scripture* is written with first-year university students in mind. It is designed as a text for an introductory course in biblical theology taught at Redeemer University College in Ancaster, Ontario, Canada. As a Christian university, Redeemer is committed to distinctively Christian scholarship that is shaped by the Bible. We want our students first to understand the true nature of Scripture: it is God's story, the true story of the world. Only when it is understood for what it is can it become the foundation for human life, including the life of the scholar. Our second goal for students is that they learn to articulate a thoroughly biblical worldview by systematically developing the most comprehensive categories of the Bible's story line: creation, sin, and redemption. This book is written to meet the first goal, sets the basis for the second goal, and quite naturally leads to it.

*The Drama of Scripture* tells the biblical story of redemption as a unified, coherent narrative of God's ongoing work within his kingdom. After God created the world and human rebellion marred it, God set out to restore what he had made: "God did not turn his back on a world bent on destruction; he turned his face toward it in love. He set out on the long road of redemption to restore the lost as his people and the world as his kingdom."[1] The Bible narrates the story of God's journey on that long road of redemption. It is a unified and progressively unfolding drama of God's action in history for the salvation of the whole world. The Bible is not a mere jumble of history, poetry, lessons in morality and theology, comforting promises, guiding principles and commands; instead, it is fundamentally coherent. Every part of the Bible—each event, book, character, command, prophecy, and poem—must be understood in the context of the *one* story line.[2]

Many of us have read the Bible as if it were merely a mosaic of little bits—theological bits, moral bits, historical-critical bits, sermon bits, devotional bits. But when we read the Bible in such a fragmented way, we ignore its divine author's intention to shape our lives through its story. All human communities live out of some story that provides a context for understanding the meaning of history and gives shape and direction to their lives. If we allow the Bible to become fragmented, it is in danger of being absorbed into whatever *other* story is shaping our culture, and it will thus cease to shape our lives as it should. Idolatry has twisted the dominant cultural story of the secular Western world. If as believers we allow this story (rather than the Bible) to become the foundation of our thought and action, then our lives will manifest not the truths of Scripture, but the lies of an idolatrous culture. Hence, the unity of Scripture is no minor matter: a fragmented Bible may actually produce theologically orthodox, morally upright, warmly pious idol worshippers!

If our lives are to be shaped by the story of Scripture, we need to understand two things well: the biblical story is a compelling unity on which we may depend, and each of us has a place within that story. This book is the *telling* of that story. We invite readers to make it their story, to find their place in it, and to *indwell* it as the true story of our world.

There are three important emphases in this book. First, we stress the comprehensive scope of God's redemptive work in creation. The biblical story does not move toward the destruction of the world and our own "rescue" to heaven. Instead, it culminates in the restoration of the entire creation to its original goodness. The comprehensive scope of creation, sin, and redemption is evident throughout the biblical story and is central to a faithful biblical worldview.

Second, we emphasize the believer's own place within the biblical story. Some refer to four questions as foundational to a biblical worldview: "Who am I?" "Where am I?" "What's wrong?" "What's the solution?" Tom (N. T.) Wright adds an important fifth question: "What time is it?"[3] He thus asks us, "Where do *we* belong in this story? How does it shape *our* lives in the present?" As part of our telling of the Bible's grand story, we will explore the biblical answers to these five questions.

Third, we highlight the centrality of *mission* within the biblical story.[4] The Bible narrates God's mission to restore the creation. Israel's mission flows from this: God chose a people to again embody God's creational purposes for humanity and so be a light to the nations, and the Old Testament narrates the history of Israel's response to their divine calling. Jesus comes on the scene and in his mission takes upon himself Israel's missionary vocation. He embodies God's purpose for humanity and accomplishes the victory over sin, opening the way to a new world. When his earthly ministry is over, he leaves his church with the mandate to continue in that same mission. In our own time, standing as we do between Pentecost and the return of Jesus, our central task as God's people is to witness to the rule of Jesus Christ over all of life.

We have also borrowed from Tom Wright his helpful metaphor of the Bible as a drama.[5] But whereas Wright speaks of *five* acts (creation, sin, Israel, Christ, church), we tell the story in terms of *six* acts. We add the coming of the new creation as the final, unique element of the biblical drama. We have also added a prologue. This prologue addresses in a preliminary way what it means to say that human life is shaped by a story.

If you are using this text for a course or Bible study, you can access resources on our website www.biblicaltheology.ca that will enhance your use of this book: a course syllabus, PowerPoint slides, a reading schedule for a thirteen-week course, supplementary reading, and more.

Projects of this scope and kind always involve contributions from many people besides the authors, and there are several to whom we here express our gratitude. First, we thank the many students at Redeemer University College who read the manuscript at various stages and offered critical comment, especially Elizabeth Buist, Elizabeth Klapwyk, Ian Van Leeuwen, and Dylon Nofziger. We appreciate the help Dawn Berkelaar provided in a small section of the book. For the diagrams and drawings in the book, we are grateful for Ben Goheen's artistic talent. Fred Hughes, formerly head of the School of Theology and Religion at the University of Gloucestershire, has been supportive of this project from its inception, has read the entire manuscript of an earlier version, and has offered many helpful suggestions. He also opened up the opportunity for Mike and Craig to work together, inviting Mike as a visiting scholar to the International Centre for Biblical Interpretation at the University of Gloucestershire during the summer of 2002, when we wrote most of the manuscript. We are also thankful for the support of Redeemer University College, which from the beginning of the project has offered support and assistance of many kinds. We are indebted to our friends and colleagues Gene Haas and Al Wolters in the Religion and Theology Department at Redeemer, and Wayne Kobes in the Theology Department at Dordt College, Sioux Center, Iowa. Both Gene and Wayne also teach first-year biblical theology courses and have been helpful with their advice. Al has been a mentor to both authors, and we have greatly appreciated his wise counsel and unflagging support.

In the United Kingdom Alan Dyer and Mark Birchall were always supportive of this project and made many helpful comments as they read the manuscript more than once. Sadly, about the time we handed the manuscript over to the publisher, Mark went to be with the Lord. He will be sorely missed. In South Africa Wayne Barkhuizen made helpful comments on the manuscript.

Jim Kinney, director of Baker Academic, has been very helpful and encouraging. He and some of his colleagues read an early draft and offered insightful criticism and counsel that significantly shaped the final manuscript. Undoubtedly, the one to whom we are most indebted is Doug Loney, our colleague at Redeemer, Dean of Arts and Humanities and a member of the English Department. Doug has given to this project much time and skill as a writer, taking our manuscript in its two different writing styles and turning it into what we believe to be a lively and coherent text. We also thank Doug's wife, Karey, and Mike's wife, Marnie, for their patience and support. We dedicate this book to our Redeemer colleagues, Doug Loney and Al Wolters, and to Gordon Wenham of the University of Gloucestershire, whose faithful work in Old Testament studies over many years has been a blessing to us both.

# Prologue

## The Bible as a Grand Story

Have a close look at this picture. What do you think is happening?

A fox compliments a crow: "My you have a lovely voice; won't you sing me a song?"

What is the meaning of this event?

**Figure 1** *Fox and Crow*

If you have a vivid imagination, you are able to concoct some story about the fox and the crow, or perhaps more than one story. But all careful readers know that unless the event sketched in this picture can be placed in the context of the story it comes from, it is hard for any reader to be sure what meaning its author (and artist) intends.

Now look at the image again, with some additional information filled in:

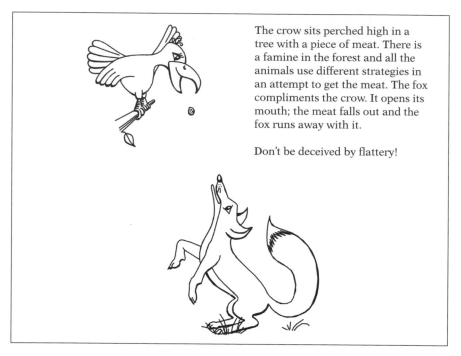

The crow sits perched high in a tree with a piece of meat. There is a famine in the forest and all the animals use different strategies in an attempt to get the meat. The fox compliments the crow. It opens its mouth; the meat falls out and the fox runs away with it.

Don't be deceived by flattery!

**Figure 2**  *Fox and Crow Revisited*

You can understand what happens between this fox and this crow only if you have some knowledge of the whole story surrounding this episode. When it is revealed that there is a famine in the forest, and that crafty animals like the fox use all sorts of devious strategies to get hold of food, then you begin to see why the fox might be flattering the crow. First you need to know something of the beginning, the middle, and the end of a story. Only then can you understand any one episode in it. This is true not only of fictional stories like this one but also of life: we need some sense of the "big story" of the world before the meaning of any event in our lives makes sense.

This brings us to another example, a story that is perhaps closer to our own experience of life than a fable about wheedling foxes and operatic crows:

**Figure 3** *Percy and Abby*

Percival and Abigail, a young man and woman, find themselves at the same table during an after-the-service social for newcomers to the church. Over coffee and the egg-salad sandwiches, they begin to talk of this and that. Eventually the others at their table have wandered away, and someone has rather pointedly removed their coffee cups and begun to stack chairs. But Percy and Abby barely notice these things. Each is beginning to think that it might be worthwhile to get to know this other person just a little better. So they arrange to meet again, at a quiet café, for dessert and (of course) more coffee. But their real reason for meeting there is that it's a much better place for private conversation than that crowded church hall. (Out of respect for this young couple's privacy, we have decided not to include another cartoon here.)

As the conversation picks up again, Abigail and Percival gradually find themselves telling each other bits and pieces of—what? Yes, of course: they begin to tell the stories of their lives. How he is the youngest of four and the only boy, spoiled rotten by three doting sisters. How she was born in New Delhi, while her parents were serving at the consulate, and spent her high school years in four different countries. Little by little, they lay down the broad strokes of the plot and begin to fill in the details: Percy's hardly been two hundred miles from the family farm (though he longs to travel). Abby speaks four languages and can understand a couple more. His childhood holidays were spent with a boatload of cousins at his grandparents' cottage in Muskoka. She once celebrated New Year's Day by snorkeling in Mauri Bay (South Africa). And so on, and on, through the memories of childhood faiths and fears, first summer jobs, education plans, and hopes for the future.

The only proper answer to "Tell me about yourself" is to tell a *story* or a series of stories. By sharing these personal narratives, we come to know one another. We want to understand not only who that other person is now, at this moment, but also how he or she came to be so. What are the experiences, ideas, and people that have shaped their lives? Their personal stories give the context and explain much about their lives. Yet as they continue their conversation, they might ask: Are we left with our own personal stories to make sense of our lives? Or is there a true story that is bigger than both of us, through which we can understand the world and find meaning for our lives? Are our personal stories—apart or together—parts of a more comprehensive story?

In order to understand our world, to make sense of our lives, and to make our most important decisions about how we ought to be living, we depend upon some story. In fact, among some philosophers, theologians, and biblical scholars, there is growing recognition that "a story . . . is . . . the best way of talking about *the way the world actually is*."[1] Just as it is hard to make sense of the first picture without the story line, so it is with our lives' isolated details. Percy needs to know something about Abby's background in order to understand what is important to her. Likewise, we need a large background story if we are to understand ourselves and the world in which we find ourselves. Individual experiences make sense and acquire meaning only when seen within the context or frame of some story we believe to be the true story of the world: each episode of our life stories finds its place there.

This does not mean that every story is as important as any other. There are a great variety of stories. Some merely entertain us; others teach what is right and good or warn us of danger and evil. But there are also stories that are basic or foundational: they provide us with an understanding of our *whole* world and of our own place within it. Such comprehensive stories give us the meaning of universal history. These have been called "grand narratives," "grand stories," or "metanarratives." Each of us (whether we're conscious of it or not) has one. To frame and give shape and meaning to our experience of life, all of us depend upon some particular story.

Lesslie Newbigin worked as a missionary in India for many years and has written extensively about the significance of these grand narratives for understanding our lives. He draws the connection between story and understanding: "The way we understand human life depends on what conception we have of the human story. What is the real story of which my life story is part?"[2] Philosopher Alasdair MacIntyre agrees, affirming that our life decisions are shaped and ordered by our sense of how they fit within this larger context: "I can only answer the question, 'What am I to do?' if I can answer the prior question, 'Of what story do

I find myself a part?'"[3] Both of these thinkers rightly assume that there is more than one basic story competing in our culture for acceptance and use in making sense of our lives today.

*Which* story a person lives out of makes a huge difference in how one interprets events in life. Take the example of divorce. Even where divorce is necessary and the right thing for a person to do, Christians will always see divorce as coming far short of the ideal that God intends for a man and a woman united in marriage. Hence, it is a tragedy. Divorce does not fit the biblical story of how our lives are meant to be lived with one another and before God. But this point of view differs sharply from that held by many people in our culture. Because of the individualism and consumerism central to the Western cultural story, divorce is often portrayed as something rather positive: no tragedy, but rather a courageous step of personal growth. We can see that these two views of divorce do not stem from a trivial disagreement. Their roots go to the foundation of the respective stories that have given the differing views their shape and substance.

While Newbigin lived and worked among the Hindus and Muslims of India, he was wrestling with the meaning of the fundamental stories shared in those cultures and of how those stories might relate to Christianity. And similarly, when he retired and returned to England, Newbigin struggled earnestly to comprehend just what life story was embodied within his own (Western, European) culture, and how it too might relate to the other comprehensive story to which he was committed—the Bible. What he came to see was that the basic story assumed in much of modern Western culture is humanistic and has its roots in the European Enlightenment of the seventeenth and eighteenth centuries. The belief that human reason is the measure of all things and that "knowledge is power"[4] permeated European society. People believed that through science and technology alone, and utterly apart from God, humankind could build a perfect world.

Newbigin adamantly maintains that this comprehensive story is unhelpful and untrue. Because it has become the foundation for human life, it also is dangerous. It is a false story, in stark contradiction to the truth of the biblical story. Ever since the Enlightenment, human thought and life in the Western world have been conforming themselves to this false view, often leading to disastrous effects. But as Alasdair MacIntyre urges us to recognize, we do have a choice. The modern Western worldview is not the only such grand story available. There is another, better, and *truer* way in which to see our world.

To be human means to embrace some such basic story through which we understand our world and chart our course through it. This does not mean that individuals are necessarily conscious of the story they are living out of or of the molding effect that such a story has had on their thought and actions.[5] For instance, many college and university students of our time are living sexually promiscuous lives. They may live this way without thinking much about *why* they do so. Hence, they are not at all likely to see that the *story* within which such conduct is approved is heavily indebted to Jean-Jacques Rousseau, Sigmund Freud, and other such thinkers of past centuries. Their views of marriage and the human person underlie the changes in attitude toward sexuality that took place in the 1960s and onward.[6]

Everyone has a basic story. How are we to relate the biblical story and the humanistic story of Western culture? In its different versions, the modern Western story has been so dominant and has so strongly asserted its right to be *the* story that it is often assumed that we should use it for understanding the grand narrative of Scripture. But biblical Christianity claims that the Bible alone tells the true story of our world.

Newbigin rightly discerns how much is at stake here: "The question is whether the faith that finds its focus in Jesus is the faith with which we seek to understand the whole of history, or whether we limit this faith to a private world of religion and hand over the public history of the world to other principles of explanation."[7] Does it really make any difference whether we use the modern Western story as the basis from which to understand the scriptural story or whether we try to understand the Western story from within the biblical story? It makes a profound difference! No building can have more than one foundation. We can have no more than one *fundamental* story as the basis for what we think and how we act. Once you make one story part of another, the nature of the first as "basic" is destroyed. The whole point of a basic story or grand narrative is to make sense of life as a whole, and such grand narratives cannot easily be mixed up with each other. Basic stories are in principle *normative*—they define starting points, ways of seeing what is true—and they are *comprehensive*, since they give an account of *the whole*.[8] As N. T. Wright says: "The whole point of Christianity is that it offers a story which is the story of the whole world. It is public truth."[9]

Think, for example, of the question about what it means to be human. This is a really important issue, which all stories address. In the twenty-first century, many of us struggle with issues regarding who we are, and there is a lot at stake in getting the answer right. Again and again we hear one answer to this question from many different directions and in many voices: "You are no more than a random product of time and chance." But this answer comes out of a story that denies the very existence of God. The answer from the biblical story is completely and utterly different, as we will see. From the Bible we learn that we are God's handiwork and the highpoint of his creation, being *made in his image.* As we seek the truth about who we are, we must decide *which* of these basic stories is true. Clearly they cannot *both* be true. They offer seriously different answers to the most important questions we have, and we must choose between them.

We believe N. T. Wright is correct in saying that the Bible offers a story that is *the true story of the whole world.* Therefore, faith in Jesus should be the means through which a Christian seeks to understand all of life and the whole of history. This is not just because the scriptural story is comprehensive, or because it happens to be the story that we have inherited, or because it is the story that works for us. We must take the Christian story seriously in this way because *it is true* and tells us truthfully the story of the whole of history, beginning with the creation and ending with the new creation. This is the way the world is, and Christians should make sure that the story of the Bible is basic in their lives. But what exactly *is* the biblical story, and how do we grasp it?

There are numerous ways in which to encounter the Christian story. Church liturgy (whether of the free charismatic type or of the more traditional sort) reminds us constantly of the story that should shape our lives. Hymns and choruses celebrate it. The creeds rehearse it as we confess our faith in God the Father, Son, and Holy Spirit. Sermons explain its importance to our lives from week to week. But the authoritative source for the Christian story is the Bible itself.

Orthodox Christianity has always maintained that Scripture is the *norm* for faith and life, the great rule and source of guidance. All of the great Christian confessions certainly say that this is so. What Christians do not always agree about is how Scripture functions to direct faith and life. Sometimes Christians have treated the Bible as if it were a systematic list of propositions like the Westminster or Belgic Confessions. But though the Bible is the ultimate source of these great documents, it clearly is not written in the same way, as a series of propositional truths, nor does it have the same purpose. Over the past few decades, one of the most exciting developments in biblical studies has been the growing recognition among some scholars that the Bible has the shape of a *story*, that it is "an immense, sprawling, capacious narrative."[10] It functions as the authoritative Word of God for us when it becomes the one *basic* story through which we understand our own experience and thought, and the foundation upon which we base our decisions and our actions.

In other words, the Bible provides us with the basic story that we need in order to understand our world and to live in it as God's people. We know that it is one thing to confess the Bible to be the Word of God, but often quite another thing to know how to read the Bible in a way that lets it influence the whole of our lives. There can easily be a gap between what we say we believe and how we live. If God has deliberately given us the Bible in the shape of a story, then only as we attend to it as story and actively appropriate it as our story will we feel the full impact of its authority and illumination in our lives.

There thus is a lot at stake in how we understand the Bible to be speaking to us. If we view it as a single unfolding story, it can be tremendously exciting. Such a story invites us—*compels* us—to get involved. Think again here of Abby and Percy, two young people telling each other their personal narratives to see if there might be room for each of them within the other's life story. If things work out for these two, they will discover a greater and more basic story. Their lives as individuals will take on new significance as parts of one whole life lived together in God's story. As we enter deeply into the story of the Bible, God will be revealed to us. We will also find ourselves called to share in the mission of God and his purposes with the creation. In this book our aim is to attend closely to the Bible as an unfolding story and to see what such a reading of the Bible yields. After all, the Bible claims to be nothing less than God's own true story of our world, and it calls us to appropriate this story for ourselves.

## Is the Bible a Single Unfolding Story?

You may have heard the old Hindu fable in which six blind men encounter an elephant for the first time. Each takes his turn in differently describing it to the others: the beast is like a wall, a snake, a spear, a fan, a rope, or a tree. Though there is only one elephant, each man has a completely different experience of it, depending on whether he happened to approach the beast by touching its side, trunk, tusk, ear, tail, or leg. The story reminds us that it is often difficult to be sure that our isolated experience has given us the complete picture of anything complicated. Trying to grasp the overall scope and shape of the Bible can be a bit like that. Depending on where we first touch the Scriptures, it may not be immediately apparent that the whole of it has the shape of a story. Thus, the reader who dips into the New Testament at 1 Corinthians finds herself reading a letter from a missionary to a struggling young church and wondering, How is this a part of the grand story? Or take the poetry of the Psalms or the fantastic images in Revelation: Where and how do they fit in the grand story?

It may be helpful to think of the Bible—as large and varied a book as it obviously is—not as if it were an elephant, but something bigger still: a huge building, a cathedral.

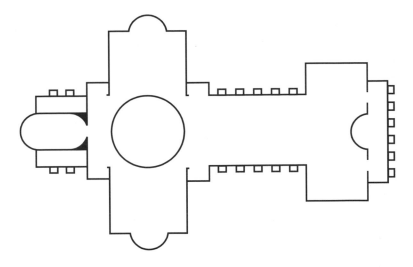

**Figure 4** *Cathedral Floor Plan*

If you have ever visited one of these magnificent churches, like the National Cathedral in Washington (D.C.), Notre Dame in Montreal (or its more famous older sister in Paris), or St. Paul's in London, you know that you can spend days exploring one of them. There are many different angles from which one can approach a cathedral. Inside are fascinating side chapels and main chapels to explore, full of stained glass, paintings, statuary, and other treasures. What at first seems to be one huge room turns out to be a multitude of rooms and corridors, towers and balconies, stairs and hidden passages. And this is only what the public sees. If you secure permission from the dean, the head of the cathedral, to explore the whole of the great church, you discover all sorts of additional ways in and out of the building and many different vantage points from which to see it.

Imagine that the Bible, with its sixty-six books, written by dozens of human authors over the course of more than a thousand years, is a grand cathedral with many rooms and levels and a variety of entrances. You can, for example, enter the Bible through one of the Gospels. Indeed, many people are encouraged to start reading the Bible with the Gospel of Mark or the Gospel of John. Many Christians begin to explore the Old Testament relatively late in their journey of faith. Few find themselves drawn again and again to the genealogies at the start of Chronicles or the long lists of dietary laws in Leviticus.

If you want to gather a sense of the cathedral as a whole, you face an important question: Where is the main entrance, the place from which you can orient yourself to the whole? A traditional cathedral usually has a main entrance through the west door, from which one can look down the long nave to the eastern end of the building, where the altar stands. In the West such churches were always built with the altar eastward, toward Jerusalem (which originated the word "oriented," now also more generally meaning "given a sense of direction"). The "cathedral" of the Bible has many themes. People have proposed various overarching themes of the Bible, and these are different doors from which we can gain a perspective on God's whole stunning revelation.

In our opinion, "covenant" (in the Old Testament) and "the kingdom of God" (in the New Testament) present a strong claim to be the main door through which we can begin to enter the Bible and to see it as one whole and vast structure. In the Old Testament, God establishes a covenant with Noah, Abraham, Israel, and King David; in Jeremiah, God speaks of a new covenant that he will make in the future. In the Gospels, it is clear that the main theme in Jesus' extensive teaching ministry is the kingdom of God. Mark (1:14–15) thus sums up Jesus' ministry: "After John was put in prison, Jesus went into Galilee, proclaiming the good news of God. 'The time has come,' he said. 'The kingdom of God is near. Repent and believe the good news!'" Taking covenant and kingdom to be the main entrance into the Bible does not deny that there are other entrances. Readers have suggested many other entrances as the best ones from which to gain a view of the whole: entrances such as "promise" and "presence." All these are helpful, but they are a bit like side chapels or side entrances rather than the main entrance. We certainly glimpse a view of the cathedral from them, but we do not gather that same overview of the whole that we obtain from covenant and kingdom.

You may ask, Are covenant and kingdom the same entrance or two different ones? This is an important question. The kingdom of God, as we explain below, is all about the reign of God over his people and eventually over all of creation. Covenant is particularly about the special relationship that God makes with his people as he works out his plans in history. In fact, covenants were relationships established by kings with their subject peoples. When God's people enter into a covenant relationship with him, they are obligated to be his subject people and to live under his reign. As we soon see, covenant also insists that we take seriously God's purposes with the whole of creation. Thus, covenant and kingdom are like two sides of the same coin, evoking the same reality in slightly different ways.

After all our study, we find covenant and kingdom to be the double door of the same main entrance to the scriptural cathedral, evoking the same reality. That is why we have used "kingdom" to structure this book. Both alert us to God as the great king over all, who wants to have a people living under his reign and spreading the fragrance of his presence all over his creation. Both also alert us to the fact that this has always been God's plan from the beginning, but that things went badly wrong. Now God is doing remedial work to restore his project and pursue his original and persistent intentions. In the covenants of the Old Testament, the focus is narrowly upon Israel and yet always for Israel to be a light to the nations. In the New Testament, "the kingdom of God" clearly has all the nations and the whole creation in view. Either way, as we enter the Bible through this main double door, covenant and kingdom alert us to the importance of the story line of the Bible. It starts with creation and moves on from there. This entrance gives us the right perspective for understanding what God is up to and what he is saying to us today.

We may not start reading the Bible in Genesis, and we may hardly ever spend loads of time in the genealogies of Chronicles and the laws of Leviticus and Numbers. But if we enter the Bible through covenant and kingdom, we soon find ourselves asking questions like these:

How does God's covenant with Abraham relate to his purposes for his whole creation?

If Jesus is our king, what about the rest of creation?

If this is God's world, what went wrong with it? How come he lost control over it?

How does the church fit in to God's kingdom purposes for his whole creation?

The only way to answer these questions is to go back to the beginning of the Bible and read the story as it unfolds in its various acts, starting with "In the beginning . . ." And that is what we are going to do in this book. So yes, provided we do not understand the matter simplistically, the Bible certainly is a single unfolding story. And in this book we are going to tell that story.

## The Biblical Drama

In the second century BC the dramatist Terence began writing plays in five distinct "acts" for performance in Roman theatres. Ever since, the Western tradition of dramatic storytelling has come to acknowledge this five-act structure as particularly suited to the careful unfolding of a long and important story. The five acts are generally organized this way: (1) The first act gives us essential background information, introduces the important characters, and establishes the stable situation that will be disrupted by the events about to unfold. (2) The first action begins, usually with the introduction of a significant conflict. The middle of the play (3) is where the main action of the drama takes place. Here the initial conflict intensifies and grows ever more complicated until (4) the climax, or the point of highest tension, after which that conflict *must* be resolved, one way or another. After the climax comes (5) the resolution, in which the implications of the climactic act are worked out for all the characters of the drama, and stability is restored.

This is the structure that Wright has in mind when he describes the biblical story as being like a five-act play, of which a large part of the fifth act is missing.[11] It is for the actors (us) to improvise a suitable second scene in act 5, preparing for the conclusion God has revealed, toward which our play must move.[12]

Wright's application of the five-act structure of drama to the dramatic story of the Bible is enormously helpful, and that is why we have (mostly) adopted that structure for our own retelling of the biblical story. Act 1, which you are about to read, gives essential information about God, humanity, and the world. It describes a stable situation, a very good creation. The human actors begin their work in the garden, and history begins. In act 2 the conflict is introduced as we encounter a mysterious enemy to God's plan. Here the fundamental problem in our world has its origin. In act 3, the conflict (between human sin and God's good purposes for the creation) intensifies and complications arise. Act 4 is the story of how the history of God's gracious dealings with his rebellious creatures comes to a climax in the death and resurrection of Jesus Christ. In act 5 we see the implications of Christ's great act of redemption worked out in the lives of his community.

And here is where, in this book, we depart from the five-act tradition (and from Wright's model). It is clear that the biblical story does not simply *end* at the conclusion of the fifth act. Nor is the outworking of act 5 a smooth resolution. While the resolution has taken place in Christ, the conflict continues and actually intensifies. God's purpose is nothing less than to reconcile the whole of creation to himself, a purpose accomplished once and for all in the death and resurrection of his Son some two thousand years ago. We have God's own tremendous promise that his grand purpose for his creation is ongoing and *not yet finished* in our world. There is much more to come in God's story. He has prepared another act, which is yet to be revealed, an act unlike anything we have seen or imagined thus far, and upon which the curtain of history will *never* close. So we have included this act 6 in our telling of the biblical story. Using the kingdom of God as our overarching theme and the six-act structure, we have identified the following main acts in the biblical drama:

Act 1   God Establishes His Kingdom: Creation
Act 2   Rebellion in the Kingdom: Fall
Act 3   The King Chooses Israel: Redemption Initiated
    Scene 1   A People for the King
    Scene 2   A Land for His People
Interlude   A Kingdom Story Waiting for an Ending: The Intertestamental Period
Act 4   The Coming of the King: Redemption Accomplished
Act 5   Spreading the News of the King: The Mission of the Church
    Scene 1   From Jerusalem to Rome
    Scene 2   And into All the World
Act 6   The Return of the King: Redemption Completed

# Act 1

# God Establishes His Kingdom

## Creation

The first five books of the Bible are called the Torah or Law of Moses. Though this does not necessarily mean that Moses wrote every word, most of it came through him, and he is certainly the central figure in the story they tell. The second book, Exodus, tells of Moses' birth and his emergence as the leader through whom God works to bring the Israelites out of Egypt. After that, Moses is in almost every chapter till the end of Deuteronomy. But that accounts for only four of the five books. Where did the first one come from, and why is it included as part of the Law of Moses when it tells a story that happened long before Moses himself was born?

### Who Is the "Lord God"?

It probably doesn't matter too much to you that "Michael" is a Hebrew name meaning "(He) who is like God" or that "Craig" is a Gaelic word that means "a rocky outcrop." In our culture, though names are important, we do not often attach special meaning to them. But in the Old Testament world we are preparing to visit in act 1, the meaning of names is often quite significant. And no names are more important than those identifying God in Genesis and the other Old Testament books.

In Genesis 1, the Hebrew word *Elohim* (translated simply as "God" in our English Bibles) is the general name for God used throughout the ancient Near East. And the Bible says that "God" brings the whole creation into existence out of nothing. But in Genesis 2:4, another name begins to be used. "God" is now called "the LORD God" (*Yahweh Elohim*). This is a highly unusual way of referring to God, and it is meant to reveal some important things about who he is.

Two key passages in the Old Testament (Exodus 3; 6:1–12) shed light on the mysterious name *Yahweh*[1] (or *Jehovah*, as in some older versions of the Bible).[2] These texts tell how God reveals himself to Moses as Yahweh when he calls Moses to lead the people of Israel out of slavery in Egypt. The name *Yahweh* is the title God chooses to identify himself as the divine Redeemer, the God who rescues his people from slavery and meets with them at Mount Sinai (Exodus 19:4).

When the names *Yahweh* (LORD) and *Elohim* (God) are joined as in Genesis 2:4, it makes the powerful point that the same God who rescues Israel from slavery is the God who has made all things, the Creator of heaven and earth.[3] "Yahweh, the God of the Hebrews, is also the God of all the earth over which his lordship shines forth through the hail and thunder."[4] The Israelites first come to know God (through Moses) as their Redeemer; only afterward do they learn of his role as the Creator. And it is not so different for us, even though we live so much further along in the biblical story. When we come to know God through the saving work of his Son, Jesus, we are meeting him first as our Savior and Redeemer—but God is still the Creator of all that was or is or shall be: He is the one eternal LORD God, Yahweh Elohim. Thus, the minute we start to witness to our faith and to tell *the Christian story* (rather than just our own personal story), we are inevitably driven back to the start of it all: the Creation itself. "In the beginning, God . . ."

## A Faith for Israel

The first scene of *any* story is worth paying attention to, and the first scene of the biblical story is no exception. The first chapters of Genesis, telling the story of creation, were written for the Israelites long ago in a culture quite different from ours. Though some aspects of the creation stories in Genesis 1 and 2 may seem strange to us, we need to remember that they made perfect sense to the people of Israel when they first heard them. This is so because the writer is using imagery and concepts familiar to his own audience. Once we read the first chapters of Genesis against the backdrop of the ancient world in which they were written, we begin to see the power of the message this story is meant to convey.

Several scholars have pointed out a strong polemical or argumentative aspect to Genesis 1 and 2. The ancient Near East had many competing accounts of how the world came into existence. These stories were common in Egypt when Israel was captive there and in Canaan when Israel began to take it over as its land. It would have been only too easy for the Israelites to adopt the stories of those who lived in the land before them or alongside them and who (after all) supposedly *knew* the land much better than they did themselves. Many of the gods worshipped by the Canaanites were closely associated with the fertility of the land. The newcomers struggling to learn how to farm there would be tempted to call out to these "gods" rather than to the LORD God.

We know quite a bit about the sort of creation stories circulating in the ancient world. It is fascinating to see how the story told in Genesis 1 and 2 deliberately contradicts certain important elements of them. For example, look at how Genesis 1:16 describes the sun and the moon. The text does not refer to the sun by its normal Hebrew name, but instead merely as "the greater light," which God made for the day. Similarly, it calls the moon "the lesser light." Why? Probably because the sun and moon were so often worshipped as gods by the people among whom the Israelites were now living. In the Genesis story readers cannot mistake the sun as a divinity to be worshipped. The Scripture clearly describes the sun as a created thing, an object placed in the heavens for the simple, practical purpose of giving light. The attention is thus all on the One who has created this marvelous light, the One whose power is so great that he can merely say a word, and an entire universe springs into being. No mere "light" in the heavens deserves to be bowed down to. God alone is divine; he alone is to be worshipped. Though the whole of creation is "very good" (Genesis 1:31), it is so because the One who has created it is infinitely superior to anything he has made.

And this transcendent Creator is *not* like the capricious gods described in the Babylonian creation story (the *Enuma Elish*), who make humankind merely to serve as the gods' servants, to wait on them and keep them happy. In Genesis, the God who creates the world sets men and women within it as the crowning touch on what he has brought into being. The creation itself is described as a marvelous home prepared for humankind, a place in which they may live and thrive and enjoy the intimate presence and companionship of the Creator himself.

## What Kind of Literature Is Genesis 1?

The creation stories of Genesis thus are argumentative. They claim to tell the truth about the world, flatly contradicting other such stories commonplace in the ancient world. Israel was constantly tempted to adopt these other stories as the basis of its worldview, in place of faith in the LORD God, who created the heavens and the earth. However, the Genesis creation narrative is more than a polemic. It also aims to teach us positively what faith in God *means* for how we think about the world he has made and how we live in it. It does this in a story form. And it is precisely this story form that we need to be sensitive to if we are not to misinterpret it.

In order to understand the Genesis story of creation, we must understand something about the kind of writing it is. Scholars themselves have difficulty in describing this. Von Rad sees it as "priestly doctrine" so rich in meaning that "it cannot be easily over-interpreted theologically."[5] Blocher sees the creation account as an example of carefully crafted wisdom literature.[6] But what scholars *do* agree on is that the story told in the first chapters of Genesis has been *very* carefully put together: the evidence of craftsmanship in the telling is clear. Hence, we need to focus as much on the *way* in which the story is told as upon the details themselves and weigh whether or not these details are meant to be read as a modern historian or scientist would read them. Indeed, this is a difficult question: the story told here is of the mysterious inauguration of history itself. But the broad outlines of the Genesis story are certainly as clear to us as they were to those who first heard it. God is the divine source of all that is. He stands apart from all other things in the special relationship of Creator to creation. The fashioning of humankind by God was intended to be the high point of all his work of making and forming. And God had in mind a very special relationship between himself and this last-formed of all his creatures.

In these chapters we are told the story of creation but not to satisfy our twenty-first-century curiosity concerning the details of *how* God made the world. For example, we wonder whether God created over a long period of time or caused all that he made to spring into existence instantly. The Genesis story is, however, given so that we might have a true understanding of the world in which we live, of its divine author, and of our own place in it. As John Stek rightly says of the creation accounts in Genesis:

> Moses' . . . intent was to proclaim knowledge of the true God as he manifested himself in his creative works, to proclaim a right understanding of humankind, the world, and history that knowledge of the true God entails—and to proclaim the truth concerning these matters in the face of the false religious notions dominant throughout the world of his day.[7]

Over against pagan religious notions dominant in Egypt and Canaan, Genesis 1 proclaims the truth about God, about humankind, and about the world. When contrasted with the ancient Near Eastern myths, the portrait of God, humanity, and the world becomes clear. This opening act introduces us to the main actors in the play—God and humanity—and the world in which the historical drama will unfold.

| Pagan myths | Genesis 1 |
| --- | --- |
| gods | God |
| humanity | humanity |
| world | world |

**Figure 5** *Pagan Myths versus Genesis 1*

## The God Who Brings All Things into Being

Reading the first chapter of Genesis is a bit like what might happen to you at a really great art exhibition. Suppose you are sitting quietly, overwhelmed by the beauty and power of the magnificent paintings. Then someone approaches you and says, "How would you like to meet the artist?" Genesis 1 is an introduction to *the* Artist. And what an introduction it is! The first three words of the Hebrew Bible may be translated: (1) "in the beginning," (2) "[he] created," (3) "God" (acting subject). In three short Hebrew words, we are transported back to the origin of everything, to the mysterious, personal Source of all that is: the eternal, uncreated God. This God, who himself has no beginning and no end, merely speaks a word of command in order to bring into being everything else that exists.

The idea of creation by the word preserves first of all the most radical distinction between Creator and creature. Creation cannot be even remotely considered an emanation from God. It is not somehow an overflow of his being, his divine nature. Instead, it is a product of his personal will. The only continuity between God and his work is his word.

Genesis 1 introduces us to God as the infinite, eternal, uncreated person who by his creative actions brings the whole of creation into existence. The "heavens and the earth" (Genesis 1:1) refers to the whole of creation. Light and darkness, day and night, sea and sky and land, plants, animals and humankind—all come from this God, from his powerful and good activity of creation. As von Rad says, "The idea of creation by the word expresses the knowledge that the whole world belongs to God."[8]

This is truly one of the points through which logic can barely wade, whereas faith can swim. "The place where the Bible begins is one where our own most impassioned waves of thinking break, are thrown back upon themselves, and lose their strength in spray and foam."[9] In the book of Revelation, one of the great causes for continual worship of God is his work in creation:

> You are worthy, our Lord and God,
> to receive glory and honor and power,
> for you created all things,
> and by your will they were created
> and have their being. (Revelation 4:11)

This hymn of praise in the last book of the Bible is set in the very throne room of heaven. This is appropriate because it echoes a truth about God implied from the beginning of the creation account in Genesis. By causing the creation to come into being by his word of power, God establishes it as his own vast kingdom. He thus establishes himself as the great King over all creation, without limits of any kind, and worthy to receive all glory, honor, and power in the worship of what he has created.

In the ancient Near East people knew all about authority. Among them, the power of even tribal or national rulers was nearly absolute. And in a variety of ways in Genesis 1, God is pictured as *the* Monarch, the royal one whose sovereignty extends by right and by power over the whole of his creation. The lightest word of a mortal king in the ancient world was to be understood as a command by anyone who heard it. But *this* immortal King speaks, and by his divine command the whole of creation springs into existence exactly as he intends. As God creates, he *names* what he creates, and this again is an expression of his sovereignty. "The act of giving a name meant, above all, the exercise of a sovereign right. . . . Thus the naming of this and all subsequent creative works once more expresses graphically God's claim of lordship over the creatures."[10]

In Genesis 1, God's word of command, the repeated phrase "Let there be . . . ," brings into existence a creation characterized by precision, order, and harmony:

> Just as God is the One who sets time in motion and set up the climate, he
> is likewise responsible for setting up all other aspects of human existence.
> The availability of water and the ability of the land to grow vegetation;
> the laws of agriculture and the seasonal cycles; each of God's creatures,

created with a role to play—all of this was ordered by God and was good, not tyrannical or threatening.[11]

God's creation is "good," and this creaturely goodness merely highlights the Creator's own incomparable goodness, wisdom, and justice. He alone is the wise King over the great kingdom of all that is.

As King, however, God does not hold himself distant from his creation. He is not the sort of monarch who rules from afar and takes no interest in his territories or his subjects. Having built his kingdom, God reigns over it in a deeply personal way. Genesis 1 and 2 portray God as highly relational. He speaks, not only to give commands, but also to express his own involvement in the making of the cosmos. There is the mysterious phrase "Let us . . ." in Genesis 1:26 (which we take to be God addressing the heavenly council of angels). This draws attention to God's personhood and his will that there should be other entities distinct from (and yet related to) himself.[12] But most dramatically, when God creates humankind, he blesses them and speaks to them directly: "Be fruitful and increase in number; fill the earth and subdue it" (Genesis 1:28). There is a personal relationship between the divine King and his human subjects. God has a particular task and invites them to participate in it with him, filling and ordering the world, which he has given them for their home. The personal character of God is shown even more clearly in Genesis 2 and 3. The LORD God (Yahweh Elohim) *walks in the garden with Adam and Eve* and shows the most intimate, personal concern for them, their needs, and their responsibilities.

## Humankind as God's Image

The highpoint of the Genesis story of creation is the making of humankind (1:26–28). In the Bible, a man or woman is a creature designed and made by God as part of God's world. However we relate God's activity of creation to scientific theories,[13] if we are faithful to what the Bible has to say about who we are, we cannot think of ourselves as merely the random products of time and chance (as do advocates of atheistic evolution). Humankind is *creaturely*, and according to Genesis (and the rest of the Bible), each human being is a special creature at that.

In Genesis 1 and 2 the teaching about humankind is rich and manifold. Unique among the creatures, which God creates, humankind is personal. God addresses only the man and woman: they enjoy a uniquely personal relationship with God. As Augustine observed long ago in his *Confessions*, we are made for God, and our hearts are restless until we find our rest in him.[14] This relationship between the creating God and his human creatures is stunningly evoked in Genesis 3:8. God is in the habit of "walking in the garden in the cool of the day" and meeting with the man and woman he has put there. Gordon Wenham has observed how Genesis portrays the garden in terms reminiscent of the tabernacle, in which God lives amid his people.[15] Men and women are made for intimate relationship with God, and our earthiness is no obstacle to that relationship. God walks regularly with Adam and Eve in the huge garden he has set aside for them. He discusses with them how this great park is developing, how its plants are growing under their care, and how the animals are getting along.

Modern scholars often refer to *two* creation stories in Genesis, seeing a distinction between what is told in 1:1–2:4a, and 2:4b–25. This is a bit misleading. Although these two sections are distinct, they are closely related. Genesis 1 looks at humankind in its relationship to the world. Genesis 2 focuses on the man and the woman in their relationships to one another and to God. The two passages use different images and metaphors because they are bringing into focus different aspects of what it means to be human.

In Genesis 1:26–28 God creates humankind *in his image*, in his likeness. Note that the words "image" and "likeness" make the same point. Though God is the infinite Creator and the humanity merely his finite creation, there is something *fundamentally similar* between them. "Image" is a metaphor. As we unpack it, we need to bear in mind that its function as a metaphor is to draw our attention to a striking similarity between humans and God while not for a moment denying that we are radically different from God. Earlier we recognized that God as Creator is radically different from everything he has created—including ourselves. But if humankind is created "in God's image," then in some way we are *like* the One who created us. This likeness is clarified in the verses that follow.

In Genesis 1:26, God says, "Let us make man in our image, . . . and let them rule . . . over all the earth." He then says to the human beings he has created, "Be fruitful and increase in number; fill the earth and subdue it. Rule over . . ." (1:28). From this it should be clear that the fundamental similarity between God and humanity is humankind's unique vocation, its calling or commissioning by God himself. Under God, humanity is *to rule* over the nonhuman parts of creation on land and in sea and air, much as God is the supreme ruler over all. As von Rad explains:

> Just as powerful earthly kings, to indicate their claim to dominion, erect an image of themselves in the provinces of their empire where they do not personally appear, so man is placed upon earth in God's image as God's

sovereign emblem. He is really only God's representative, summoned to maintain and enforce God's claim to dominion over the earth. The decisive thing about man's similarity to God, therefore, is his function in the nonhuman world.[16]

In God's kingdom, which he has set up by creating it, the special role he has assigned to humanity is that we should serve as his "under-kings," vice-regents, or stewards. We are to rule over the creation so that God's reputation is enhanced within his cosmic kingdom.

Genesis 1:26–28 has become notorious in some environmentalist circles because of Lynn White's argument that this teaching has been used to justify much of the environmental destruction characterizing the modern world.[17] This passage does understand humankind's vocation as one of rule or dominion, but it is incorrect to read it as legitimizing a ruthless mastery over nature and exploitation of it. In God's own creative work, he acts for the good of what he has made and not for his own selfish pleasure. For example, he creates a perfect home for humankind. And at every point in God's work within it, the creation is described as "good" and "very good." Over this good creation, God calls the human "ruler" to serve as steward or under-sovereign, to embody God's own care for, and protection of, his good creation in his own sovereign rule over the earth. Psalm 8:6 expresses this wonderfully: the glory of human beings is that God has made them "ruler over the works of [his] hands." It is impossible to read this as suggesting that humans are free to do what they like with God's workmanship. Above all things, the human caretakers are accountable to the divine Creator of the world entrusted to their care.

To be human means to have huge freedom and responsibility, to respond to God *and* to be held accountable for that response. Thus, a better way of expressing the concept of humankind's "dominion" over creation may be to say that we are God's royal stewards, put here to develop the hidden potentials in God's creation so that the whole of it may celebrate his glory.

Imagine that you are a fifteenth-century sculptor and one day receive an email from Michelangelo asking if you would be willing to come to his studio to complete a piece of work he has begun. He mentions that you are expected to continue his work in such a way that Michelangelo's own reputation will be enhanced by the finished product! God's call to us to "have dominion" over his creation entails this sort of compliment to what we are capable of achieving as his stewards. It also brings a correspondingly heavy responsibility for what comes out of our stewardship. If this is what being "in the image of God" involves, then clearly our service for God is to be as wide as the creation itself and will include taking good care of the environment. The passage that begins in Genesis 1:26 is often helpfully referred to as the "cultural or creation mandate." It enjoins us to bring every type of cultural activity within the service of God. Indeed, there is a dynamic element to "the image of God." God himself is revealed or "imaged" in his creation precisely *as* we are busy within the creation, developing its hidden potentials in agriculture, art, music, commerce, politics, scholarship, family life, church, leisure, and so on, in ways that honor God. *As* we take God's creative commands of "Let there be . . ." and develop the potentials in them, we continue to spread the fragrance of his presence throughout the world he has made.

Genesis 1 describes humankind not as tyrants exploiting the earth, but as stewards ruling *coram deo*, before the presence of God. The nature of our relationship with God is expressed in how we look after his good creation. And we do this not merely as individuals, but as partners.

In Genesis 1, humans are made "male and female." A gender distinction is built into creation so that God's image bearers are always male or female, man or woman. That is, we always stand in relationship to one another, as well as in relationship to God. None of us can be fully human on our own: we are always in a variety of relationships. Humans are made for God. Genesis 2 focuses more closely on this and the other relationships in which humans live out their lives by virtue of the way God has made the world. Genesis 2:18–25 tells the story of God's creation of Eve as a suitable helper and companion for Adam, illustrating once again the special nature of God's love for his creatures. God expresses his love by providing what is best for the human persons themselves. Adam's rule over the earth is embodied in his naming of the animals: just as (in Genesis 1) God named the creation as he formed it, so here Adam is permitted to name the animals God has made. Adam thus has one relationship to God and another to the animal world. But Adam is also made for *human* companionship. This is expressed at the deepest level in his relationship of marriage with Eve, a union whose intimacy is captured in the observation that these two individuals become "one flesh" (2:24).

Adam and Eve's call to rule the creation manifests itself in Genesis 2 in their responsibility to work in the garden and care for it (2:15). From the description given in Genesis 2:8–14, this "garden" is more like a major national park than one of our household gardens. It is large, with rivers running through it and lots of trees and animals. Adam and Eve thus are the first farmers and conservation officers. Once more we see that to be human is to be in relationship in some way to the creation, as one who works within it, explores its potential, and cares for it. Humans are made for God, and also for one another and for the creation, to be at work within it. According to Psalm 8, it is our *glory* to work and so to present the image of God.

The different relationships in which Genesis 1 and 2 envisage humankind can be shown as follows:

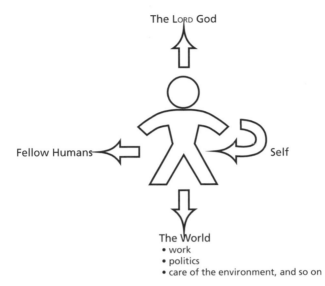

**Figure 6**  *A Biblical Understanding of Humanity*

## The World as God's Kingdom

Though Christianity has often been accused of being otherworldly, it should be clear by now that the beginning of the biblical story does *not* encourage anyone to feel detached from, or somehow superior to, this world of space and time and matter. The Bible depicts this created, material world as the very theater of God's glory, the kingdom over which he reigns. These early chapters of Genesis are very positive about the world. Though it is *created* (and therefore must never be put on the same level as the uncreated God), it is always described as "good." Through Genesis 1 the repetition of the word "good" is a reminder that the whole creation comes from God and that in its initial state it beautifully reflects his own design and plan for it. Creation has great diversity: light and darkness, land and sea, rivers and minerals, plants, animals, birds and fish, human beings both male and female. This bounty is part of God's intention, suggesting a marvelous harmony of created things. Like an orchestra, it produces a symphony of praise to the Creator. There is an order to this diversity; God's creative word gives it structure.

Genesis also reveals our world as existing within time. God is the one who creates the day and the night, and he names them. In these early chapters little is said about how God intends his creation to develop *through* time, but clearly he intends for development within what he has made. The man and the woman are to produce children from their one-flesh union, and these future generations will spread out to subdue the earth. The story of Genesis 2:4 begins with the phrase, "This is the account of the heavens and earth . . . ," suggesting that history is an integral part of creation.[18] The work of Adam and Eve in the marvelous park made by God marks the beginning of a long process by which their children and their descendants are to develop the riches of the creation. Adam and Eve's royal stewardship of Eden is to be a small version of what God intends to happen to the whole creation as history unfolds.

# Act 2

# Rebellion in the Kingdom

## Fall

A major feature of any story is its central conflict, the thing that goes wrong and needs to be fixed. Eugene Peterson describes it thus: "A catastrophe has occurred. We are no longer in continuity with our good beginning. We have been separated from it by a disaster. We are also, of course, separated from our good end. We are, in other words, in the middle of a mess."[1] And the entrance of sin into God's perfect world is that cosmic conflict that Genesis describes. This calamity comes upon the creation soon after God forms it, threatening to mar the goodness of creation itself and to touch with evil every event coming after it. Genesis 3 describes this element of the biblical story, often called (simply and ominously) the story of "the fall."

As we saw with the first and second chapters of Genesis, it is important to explore the *type* of literature we are dealing with. When discussing the fall, some scholars too quickly resort to terms like "myth" and "legend." But this narrative is part of a larger structure (Genesis 2:4–3:24) introduced with the important phrase, "This is the account of . . . ," suggesting that, for the author, what follows has to do with *what really happened*. Thus, we need to take seriously the events recorded in Genesis 3, even while we recognize that the details—including a talking serpent and symbolic trees—are unlike those of any historical text we are used to. In our view, the third chapter of Genesis does tell us reliably about the mysterious origin of evil in God's world. It was rooted in the mutiny of the first human couple. They were tempted, and they succumbed, with catastrophic consequences.

It is clear from the first two chapters of Genesis that human beings are *good* as God creates them. And even the name of the park in which God places Adam and Eve—*Eden*—is meant to evoke pleasure and delight.[2] Eden is fertile and rich in minerals. Several scholars have noted that the description of Eden shows it to be a place where God himself dwells. This is confirmed in Genesis 3:8, which says that the LORD God walks in Eden and communes there with Adam and Eve. At its beginning the creation is redolent with *shalom*, the Old Testament word for peace, meaning the rich, integrated, relational wholeness God intends for his creation. The life of Adam and Eve is the life of *shalom*. They walk with God, they have each other, the garden provides all they need as they till its fertile soil and prune its burgeoning plants. There is no storm cloud on *this* horizon, no hint of trouble to come. What could possibly go wrong?

We all know from our own experience that the world we live in is deeply wounded, but what has caused it to be so? When we read about life in Eden, we long for our own lives to be like that. Why is *our* experience so different? Genesis 3 answers this question, though perhaps without giving us all the information we would like to have. We are not told where the talking serpent comes from or who he is. (Only later in the Bible do we learn that this "creature" is also known as Satan; see Revelation 12:9.) How could such a creature disrupt God's good creation? These questions are *not* answered, and they alert us to the mystery that surrounds the origin of evil in the creation. We should take this mystery seriously.

Part of being human is the freedom to choose. Even in God's good creation, Adam and Eve's freedom to love means that they may also choose *not* to love; hence, they may experience temptation. But what would temptation involve for them? The answer is found in the mysterious "tree of the knowledge of good and evil" (Genesis 2:9). The serpent tempts them to eat from this tree, contrary to what God has told them to do (2:17; 3:1–5). But what does this mean? This story is the only place in the Bible where such a tree is mentioned, and it is vital to see that it represents the temptation to be autonomous (from the Greek words *autos*, "self," and *nomos*, "law").

Adam and Eve can obey God or they can defy him. They can yield to God's law and enjoy life, or they can try to find their own way apart from his instructions and experience death. Adam and Eve are created beings, fully and wonderfully human as they live out their freedom under God's reign, according to his rule of life. The temptation they face through the serpent is to assert their autonomy: to become a law unto themselves. *Autonomy means choosing oneself as the source for determining what is right and wrong, rather than relying on God's word for direction.* The serpent subtly casts doubt on God's words to Adam and Eve and doubt even on God's own inherent goodness. It suggests that God is *afraid* that his human creatures might become his equals once they know good and evil experientially, through eating fruit of the tree. God has said that if they eat of it they will die, but the serpent suggests rather that to eat of it is to find the path to true life. In the light of these suggestions, the woman and the man see the tree differently—and they take and eat.

Strangely, at first, the serpent seems to be right: Adam and Eve do *not* immediately die. Or do they? One of the things this story should do is to make us reflect long and hard on just what "death" means. The physical life of Adam and Eve does not stop in the instant they taste the fruit: this isn't the poison apple of the fairy tale. But something in them and between them *does* die. Their sense of themselves and their relationship with each other is shattered. They become morbidly self-conscious and thus try hurriedly to cover up their nakedness. For the first time they feel shame. And (what is even far worse) their relationship with the LORD God is also broken: they *hide* from him in fear and shame. God confronts Adam and Eve and declares judgment. The serpent is cursed, childbirth for the woman is made much harder, and the ground itself is stricken so that work is made difficult for the man and far less pleasant. Adam and Eve are driven out of Eden, and the entrance to the garden is barred.

This story is so rich in meaning that it gives us a great deal to think about. The "fall" into sin remains a mystery, but the story of Genesis 3 illumines the fundamental nature of sin. It is a quest for autonomy, a desire to separate ourselves from God. The *consequences* of sin are also clearly demonstrated. Just as Genesis 2 shows humankind in our created and unfallen relationships, so Genesis 3 focuses on the breakdown of those relationships following the human mutiny against the divine King. We humans are made for relationship, but sin's effect is to drive us apart. Above all, humankind is made to enjoy relationship with God, but the sin of Adam and Eve causes them to flee from him and be afraid, ashamed, and alone. Adam blames Eve, Eve blames the serpent, and Adam and Eve both seek to cover their nakedness.

All these actions show that sin has undermined both the sense of self and the sense of belonging to another. God's judgments suggest that the social and work dimensions of their lives have similarly been twisted out of shape. Although the man and woman do *not* die physically—at least not right away—we see from this story that "death" can mean much more than the end of physical life. Death means the distortion of relationships in general, and particularly the end of that one vital relationship with God:

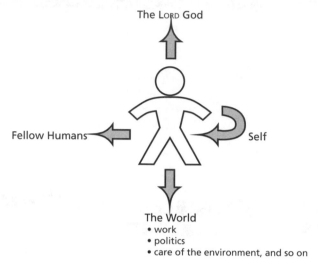

**Figure 7** *A Biblical Understanding of Humanity—The Effects of Sin*

Is the story of the world to end so soon and so sadly? By no means. Even in the tragic tale of sin's entrance into the world, God does not give up his purposes for his creation and his kingdom. Though Adam and Eve flee from him, God graciously takes the initiative to seek them out. In declaring judgment, God curses the serpent and promises to put enmity between the serpent's offspring and that of the woman (Genesis 3:15). The woman's offspring will crush the serpent's head: God promises to extinguish the evil forces Adam and Eve have unleashed. This is the first biblical promise of the Gospel: Christ is to be "the seed of the woman" and will defeat Satan, though at great cost to himself, in the "wounding" of his "heel." In Genesis 3:20, God provides for Adam and Eve's shame, clothing them with skins of animals. In the Old Testament, to remove someone's clothes could signify their disinheritance; God's provision of clothes for Adam and Eve is a sign to them that he has *not* given up on his purpose for them. They are still to bear his image in this world. They are still to "inherit the earth."[3]

As Adam and Eve leave Eden, their future seems most uncertain. (True, they have not immediately and physically died from eating the fruit. Ironically, in this one respect, the serpent has been right. But in everything else he has been quite wrong.) Disobedience has brought catastrophe. That wonderful garden now lies closed behind them, and an uncertain and dangerous world looms ahead. How awful it had been to face the LORD God when he had at last found them! How hard to look him in the face! And yet he has given them clothes to wear. And there is also that mysterious promise to consider, in which he has spoken of Eve's offspring, who will crush the serpent's head.

# Act 3

# The King Chooses Israel
## Redemption Initiated

**Scene 1: A People for the King**

*Genesis: The Origins of Israel*

### THE UNLEASHING OF SIN—AND GOD'S RESPONSE

When the gates of Eden close behind Adam and Eve, they do not cease to be what God has created. The effect of the fall on all of us is *not* that we stop being human—we remain in the image of God (Genesis 5:1; 9:6). But our rebellion has deeply affected *how* we are human. Thus, Adam and Eve remained married even after their sin, and Eve gives birth to two healthy sons. These four are a family, as God has planned before the fall. But after the fall, as soon as we move into the story told in Genesis 4, the terrible change becomes apparent.

Cain and Abel are the first brothers, but Abel's name, with its allusion to vanity (a theme explored in detail in Ecclesiastes), suggests the trouble that is to come.[1] Cain is a farmer, Abel is a shepherd. But instead of enjoying each other's companionship and supporting each other in their different jobs, Cain becomes jealous of Abel. Things come to a head when each of the brothers makes an offering to God. Abel's is accepted, but Cain's is rejected because of the evil that is inside him. God graciously tells Cain that if he does what is right, his offering will also be accepted—and then warns him that, if he is not careful, sin will leap on him like a wild animal and possess him. But Cain's resentment festers. He invites Abel to go for a walk in one of his fields, and there Cain murders his brother. The unthinkable has happened. The family that God means to be a source of companionship and joy has become a place of jealousy, rage, and murder.

Such is the horror of this killing that we might expect God to destroy everything immediately. But he does not. The good order that God has established for his creation remains. Cain marries and has a son named Enoch, then builds a city and names it after his son. Cain and his family are still humans in the image of God. But the story demonstrates clearly that humans now, after their fall into sin, have a terrible capacity to misdirect their lives. Family life and God's other good gifts can become sources of pain and vengeance.[2] It is against this background that we need to understand the events that follow: Cain builds a city, and people begin to develop culture in many different directions (Genesis 4:17–22).

"Culture" is the name we give to organized activities within society, such as making things like music or building houses or founding economic or political structures. Genesis 1:26–28 is sometimes described as *the cultural mandate* because the human task there commanded, to exercise royal stewardship over God's good creation, involves developing the hidden potentials of God's creation. Then the whole of creation may more and more declare God's glory, like a great symphony. Royal stewardship thus includes exploring and developing what can be achieved in architecture, farming, art, and family life. God has always intended that we should be involved in this kind of work.

In Genesis 4 we read about Cain (who built a city called Enoch), Jabal (the ancestor of those who live in tents and keep livestock), Jubal (the ancestor of those who play the lyre and pipe), Tubal-Cain (who made all kinds of bronze and iron tools), and Lamech (who wrote poetry). We thus must not assume that all this cultural activity is a result of sin. On the contrary, these cultural achievements come about when men and women develop the potentials that God has built into his creation. Such pursuits are essentially *good*, not evil. This is what Hans Rookmaker means in his small book *Art Needs No Justification*.[3] Rookmaker did not mean that we should embrace art for art's sake. The justification for art is that God has made the world with the human potential for imaginative, artistic activity. Cultural activity is a fundamental way in which we may serve and glorify God.[4] In the context of Genesis 4, however, we are reminded that sinful humans misdirect such good, cultural activities.

Knowing what we do know about Cain, our hearts sink as we think of him building and controlling a city, even though building a city is one important part of developing potentials hidden in creation. It is wrong to think that God's goal for creation is that it should be only a pristine, rural park. God's intention is for cities to be developed as well. Urbanization is not necessarily evil: cities can be wonderful places in which humans may flourish and God may be glorified.[5] But the fact that Cain is the one who develops the first city makes us wary of the possible corruption of God's intention. Cities, as we know too well, can become places of squalor and oppression. How will Cain's jealousy and rage affect city life in and around the city called Enoch?[6] The cultural development of the city thus begins—in itself, potentially a good outworking of humankind's mandate to develop the creation—but it begins with a man who has already shown his contempt for God's supreme rule.

Poetry is a wonderful gift from God, and the Bible contains many songs and poems that develop the beauty and power of language in obedience to God's order. Lamech is the first poet in the Bible. But in his poem, God's wonderful gift has already been distorted, twisted into an instrument to threaten with revenge and violence: "If Cain is avenged sevenfold, truly Lamech seventy-sevenfold" (Genesis 4:23–24 NRSV). Again, a good gift (poetry) is used, but in a way that ignores or denies God's rule for the creation and his role as the Giver.

Through a genealogy the fifth chapter of Genesis tells a story of the development of the human race from Adam to Noah (Lamech's son). Noah means "rest," and Lamech's great hope is that God through Noah will grant rest to humans from the difficulties of work in the fallen creation (5:28–29). Lamech knows only too well that the fall has implications for all of life, not least for work, and with Noah's birth he is hoping that things will get better. But things did not get better for the creation—at least not at first. Genesis 6–9 tells the story of Noah and the catastrophic flood. Though Lamech hopes for rest and relief, what comes with the flood is a terrible judgment.

Genesis 6:1–4 is a perplexing episode in which the sons of God (some kind of heavenly creatures) have intercourse with the daughters of humans, and their offspring are the so-called Nephilim—giants or monstrous men of some kind.[7] The significance of this story is that again (as in Genesis 3) God's order for creation has been transgressed in catastrophic ways, which again brings God's judgment. This crossing of forbidden boundaries (in the mating of humans with something not human) is a symptom of the underlying disease of sin, and Genesis

6:5–8 indicates how serious the situation has become. Evil has taken a stranglehold on human life.

Things have reached such a low point that God decides to destroy the world through a great flood and then begin anew.[8] Noah will be like a new Adam. He will bring a new possibility of rest as Lamech hoped—but only after terrible judgment. The flood God sends upon the earth is catastrophic and universal, a sort of "uncreation." Huge amounts of water are unleashed on the earth as "the springs of the great deep burst forth," and it rains steadily for forty days (6:11–12). But though the judgment against sin is terrible, once more God's gracious commitment to his original purposes for creation is manifest. God tells Noah what he is going to do and instructs Noah to build an ark in which Noah, his extended family, and several of each kind of animal on earth will be delivered from judgment. This is such a good Sunday school story that we often miss its creationwide significance. Why take these *animals* into the ark? Because God is concerned for the *whole* of his creation—including the animals. Salvation does not stop with humankind: it embraces the whole creation (see Romans 8:21).

> Man's salvation and perdition, his joy and sorrow, will be reflected in the weal and woe of this animal environment and company. Not as an independent partner of the covenant, but as an attendant, the animal will participate with man (the independent partner) in the covenant, sharing both the promise and the curse which shadows the promise. Full of forebodings, but also full of confidence, it will wait with man for its fulfilment, breathing freely again when this has taken place provisionally and will take place definitively.[9]

We often ignore this emphasis in Scripture because of our narrow view of salvation.[10]

The story of the flood reveals a God who is both a holy Judge and a gracious Redeemer. When Noah and his family come out of the ark, God makes a number of promises to Noah that comprise his *covenant* with Noah (Genesis 9:8–17). "Covenant," the word that describes the relationship between God and his people, is helpfully defined by O. Palmer Robertson as a "bond in blood sovereignly administered."[11] Let us consider the three main elements in this definition:

1. *A bond.* The covenant speaks of a deeply personal relationship between God and his people, a relationship so close that God may be thought of as *binding* or tying himself to them, and them to him. In later covenants with Israel, a favorite expression is, "I will be your God and you will be my people" (as in Jeremiah 7:23).

2. *In blood.* A covenant is a serious, legally established relationship, like a marriage (also described as a "covenant" in the Old Testament).[12] The serious, public nature of a covenant is symbolized in rituals involving sacrifice and the shedding of blood (as in Genesis 8:20–22).

3. *Sovereignly administered.* This covenant is not a relationship between equal partners who hammer out mutually agreeable terms. God is the sovereign Lord, and he alone can establish the terms of the covenant relationship.

Dumbrell rightly makes the point that when (in Genesis 6:18) God tells Noah that he *will establish his covenant with him*, "covenant" here refers to an *already existing* relationship.[13] In Genesis 9, Dumbrell argues, God is renewing his covenant *in creation* and doing so with Noah. The evidence for this relates to the way in which Genesis 9 depicts Noah as a second Adam. Noah is commissioned in the same way as Adam was—and in virtually the same words. God says, "Be fruitful and multiply, and fill the earth" (cf. 1:28; 9:1, 7 NRSV).[14] God is making a new start with Noah, but his purposes for his creation remain the same: Noah is commissioned as a second Adam. Furthermore, the content of God's covenant with Noah extends to the whole of creation. In 8:21 the LORD says that he will never again curse the ground or destroy every living creature. In 9:8–17 God is quite clear that his covenant is with Noah and his descendants and with every living creature. The rainbow is a sign of this gracious covenant established between God and "all flesh that is on the earth" (9:17 NRSV).

The covenant with Noah, therefore, refers to the special relationship God enters into with Noah and his family. Underlying this is God's covenant with creation. Hence, God is really acting in and through Noah to fulfill what God has always intended for the whole of his creation.

But alas, God's new start does not bring the fullness of rest that Lamech hoped for. The whole of the earth is peopled from Noah's three sons, Shem, Ham, and Japheth (9:18), but sin is soon showing itself again in the family life of Noah and his sons (9:20–28). Once more, cultural development is ambivalent. On the one hand, agriculture does advance. Noah is the first to plant a vine and to develop the wonderful, God-given art of winemaking (9:20). What would life be without Cabernet Sauvignon, Pinot Gris, and Merlot? But while wine itself and the craft of making it are good gifts in themselves, they can also be misused sinfully. The world's first vintner becomes drunk and disgraces himself and his family, lying openly naked in his tent to sleep it off, where his son Ham discovers him. It is hard to be sure what the problem is in his son's response to Noah's behavior—is there a sexual offense involved, or is Ham's gossip about his father's nakedness an act of sinful disrespect? Either way, there is further family breakdown here. Noah curses

Canaan, the son of Ham (thus cursing the people who will descend in this line of his own family), and he blesses Shem (from whose line the Israelites will descend).

Genesis 10 tells of the world's nations emerging from the sons of Noah. This is a positive fulfilling of God's command to Adam, which he then has repeated to Noah: "Be fruitful and multiply, and fill the earth." However, at this stage in the story we are not surprised to learn that this positive development—a great expansion in population and cultural progress—has a negative side to it as well. The next chapter of Genesis tells the story of the tower of Babel. This episode in the Genesis story represents the high tide of sin to this point in the biblical drama. Babel is a monumental, communal attempt by Adam's race to wrest human autonomy from God once more.

As already noted, the impulse to build a city is part of normal cultural development within God's world. But this impulse can be misdirected, and in the story of Babel we have misdirection on a massive scale. As people migrate eastward, they build a city with a huge tower. This is their way of asserting their own will against God's desire that humans should be spread and scattered throughout the world ("fill the earth"). The tower they build is probably a ziggurat, the most prominent part of a temple devoted to worship of "the gods" in ancient Mesopotamia. The name "Babel" hints at what this particular city and tower have in mind. *Babel* means "gate of God."[15] In ancient Mesopotamia, a ziggurat was constructed to serve as a staircase by which the god or gods could descend from heaven to a city and bless it. At its top was a small room with a bed, a table, and some fresh food so the god could refresh himself as he descended.

However, as Genesis 11 tells of Babel, the storyteller reminds us that "Babel" is related to another Hebrew word meaning "mixed up" or "confused." For the storyteller, "the name 'Babel/Babylon' does not mean 'gate of the god,' as the Babylonians held, but 'confusion,' and it evokes the similar sounding words 'folly' and 'flood.' Far from being the last word in human culture, it is the ultimate symbol of man's failure when he attempts to go it alone in defiance of his creator."[16] Though God has commanded humankind to spread out over the whole earth, this group in Mesopotamia has chosen rather to establish for themselves a secure center from which to control their own environment and protect themselves. Instead of a God-given unity and identity, they seek a false, autonomous collectivism and a reputation of their own devising. Here we have a repetition of the eating from the tree of the knowledge of good and evil, but now performed on a grand social scale. By building this tower, they arrogantly challenge God to come down and bless *their* endeavor.

In a statement full of wonderful irony (11:5–6), God does indeed come down to see what these rebellious city-builders are up to. Although they think of their tower as a wonderful achievement, a stairway to heaven itself, God has to descend from heaven just to be able to *see* the thing! Far from blessing this project, God condemns the arrogance that has inspired it. He judges the people by confusing their language and scattering them abroad. God thus forces them to fulfill his will for them, to spread out across the face of the earth.

Babel stands as a monument to the perennial human desire to build our *own* kingdom apart from God. But God will have none of this false center for human existence, and so he scatters the builders of Babel. *Name* in Scripture stands for identity. With this city and tower, the people have sought a false identity, a reputation built on human autonomy (11:4). God's response is to judge their sin for what it is and to put a stop to their ambitious, idolatrous building program. But as we have seen again and again, judgment is accompanied by mercy. Though Genesis 11 marks a climax in the advance of human sinfulness within the creation, Genesis 12 marks yet another new beginning as God steadfastly pursues his purpose for his creation.

### THE ABRAHAMIC COVENANT: BLESSED TO BE A BLESSING

Thus far, the biblical story has encompassed the lives and acts of the whole of humankind. But now, in response to the catastrophe of Babel, the highwater mark of sin in God's good creation thus far, God takes the initiative once more and turns his attention to one man, Abraham. Indeed, Abraham and his descendants are the major concern of the rest of Genesis.[17]

God calls Abraham to leave his country (Ur), his people, and his father's household, to go to the land that God will show to him (12:1–3). This is a radical call. Even for us in the twenty-first century, with all our conveniences of travel and communication, it is hard to contemplate moving from one country to another. We can only dimly guess at what it must have meant to a person like Abraham to be asked to leave absolutely everything he knows—family, tribe, home, and country—for a long and uncertain journey to a mysterious destination. Abraham is asked to give up all the symbols of security and autonomy with which the builders of Babel sought to shore up their own identity. But wonderfully, Abraham *does* give them up, for the sake of obeying God. To follow where God will lead, he sets out with his wife (Sarah), his nephew Lot, and their extended family.

What is God up to in all of this? By narrowing his focus to Abraham, has he given up on all other peoples? The first three verses of Genesis 12

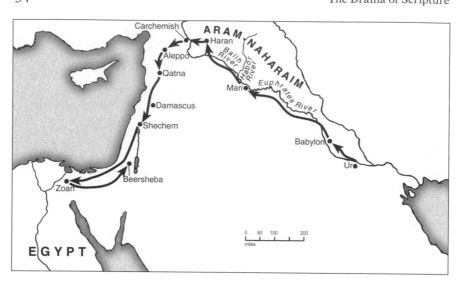

**Figure 8** *Abraham's Journeys*

spell out for Abraham what God plans to do through him—and the plan
is remarkable. God promises (1) to make Abraham into a great nation,
(2) to bless him, (3) to make his name great, (4) to make him a blessing,
(5) to bless those who bless him and curse (or judge) those who judge
him, and (6) ultimately to bless all peoples on earth through him! The
peoples of the earth have sought to make a name for themselves with
the construction of the tower of Babel, but God rejected their ambitious
plan to do things their own way. Now, however, God promises that he
will make Abraham's name great and make him into a great nation. The
trophies that the people of Babel attempted to take for themselves—fame,
security, and a heritage for the future—are God's free *gift* to Abraham.
Here we start to see how God will respond to what has gone wrong in
his creation. Through Abraham he will bring into being a nation, Israel,
which is to be God's own people among all the other peoples of the world.
And through this nation God will bring blessing to all the other peoples
of the earth (18:18–19).

    From this point on in the Old Testament story, the narrative focus
narrows to consider Abraham and his descendants. But even here in
God's very personal promises to this one man and his family, God does
not forget his purposes for all the nations of the world. This is made
clear in the words chosen for the promises of 12:1–3. Some form of
the word "bless" is used five times, and this is a very significant term
in the first chapters of Genesis.[18] The dynamic word "bless" expresses
God's purpose to give his creatures all they need to fulfill their lives in

his creation as he intends for them. The word "curse," by contrast, expresses God's awful judgment on his creatures when they rebel against his purposes for them.

God's words of blessing on Abraham in 12:1–3 suggest in yet another way what God is planning to do through this man. The fivefold repetition of the word "bless" is deliberately set in opposition to the fivefold occurrence of the word "curse" in Genesis 1–11.[19] God's curse or judgment on humankind has meant their loss of freedom (3:14–16), their alienation from the soil (3:17–19), their estrangement from one another (4:11), and their moral and spiritual degradation (9:25).[20] The repetition of "bless" in Genesis 12:1–3 declares that through Abraham, God is at work to reverse the effect of judgment on his creation. Though sin has brought God's curse on creation, God is still at work to recover his purpose of blessing for all that he has made, and Abraham is to be the medium of divine restoration for the whole world.

Through Abraham, "all peoples on earth will be blessed."[21] This final clause of Genesis 12:3 is the climactic conclusion of these verses and points to the ultimate result of God's choosing Abraham.[22] God narrows his redemptive focus to one man, one nation. But his ultimate purpose is to bring redemptive blessing to the whole creation. God's promise to Abraham is God's answer to sin, which has corrupted the whole creation: God will restore his world. "Gen[esis] 12:1–3 is the rejoinder to the consequences of the fall and aims at the restoration of the purposes of God for the world to which Genesis 1–2 directed our attention. What is being offered in these few verses is a theological blueprint for the redemptive history of the world, now set in train by the call of Abram."[23] As Gordon Wenham helpfully says,

> The promises to Abraham renew the vision for humanity set out in Genesis 1 and 2. He, like Noah before him, is a second Adam figure. Adam was given the garden of Eden: Abraham is promised the land of Canaan. God told Adam to be fruitful and multiply: Abraham is promised descendants as numerous as the stars in heaven. God walked with Adam in Eden: Abraham was told to walk before God. In this way the advent of Abraham is seen as the answer to the problems set out in Genesis 1–11: through him all the families of the earth will be blessed.[24]

From the beginning God's people are to be "missionary." They are chosen to be a channel of blessing to others.

God's relationship with Abraham is described as a *covenant* in Genesis 15 and 17. In chapter 15, God promises that Abraham's reward will be very great. Abraham asks how this can be, since he has no children to inherit these blessings. God promises Abraham that his descendants will indeed one day be as numerous as the stars of the sky. He also promises that he will give Abraham's descendants the land. They will be aliens in a foreign land for four hundred years, but then God will bring them back to inherit the land of promise, Canaan.[25] When Abraham questions God's promise, God initiates a covenant ceremony. Abraham halves three animals and arranges them to have an aisle between the halves. God passes through the animals in the form of a smoking firepot. In this well-known covenant ceremony, God signifies that if he does not keep his promise, he will be torn limb from limb like these animals (cf. Jeremiah 34:18–20). With that, the LORD makes a covenant with Abraham.

Some time later God appears to Abraham again, who is ninety-nine years old and still childless. Abraham falls face down before God, and God confirms his covenant. As for God, he promises Abraham that he will be given numerous descendants (17:4–6) and a land and home for his people (17:8). Furthermore, God himself will be the great King of the nation that will descend from Abraham (17:7). God's covenant is with Abraham and his descendants, and in Genesis 17:9 the mark of circumcision is introduced for all males belonging to Abraham's line. In the ancient Near East, circumcision was practiced by most of the nations. Here God radically changes, for his own people, the meaning of this common cultural practice. For the Israelites, it becomes a sign of the covenant between God and Abraham and his descendants. The permanent marking of the body in this way is probably meant to signify the permanence of God's relationship with this people who will come from Abraham.[26]

There thus are three main elements in God's covenant with Abraham. God promises personal relationship, the growth of a family into a nation, and land. These promises are always with a view to blessing all nations.[27] The rest of the story in the Pentateuch (the five "books of Moses," Genesis through Deuteronomy) is about the partial fulfillment of these promises and the formation of God's people. Clines helpfully defines the theme of the Pentateuch as "the partial fulfilment—which implies also the partial non-fulfilment—of the promise to or blessing of the patriarchs. The promise or blessing is both the divine initiative in a world where human initiatives always lead to disaster, and a re-affirmation of the primal divine intentions for man."[28]

At Babel, people had sought to make a name *for themselves*, but God promises that *he* will make a great name for Abraham and his descendants through their involvement with him and dependence upon him. But as the story told in Genesis 12–25 demonstrates, this sense of trust in God and dependence upon God's promise is hard to achieve and even harder to hold on to. Abraham does demonstrate remarkable faith in God by following his call to leave country and kindred and go to the land that God will show him (12:1). Yet the same longing for autonomy that we saw in Genesis 3 and 11 remains present in Abraham. He will have to undergo some extraordinarily tough reeducation to learn better.

Abraham is told that he himself will not see his descendants inherit the promised land (15:15). He has to learn to trust God against all odds, and to his credit, at times he really does (15:6).[29] But the stories of Abraham and Sarah reveal how difficult such trust is to achieve. God has made wonderful promises to Abraham and Sarah about their descendants, the land, and great blessings to come. But years roll on and Sarah is not pregnant. Eventually God does bless her with the child of promise. By this time, Abraham is already one hundred years old (21:5). Abraham's tests of faith reach their climax in Genesis 22, when God tells him to take his "only son Isaac" and sacrifice him on Mount Moriah. All these years Abraham and Sarah have waited for a son, and now Abraham is told to take Isaac and kill him. But at the last moment he is told to stop, and a ram is provided in Isaac's place. Kierkegaard comments movingly on this event in *Fear and Trembling*:

> Venerable Father Abraham! When you went home from Mount Moriah, you did not need a eulogy to comfort you for what was lost, for you gained everything and kept Isaac—was it not so? The Lord did not take him away from you again, but you sat happily together at the dinner table in your tent, as you do in the next world for all eternity. . . . Forgive the one who aspired to speak your praise if he has not done it properly. He spoke humbly, as his heart demanded; he spoke briefly, as is seemly. But he will never forget that you needed 100 years to get the son of your old age against all expectancy, that you had to draw the knife before you kept Isaac; he will never forget that in 130 years you got no further than faith.[30]

We should not underestimate how hard it must be at times for Abraham to trust God. Abraham's trust in God through this remarkable episode is rewarded in God's strong reaffirmation of the covenant between Abraham and himself (Genesis 22:16–18).

### ISAAC, JACOB, AND JOSEPH: PATRIARCHS OF GOD'S PEOPLE

Genesis 25–36 narrates the stories of Isaac and his sons, Esau and Jacob. From Jacob's sons the twelve tribes of Israel emerge. Although God's purpose in calling Abraham was to bring blessing to the whole world, for the time being the biblical story focuses on the family line through whom this blessing will come: the twelve sons of Jacob, whose families are to become the twelve tribes of the nation of Israel.

Three elements are particularly noticeable in these stories. The first is that God's promises to Abraham are reaffirmed to his son and grandson,

so that God comes to be referred to as "the God of Abraham, Isaac and
Jacob" (Exodus 3:6). In Genesis 26:1–4, Isaac must have been tempted
to move elsewhere to escape the famine in Canaan. Yet God appears to
Isaac and tells him not to go down to Egypt but to remain in the land
of Canaan. God assures Isaac that he will give these lands to him and
his descendants, make them as numerous as the stars, and through
this nation bless all the nations of the earth. This promise is repeated
in 26:23–25. It is similar with Jacob, a complex character who deceives
his father, Isaac, into giving him (rather than Esau) the blessing due the
firstborn son (Genesis 27). Because of this trickery, Esau hates Jacob
and plans to kill him, and Jacob has to flee for his life. Despite this
manipulation and intrigue, God meets with Jacob at Bethel through a
dream. On his journey a tired Jacob takes a stone for a pillow and while
sleeping dreams of a ladder stretching between heaven and earth, with
angels going up and down on it. Above it stands the LORD, who identifies himself as the God of Abraham and Isaac and reaffirms to Jacob
the promise to give him land and numerous descendants. Importantly,
Jacob is also assured that "all the families of the earth shall be blessed
in you and in your offspring" (28:14 NRSV).

The second characteristic of these stories, especially those about
Jacob and Joseph, is the repeated theme of bitter breakdown in family relationships. The feuding between Jacob and Esau plays itself out
in a variety of ways and pollutes the lives of their children after them.
Joseph (before Benjamin is born) is Jacob's spoiled youngest son, who
antagonizes his brothers by telling tales on them and by telling them his
dreams of being served by them. The brothers sell Joseph into slavery
and then pretend to Jacob that Joseph has been murdered. In all these
ways, the catastrophic pattern of breakdown in relationships that has
begun with the sin of Adam and Eve manifests itself again and again
in the "chosen line" of humanity. These stories do not condone such
behavior, but they do confront us with the stark truth concerning the
character of those whom God chooses. God will work *through* such
people to bring blessing to the world, but first he has to work *in* them
and *with* them, to bring reconciliation and maturity. As Wenham says,
"Essentially both the Jacob cycle (25:19–35:29) and the Joseph story
(37:2–50:26) are stories of family reconciliations."[31] In the Joseph story
we see the development in Joseph from a spoiled, selfish, and alienated
young man, to a mature, selfless political leader fully reconciled with
his family.[32]

The third element common to these narratives is God's providential
care of his people in the face of the many obstacles to his plan for them.
The patriarchs' wives are barren or are taken into other men's harems.
Natural disasters such as famine threaten to overtake the families. Time

and again the stupidity and sinfulness of the patriarchs themselves put them and those who come after them—and God's purposes—in peril. And yet, through all of this human turmoil, there is one constant: *God remains faithful to his promise to Abraham*. This theme is probably related to one of the names for God in these patriarchal narratives: *El Shaddai* (17:1; 28:3; 35:11; 48:3; "God Almighty" in many English versions). In Exodus 6:3 God speaks of having revealed himself to Abraham, Isaac, and Jacob by this name, the precise meaning of which is unclear. *El Shaddai* probably "evokes the idea that God is able to make the barren fertile and fulfill his promises."[33] God's providence is a particularly clear theme in the Joseph story. In Genesis 45:5–7, Joseph recognizes that all that has happened to him has been ordained by God to "preserve for [his father's offspring] a remnant on earth and to save [their] lives by a great deliverance." And in 50:20 Joseph reassures his brothers after their father's death: "You intended to harm me, but God intended it for good to accomplish what is now being done, the saving of many lives."

By the end of the Genesis story, God's promise to Abraham that he would have many descendants has been partially fulfilled (47:27; Exodus 1:6–7). Jacob's children have now become a large, flourishing group in Egypt. But "a new king arose over Egypt, who did not know Joseph" (Exodus 1:8 NRSV). This ominous note signifies the start of a chain of events that will lead the Israelites out of Egypt and into their own promised land—the home that God has also promised to Abraham.

### Exodus: Formation of a People

#### ISRAEL IS FORMED BY A MIGHTY ACT OF REDEMPTION

As the biblical story resumes in Exodus four hundred years after Abraham, we are still in Egypt. Joseph and his brothers have died, but their descendants have multiplied until they are a substantial part of Egypt's population. God's promise to Abraham concerning a great number of descendants has been partially fulfilled. But what of God's other promises—to provide a relationship with himself and to give his people a land of their own? As the Exodus narrative begins, it seems that these promises are a long way from being fulfilled. A new pharaoh has arisen who does not know Joseph, fears the numbers of Israelites, subjects them to brutal slave labor, and embarks on a vicious policy of killing all newborn male Israelites. Though this oppression seems to be an obstacle to God's fulfilling his promises, it paradoxically becomes the impetus for the Israelites' escape from Egypt.[34] When they cry out to God amid their suffering and oppression, "God [hears] their groaning

and he [remembers] his covenant with Abraham, with Isaac and with
Jacob" (Exodus 2:24).

Moses, the one who is to become Israel's liberator, is born. In desperation lest he be slaughtered, too, along with the other baby boys born to
the Israelites, Moses' mother puts him in a waterproof basket and places
it among reeds at the edge of the Nile River. Moses' elder sister keeps
an eye out to see what will happen. Amazingly, when Pharaoh's own
daughter comes down to the river to bathe, she finds the baby and adopts
him as her own child. Ironically, Moses thus receives the best education
Egypt can offer—in the heart of Pharaoh's own household.[35]

As a young adult Moses is sensitive to the sufferings of his people.
On one occasion he observes an Israelite being beaten by an Egyptian.
Enraged, Moses kills the Egyptian and then has to flee because he was
observed. Pharaoh tries to have him killed. Moses flees to Midian and
becomes a shepherd (Exodus 2:11–17).

While caring for the flocks of his father-in-law near a mountain named
Horeb,[36] Moses has an astonishing encounter with God, who speaks to
him from a burning bush (Exodus 3). Though the bush burns, it is not
consumed. God tells Moses to take off his sandals because the ground
he is standing on is holy, and he identifies himself to Moses as the God
of Abraham, Isaac, and Jacob. God tells Moses that he has heard the
cry of his oppressed people and is now sending Moses to Pharaoh to
bring his people out of Egypt into the land he promised them. But Moses
responds reluctantly, wondering how *he* can convince the Israelites
that it is really God who has sent him. In response to this, God says to
Moses, "I AM WHO I AM. This is what you are to say to the Israelites: 'I
AM has sent me to you'" (3:14).

In this episode we are introduced to the most common and distinctive
name for God used in the Old Testament, *Yahweh*, generally translated in
English versions of the Bible as "LORD." The name Yahweh occurs some
6,800 times in the Old Testament, and much has been written about its
precise meaning.[37] Numerous translations and suggestions have been
made about this name and about the phrase it comes from (in 3:14).
Some suggest that the mystery of this expression is that God is refusing
to reveal his name. But it is hard to relate this to the recurrence of the
name itself in the text of the Bible and to God's continuing revelation of
himself to his people in the Old Testament. Alternative suggested translations are "I will be who or what I will be," or "I will cause to be what I
will cause to be." But perhaps the best translation of this expression is
"I will be who I am." Understood this way, the name Yahweh indicates
not just that God is present *now*, but also that he will be "faithfully
God for [his people] in the history that is to follow. . . . Israel need not
be concerned about divine arbitrariness or capriciousness. God can be

counted on to be who God is. Israel understands its history from this name and this name from its history. The name will shape Israel's story, but the story will also give greater texture to the name."[38]

God has made promises to Abraham, and now he demonstrates his faithfulness to those promises by rescuing the nation descended from Abraham, taking them out of slavery, and placing them in the land he has promised them. His name, Yahweh, is particularly associated with this marvelous act of deliverance from slavery in Egypt. Exodus 6:6–7 brings all these elements together as the LORD commissions Moses:

> Therefore, say to the Israelites: "I am the LORD, and I will bring you out from under the yoke of the Egyptians. I will free you from being slaves to them and will redeem you with an outstretched arm and with mighty acts of judgment. I will take you as my own people, and I will be your God. Then you will know that I am the LORD your God, who brought you out from under the yoke of the Egyptians."

The big obstacle to the Israelites' leaving Egypt is Pharaoh, who regards his own power as absolute. When Moses and Aaron ask Egypt's king to let the Israelites go so that they can hold a festival to the LORD in the desert, Pharaoh replies: "Who is the LORD, that I should obey him and let Israel go? I do not know the LORD and I will not let Israel go" (5:2). And thus "Pharaoh and [Yahweh] face off. Both claim Israel. Both demand Israel's service and allegiance for themselves. . . . The course of the plagues makes it evident who really possesses supreme power."[39]

God sends Moses (and Aaron, Moses' spokesman) to confront Pharaoh, who hardens his heart and refuses to acknowledge the LORD or to let the Israelites go. Through a series of ten plagues, Pharaoh is confronted with the fact that the LORD is God. The first nine are blood in the Nile, frogs, gnats, flies, diseased livestock, boils, hail and thunder, locusts, and dense darkness. Finally a deadly plague comes upon the firstborn males in the whole of Egypt, both human and animal—except for the Israelites.

Several suggestions have been made about how to understand these plagues. Some observe, for example, that the plagues can be understood as related to natural catastrophes that we know happened from time to time in Egypt.[40] Greta Hort has thus suggested that the first six plagues result from a high Nile (during summer months, July–September) infected by flagellates. These flagellates could account for the characteristics of the first plague: the blood-red color of the Nile, the death of its fish, its horrible smell, and its being undrinkable (see 7:20–21). In Hort's view, the next five plagues result from this first one. Frogs are known to invade Egypt toward the end of the Nile's flood stage, in September and October. The sudden death of the frogs could have been caused by *Bacillus anthracis* (anthrax) breeding in the decaying fish. Hort takes the "gnats" to be a type of mosquito, swarms of which inevitably accompany the flood season in Egypt. The flies of the next plague may have been dog flies, known for their bites. The plague of the livestock Hort relates to the anthrax spread from the dead frogs. Hort believes the "boils" may refer to the bites of flies that carried this bacteria. She thus sees the insects of the fourth plague as responsible for the boils of the sixth plague. In this way, "the first six plagues form a natural sequence of interdependent events resulting from a high Nile inflected by flagellates, whereas plagues seven through ten were not connected to the first six."[41]

Concerning the hailstorms of the seventh plague, Hort notes that Egypt does experience violent storms from time to time and that these can cause major damage to crops (cf. 9:31). Hail is not common in Egypt and would terrify the Egyptians. Locust plagues *were* known throughout the ancient Near East, and so there is no problem in finding a natural parallel to plague 8. Humphreys suggests that the damp ground left by the storms (of plague 7) would provide ideal breeding grounds for locusts.[42] The ninth plague, darkness, Hort associates with desert sandstorms. In Hort's view there is no natural explanation for the tenth plague: from her perspective, it is quite exceptional. However, Humphreys builds on a suggestion from Marr and Malloy and does propose that a natural agent may be seen in the final plague.[43] He suggests that, by the end of the nine plagues, the Egyptians must be in a desperate state. In particular, they must be short of food and may have made the terrible mistake of storing wet grain left after the storms and then of feeding this to their firstborn sons and animals. The wet grain would contain poisonous mycotoxins, produced by fungi growing on substances like wet crops.[44]

It may well be that this kind of understanding of the plagues is correct. What we must *not* do, however, is to resort to a merely *naturalistic* understanding of them, in which God is brought in only to explain what cannot be explained naturally. God sustains the whole of creation in existence, and the laws of nature are part of his order for creation. As Spykman says,

> On a biblically directed, holist worldview, God and the world are not competing forces. Accordingly, in what we call miracles God does not eliminate the instrumental agency of his creatures. They remain his servants responding to the commanding power of his Word. These mighty acts of God, therefore, neither contravene nor supersede his dynamic yet stable order for creation. . . . There is nothing arbitrary or capricious about them.

> From our perspective they may appear as surprising, unexpected, extraordinary interventions of God's hand in history. For God, however, miracles are not miracles as we perceive them. They are rather the outworkings of his will in other ways, ways which appear to us unusual and exceptional, ways which are, however, consistently at God's command.[45]

Thus the important thing to understand about the plagues is that, in these extraordinary events, *God* is at work manifesting his power over the whole creation to Pharaoh and the Egyptians. It is this religious aspect of the plagues that is most important.

Scholars who have focused on the religious aspect of the plagues make various suggestions about how to understand them. Some argue—especially in light of 12:12: "I will bring judgment on all the gods of Egypt"—that the plagues are directed against different Egyptian gods. Thus, like the miracles of Elijah and Elisha recorded in the books of Kings, the Exodus plagues show that what the Egyptians *think* to be true of their gods is *actually* true only of the LORD God of heaven and earth. It is certainly possible that some of the plagues evoke particular gods in the minds of the Egyptians. The flooding of the Nile, for example, is associated with the god Osiris and his resurrection. "Thus, the blood-like waters might signal his death rather than his resuscitation, death for Egypt's agriculture rather than verdant fields, a frightful prospect for the Egyptians."[46]

We may not be able to relate each plague to a polemic against a particular god or gods, but this approach seems to be on the right track. This especially makes sense because in Egypt Pharaoh *himself* is regarded as divine: he is supposed to be the son of the sun god, Re. As a god, Pharaoh is responsible for maintaining what the Egyptians called *ma'at*, or order in the cosmos or creation. When cosmic order goes wrong, nature behaves strangely—and clearly this is evident in the plagues. "What the plagues of Exodus show is the inability of the obstinate king to maintain [*ma'at*]. Rather, it is Yahweh and his agents Moses and Aaron, who overcome in the cosmic struggle, demonstrating who really controls the forces of nature."[47] The LORD's confrontation with Pharaoh demonstrates the LORD's power so that his "name might be proclaimed in all the earth" (9:16).

Defeated at last, Pharaoh lets the Israelites go. According to Exodus 12, this deliverance is the basis for the annual Feast of the Passover, in which Israel is to remember God's mighty act of deliverance. The term "Passover'" comes from the final plague, in which God destroys the Egyptians' firstborn male children and animals but "passes over" the Israelites. In years to come, this experience of deliverance from oppression and slavery profoundly shapes the memory of the Israelites. They are free and a people only because God is their mighty Liberator. God instructs the Israelites that the month of their deliverance is to be the first month of their year (12:2). It is to represent for them what Sunday represents for Christians: the day of resurrection and new life. In their new life as God's liberated people, the Israelites order their calendar to commemorate God's mighty acts of deliverance for them.

Pharaoh does make one last desperate attempt to restrain the Israelites, sending his armies after them as they flee Egypt. But the sea, that great symbol of power but under the LORD's control, overwhelms Pharaoh's armies (Exodus 14). Exodus 15 records the victory song of Moses and the Israelites. God is pictured as a mighty warrior who has won the battle for his people and will reign forever. The hymn expresses confidence that God will continue to direct his newly redeemed people. He will lead them to the land he is giving them and plant them there on "the mountain of his inheritance." The Israelites' new home is the place that God himself has chosen for his dwelling, the sanctuary he has established (15:13–18). All these phrases indicate that the land is like a second Eden, a place in which the LORD will dwell among his people. In the ancient Near East, the gods were traditionally thought of as living upon mountains. Here, however, the whole land is pictured as the LORD's mountain, his dwelling, his sanctuary. God's planting of the Israelites in the land will be a major step on the way toward the recovery and restoration of the creation.

### ISRAEL IS BOUND TO GOD IN COVENANT

And so Moses leads the Israelites out of Egypt and into the wilderness. Three months after leaving Egypt, the Israelites arrive at Mount Sinai, the same area where Moses has first met God. But there is a difference: *then*, God speaks to one man from a burning bush; *now*, the whole mountain is ablaze (19:16). God is calling an entire people to be his, not just an individual. God reveals himself to the Israelites in thunder and lightning on the mountain, in an awesome reminder of whom they are dealing with. This too is holy ground.

Through Moses, God reminds the Israelites of what he has done for them and what his purpose is for them (19:3–6). God says he has brought them out of Egypt like an eagle carrying its tired young on its wings. Israel's formation as God's people is utterly dependent on God's gracious acts on their behalf. The deeply relational nature of God's saving activity is beautifully captured in the phrase "brought you to myself." God's intention is to have a people with whom he is in relationship.

But why has God chosen *them*? The answer of 19:5–6 is deeply significant. God has called Israel for a special purpose. Out of all the nations,

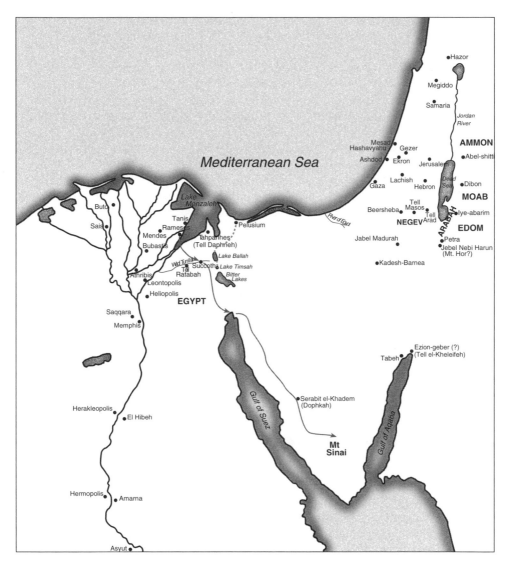

**Figure 9** *The Exodus*

*they* are chosen to be God's own treasured possession! But (as we noted with Abraham) election is not just for privilege: it is for service, for the sake of the nations. If they live under his reign, they will be a "kingdom of priests" and a "holy nation."

Holiness is one of the most important attributes the Bible ascribes to God. It tells us that God is special, different from all that he has created, and full of goodness. Israel is called by God to be holy, to be different from the other nations, to be God's own special people. The Israelites will really be different only if they live in a way that fits this aspect of God's own character. If Israel does this, its special role, to be a royal priesthood among the nations, will be fulfilled. The role of the priests within Israel is to mediate between God and the people. Thus, on an international scale, Israel is called to mediate between the LORD and all the nations. Israel is to be "a display-people, a showcase to the world of how being in covenant with Yahweh changes a people."[48] As the Israelites obey God, they will demonstrate what life under God's reign looks like. The nations will be able to catch a glimpse of God's plan for all peoples. The whole of Israel's experience, including family life, law, politics, economics, and recreation, will reflect God's character and God's original creational intention for human life. Israel's life under God is to testify to the living presence of God within God's people. It is to be such a full and rich human life that the nations of the earth will be drawn to it.[49] In this way Israel will fulfill the Abrahamic covenant to bless all nations. Faithfulness to the call to be a holy nation and a priestly kingdom is the "way in which Israel will continue to exercise her Abrahamic role, and thus to provide a commentary on the way in which the promises of Genesis 12:1–3 will find their fulfillment."[50]

God's rescue of the Israelites comes about because of his gracious love for them, not because they deserve to be rescued or have earned it in any way by their obedience to God (Deuteronomy 7:7–8). But the Israelites' destiny *after* their deliverance, to become a royal priesthood and holy nation, will be achieved only if they do obey, choosing an active life of obedience under God's reign.

Dumbrell captures the significance of this call for the rest of Old Testament history: "The history of Israel from this point on is in reality merely a commentary upon the degree of fidelity with which Israel adhered to this Sinai-given vocation."[51] The remainder of the Old Testament narrates how faithful or unfaithful Israel is to this call.

Israel's vocation is given in the context of a covenant. In Exodus 19–24, God establishes a covenant relationship between himself and the Israelites at Mount Sinai. Scholars have long noted the similarities between ancient Near Eastern vassal treaties and this Sinai covenant. A vassal treaty was a contract established between a great conquering king and a nation coming under his control. Around the time of Moses, this was the means by which the Hittite kings administered their empire. The shape of the covenant in Exodus is much like one of these vassal treaties. It is clearly not a treaty between equals: God is the great King, and Israel the subordinate nation. In this case Israel has come under God's control and become his people not through his *conquest* of them

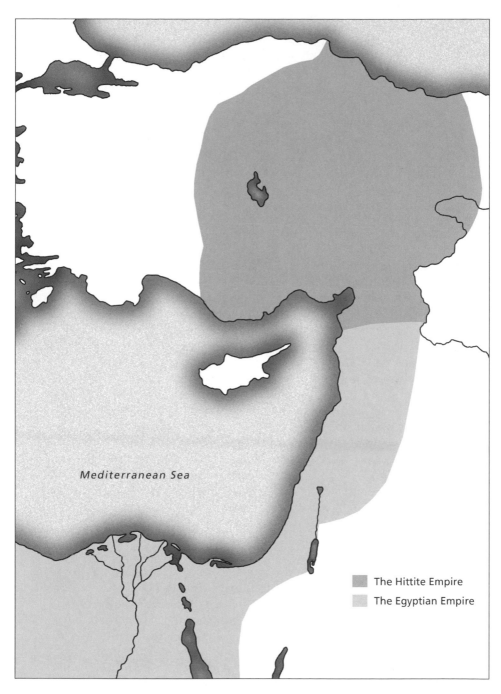

The Hittite Empire
The Egyptian Empire

Mediterranean Sea

**Figure 10** *Hittite and Egyptian Empires, c. 1500 BC*

(as the Hittite kings would conquer neighboring tribes), but because he has delivered them from slavery in Egypt.

There were six main elements in a Hittite vassal treaty: (1) a preamble, (2) a review of the history of the relationship between the king and the subordinate nation, (3) principal stipulations governing the relationship, (4) detailed stipulations, (5) witnesses to the covenant, and (6) blessings and curses for obedience or disobedience. Each of these elements is found in Exodus 19–24 and in Deuteronomy.[52] These Scriptures imply that God is a great, conquering king—something like the powerful Hittite conquerors and yet incomparably greater. This image of God's status gives us important insight into how the Israelite nation becomes God's own people. Just as a conquering king takes seriously every aspect of the life of the nation to become his vassal state, so God intends to exercise his rule over every aspect of the life of Israel. God is every bit as interested in politics, economics, and law as any other great vassal king in the ancient Near East.

This interest of God in the details of his people's experience is shown clearly in the instructions God gives to regulate and shape every aspect of their lives under his rule. We generally refer to these instructions as "law," and such law is not entirely new to the Israelites. They have had ample experience of law during their time as a subject people in Egypt. Indeed, it is possible that what God does on Mount Sinai is not to give his people a wholly new law, but to take what they know already of law and reshape it, rejecting some parts of it and developing others. The law God gives to Moses for the Israelites bears all the marks of being genuine ancient Near Eastern law. God is not calling his people to live in an eccentric, unhistorical fashion: they are to be genuine people of their own historical time and place. And yet God recasts common law to reflect his own character and creational intentions, and so it has some quite distinctive elements. For example, while some law of that time valued property above people and made the punishment for stealing greater than that for murder, Israel's law *always* places the value of people above that of mere property, for only *people*, of all God's creations, have been fashioned in his own image.

The Ten Commandments (the "Ten Words" of Exodus 20 and Deuteronomy 5) are the general stipulations for Israel in covenant relationship with God. The instructions that follow the Ten Words develop detailed applications of the general principles, which touch every aspect of Israel's life before God (Exodus 20–22). The Ten Words thus articulate the core principles that God intends and are to shape the lives of his people so that their lives will reflect his character. Only as the Israelites obey God fully will they truly be a royal priesthood and a holy nation. Only as God's law shapes their whole lives will they fulfill their calling and be a blessing to the nations.

Much has been written about the Ten Words. Though each of them (except the fourth and fifth) is expressed in a negative form, all have positive implications. The first commandment not only prohibits the inclusion of any other "gods" in Israel's formal worship, but also positively directs Israel to serve the LORD alone. The second commandment is exceptional for Israel's time and place, forbidding the people to make any image of the LORD or any other god. In the ancient Near East, only the Israelites have no concrete image of their god to bow down to. This command alone would astonish Israel's neighbors and raise the most profound questions about the nature of Israel's God. In that time, to have no image in one's sanctuary would be taken to mean that one believed in no god at all. But this prohibition of worshipping an image is extremely important. The Israelites have to realize that theirs was no ordinary "god," but the very LORD of heaven and earth himself. Similarly, though he has revealed himself to Israel as Yahweh, they are forbidden to *use* that name in an attempt to exercise magical power. The third commandment thus teaches that the LORD is to be respected, and the people must make no attempt to manipulate his name for their own purposes. The fourth commandment commends work as worthy and necessary—"Six days you shall labor"—but it also firmly places work within the context of the people's relationship to God, lest work become an end in itself.

The fifth to tenth commandments regulate relationships among God's people. Within healthy family structures, new generations are to be inducted into life among God's people. The fifth commandment insists on parental authority and responsibility. In the remaining five "words," God forbids murder, adultery, stealing, false testimony, and coveting among his chosen people. Theirs is to be a community in which the divine *shalom* of peace and harmony characterizes life within the family and among neighbors.

The Ten Commandments are good news. They tell Israel how to live so as to please God and display to the nations God's creational purposes for humanity. Because the LORD is the Creator, his instructions fit with the way he has made the world. This is particularly clear in the fourth commandment, which links the human pattern of work and rest to God's own work and rest in making the world: the lives of his people are to mirror his own life. The commandments are thus the keys to living fully human lives; they are certainly not intended as horrible constraints to make life difficult. We must remember that they were given first to the Israelites living in the ancient Near East, and our own interpretation of their meaning should account for this context. They remain profoundly relevant to our lives before God, but we cannot necessarily apply them in the same ways in which the ancient nation of Israel was to observe them. In that context, there were severe penalties for breaking the commandments: for example, anyone who worshipped another god would be put to death. Though we continue to learn from this that God takes idolatry extremely seriously, we must recognize that in our own pluralistic twenty-first-century context, it would not be a good idea to *legislate* in this way. Similarly, Christians themselves differ as to how the fourth commandment (keeping the Sabbath) should be honored in our own day.

In 20:22–23:33 many detailed stipulations follow from the general commands. These deal with a variety of subjects such as worship, slavery, assault, kidnapping, sexual offenses, economic activities, religious festivals, and the care of animals, among many others. All of life comes within the scope of the LORD's reign over his people. It is fascinating to see just how wide-ranging these laws are. Take 23:5, for example. If you spot the donkey of a person you hate, and it is unable to get up because of its burden, you must not ignore it but must help it get to its feet. The law shows genuine concern for animal welfare, amid a realistic sense of how easily we can fall into quarrels with our neighbors. God is under no illusion that his people are perfect.

In Exodus 24 the covenant is ratified with a ritual ceremony as the Israelites commit themselves to obeying it. Moses recites the laws that the Israelites are agreeing to and then writes them down. Next, he builds an altar and sets up twelve pillars, which stand for the twelve tribes of Israel. The covenant is with the *whole* people of God and, like the pillars, it is to be permanent. Finally, Moses dashes half of the blood from the sacrifices against the altar and sprinkles half on the people. Sacrifice is necessary for sinners to come into God's presence. The blood is referred to as the "blood of the covenant," and this is a phrase that Jesus will use at the Last Supper. The blood also signifies the seriousness of the relationship: it is a way of saying, "May this happen to us, may our own blood be poured out, if we fail to keep the terms of the agreement." As the ratification ceremony ends, the seventy elders—along with Moses and Aaron, Nadab and Abihu—go up the mountain (24:9–11). There they have an extraordinary experience, for they are permitted to *see* "the God of Israel." This privilege is a tremendous confirmation of the relationship with God that is central to the covenant. As in other biblical accounts of people "seeing" God (*theophanies*), we are not told about the appearance of God himself, whom no one has seen (cf. 33:23; John 1:18; 1 John 4:12). Rather, the text describes certain elements that surround the vision of God's person—in this case the pavement under his feet. The communion between God and his people that is central to the covenant is wonderfully enacted in Exodus 24:11: the elders see God, and they eat and drink. God has promised a relationship with his people, and here we see that promise well on its way to being fulfilled.

## GOD COMES TO DWELL WITH HIS PEOPLE

Though the elders' vision of God is transitory, God does intend for his presence to become a permanent part of the life of Israel. He instructs Moses to gather from among the Israelites the materials required to build a complex tent structure, the tabernacle, and then gives detailed instructions for its construction. The formal worship life of Israel is to take place here. The priests and Levites will be in charge, officiating over the sacrifices and offerings of the Israelites. But the main point of the tabernacle is that it is a portable sanctuary, God's personal residence among his covenant people:

> Then I will dwell among the Israelites and be their God. They will know that I am the LORD their God, who brought them out of Egypt so that I might dwell among them. I am the LORD their God. (29:45–46)

Nearly a third of Exodus is taken up with the detailed plans for the tabernacle, and then these details are repeated as it is actually being built. As Fretheim notes, "Thirteen chapters having to do with the tabernacle is a long stretch of non-story that can be wearisome reading."[53] But these exhaustive details make an important point: such a residence cannot be taken lightly. God himself is coming to live among his people, and it is worth pausing to look over the shape and nature of his official residence. Another reason for this "delay" in the story is that the worship of God is what Israel is all about. Exodus charts the course of this nation from slavery to worship, and servants of the great King will want to know every detail of his life in their midst. Once they were forced into building for the Pharoah in Egypt; now they willingly donate their materials and expertise to build God's house in their midst.

A further reason for duplicate descriptions of the tabernacle in Exodus is that between the two accounts is the record of a rebellious episode among the people against God and his servant Moses (Exodus 32). This outbreak of apostasy threatens the covenant relationship itself. The Israelites are waiting for Moses to descend the mountain, where he is speaking with God. They become impatient and make for themselves a golden calf, even while God is giving Moses instructions for the construction of his dwelling place. Calf images were common in the ancient Near East at this time. This golden calf is intended to be a completely different god or an image of the messenger of the LORD; either way it is a catastrophic error, comparable to Adam and Eve's mutiny in Genesis 3. The making of the calf is completely at odds with God's revelation of himself when he instructs Moses on making the tabernacle: (1) The people seek to make what God has already provided or will provide.

(2) The idea to make the image is a human initiative. (3) The materials for it are demanded (not given voluntarily), reminding readers of the old life of slavery in Egypt. (4) It is a quick, human job, without the careful preparations befitting the Holy One of Israel. And (5) the LORD, the invisible, holy God, is turned into a visible object that can neither speak nor act. "The ironic effect [of making the calf] is that the people forfeit the very divine presence they had hoped to bind more closely to themselves."[54] The Israelites thus violate the first and second of God's commandments. Only as a result of Moses' appeal to God (on the basis of God's own reputation and promise) is disaster avoided. The second account of the tabernacle details (following the story of the golden calf) indicates that God remains graciously committed to his covenant with Israel.

Exodus concludes with God's coming to his tabernacle to dwell there (40:34–38). God's occasional appearances to Israel have now yielded to his permanent presence in their midst. And the tabernacle *moves with them* wherever they go; God journeys with his people. But the tabernacle suggests much more than this: it is an emblem of the full restoration of God's presence within the whole of his creation, just as he originally intended:

> At this small, lonely place in the midst of the chaos of the wilderness, a new creation comes into being. In the midst of disorder there is order. The tabernacle is the world order as God intended writ small in Israel. The priests of the sanctuary going about their appointed courses is like everything in creation performing its liturgical service—the sun, the trees, human beings. The people of Israel carefully encamped around the tabernacle in their midst constitutes the beginnings of God's bringing creation back to what it was originally intended to be. The tabernacle is a realization of God's created order in history; both reflect the glory of God in their midst.
>
> Moreover, this microcosm of creation is the beginning of a macrocosmic effort on God's part. In and through this people, God is on the move to a new creation for all. God's presence in the tabernacle is a statement about God's intended presence in the entire world. The glory manifest there is to stream out into the larger world. The shining of Moses' face in the wake of the experience of the divine glory . . . is to become characteristic of Israel as a whole, a radiating out into the larger world of those glorious effects of God's dwelling among Israel. As a kingdom of priests, . . . they have a role of mediating this glory to the entire cosmos.[55]

As the story of Exodus reaches its end, considerable progress has been made toward the formation of God's people. They are established in formal covenant relationship with God, and they have both the law and the tabernacle. Their life has been given both an ethical shape and a liturgical shape.[56] What they need now is a place of their own.

However, having God living in this people's midst is not going to be easy or straightforward. How are these sinful mortals going to cope with this awesome and holy reality among them? After the golden calf incident, God does reveal himself to Moses as compassionate and gracious, slow to anger, abounding in love and faithfulness, maintaining love to thousands, and forgiving wickedness, rebellion, and sin (34:6). But he also says that he does not leave the guilty unpunished. Indeed, the people's sin and its effects will reverberate to the third and fourth generations.

### Leviticus: Living with a Holy God

This is precisely where Leviticus fits in. Leviticus is all about protocol for maintaining a right relationship with the King, whose royal residence is within the Israelites' camp. The first seven chapters of Leviticus deal with different kinds of sacrifices and offerings an Israelite can bring to the tabernacle and how these rituals are to be performed. So, for example, one who sins unintentionally is to take a sin offering to the tabernacle and offer it there. By this act, atonement is made for the offending party, and God gives forgiveness (Leviticus 4:27–35). An Israelite who wants to thank God for something can offer a fellowship offering (7:11). Leviticus 8 and 9 describe the people whom God appointed to work in the tabernacle, how they are ordained to their tasks, and how they begin their work. Thus, as God takes up residence among his people, he graciously provides a comprehensive apparatus for maintaining the relationship between him and them.

God is present within the tabernacle and its structured worship at a particular place among the Israelites. "God chooses a place because God has entered into history with a people for whom place is important."[57] The tabernacle provides order for Israel's worship and "a tangible aspect for the divine presence."[58] But this was never meant to detract from God's intention that his presence should pervade the entire life of the people. God's pervasive presence is what the next chapters are all about. In 10:10 (NRSV) the LORD alerts Aaron to the priestly responsibility to "distinguish between the holy and the common, between the unclean and the clean" in relation to animals, birds, different kinds of food, and various medical conditions.

For the modern reader, this presents a most unusual way of regulating one's life, but the best way to understand all these regulations has emerged from studies of how ancient cultures structured their lives. What appear to us to be random and strange regulations have profound *symbolic* significance for the Israelites. Gordon Wenham notes, for instance, that among both the birds and animals there are "clean" and "unclean" species; all the "clean" birds and animals may be eaten, but only some may be used for sacrifice:

> This threefold division of the bird and animal kingdoms corresponds to the divisions among human beings. Mankind falls into two main groups, Israel and Gentiles. Within Israel only one group, the priests, may approach the altar to offer sacrifice. This matches the law's understanding of sacred space. Outside the camp is the abode of Gentiles and unclean Israelites. Ordinary Israelites dwell inside the camp, but only priests may approach the altar or enter the tabernacle tent.
>
> These distinctions served to remind Israel of her special status as God's chosen people. The food laws not only remind Israel of her distinctiveness, but they also served to enforce it. . . . The food laws symbolize that Israel is God's people, called to enjoy life, while Gentile idolaters are by and large opposed to him and his people, and face death.[59]

Indeed, this kind of symbolism permeates Israel's life. Each week Israel keeps the Sabbath day as a reminder of what its life is really all about. And the Israelite year is punctuated by regular festivals during which Israel pauses before God to remember and to celebrate. An example of these festivals is Passover, when Israel would recall before God its deliverance from slavery in Egypt. Another major festival was the Feast of Weeks, celebrated at the end of the grain harvest. Its New Testament name, Pentecost, comes from the fact that it was celebrated fifty days after the first sheaf had been offered to God. God gives all these rituals to the Israelites as a means of grace to regularly recenter their lives in him and all that he had done for them (see Leviticus 23 for a list of festivals).

### Numbers: Journeying to the Land

At the conclusion of Leviticus, Israel is still at Mount Sinai. Numbers tells the story of their journey from there to the plains of Moab, just outside the promised land. Before they set off, at God's instruction a census is taken of Israelite men in each tribe who are over the age of twenty and able to serve in the army. The group of slaves brought out of Egypt is being shaped into a well-ordered unit ready for military conquest of the promised land. The total number of men is given as 600,000, which would mean that the total number of Israelites was over two million. God has promised to make a great nation out of Abraham's descendants, and Israel now shows every sign of such emerging greatness.[60]

Initially, preparations for the journey go well. The first ten chapters of Numbers are full of optimism as final preparations are made. This optimism is wonderfully captured in the priestly blessing that the LORD gives to Aaron and his sons as his own blessing upon Israel:

> The LORD bless you and keep you;
> The LORD make his face shine upon you and be gracious to you;
> The LORD turn his face toward you and give you peace. (6:24–26)

In the Hebrew, each line of this blessing is longer than the previous one, and the last line ends upon the word "peace" (*shalom*). There is every optimism that this is the goal of Israel's journey as the people set out for the promised land, their God himself going with them to lead the way.

Sadly, such optimism again is blunted. Wilderness travels are not easy, and despite having God in their midst, some of the Israelites soon start moaning about their new hardships, until God reacts in anger (Numbers 11). Fire burns out from the tabernacle and consumes parts of the camp. The Israelites call out to Moses for help. Only when he intervenes for them, crying out to God on their behalf, does the fire die down. Even after such a warning, the people continue to grumble, even complaining about the menu and the lack of meat! Then there are leadership difficulties: Miriam and Aaron start to mutter about Moses' leadership and to gossip about his marriage (Numbers 12).

The biggest crisis in the story of the early wilderness journey comes with the Israelites' response to the report of the spies who have been sent ahead to scout out the promised land (Numbers 13–14). They say that the land is wonderfully fertile and would make a fine homeland for Israel, but its people are powerful and their cities well fortified. The reported strength of the enemy engenders fear, and the Israelites' faith in the LORD collapses. They become depressed and disgruntled, complaining that God has brought them this far only to kill them. Once again, only Moses' intercession prevents God from destroying all of them. God stays his hand but vows that none of this unbelieving generation will enter the promised land. The result is that, rather than proceeding forthwith to the land, the Israelites wander in the wilderness around Kadesh for forty years until the faithless first generation has indeed died out.

After these forty long, tiring years, the Israelites are led onto the plains of Moab, just east of the promised land (Numbers 22). There another census is taken, to count the new generation of Israelites (Numbers 26). The area west of the Jordan River is conquered and distributed among certain of the tribes (Numbers 32). Israel is now poised to take possession of the promised land lying on the other side of the Jordan.

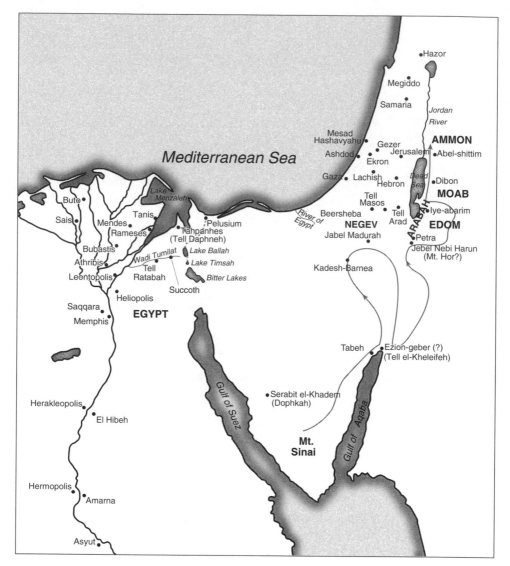

**Figure 11** *Wilderness Wanderings*

## *Deuteronomy: On the Borders of the Land*

Clearly, even for this new generation of Israelites, it is going to be no easy task to live up to God's covenant standards. The land lies ahead, and with it lies the possibility of rest and of the fulfillment of God's promises to Abraham. Deuteronomy records the sermons of Moses to the Israelites as they prepare to enter the land. Moses himself will not enter the promised land, but in Deuteronomy we have a record of the speeches he makes to prepare the people for their new task:

> Their immediate situation is outside the land, poised to enter it. In that pause, the possibility of divine blessing spread before them, lies the dramatic power of the book. Israel is in a moment of "decision." . . . Between their beginning and their end consists the immediate challenge to live in the promised land, according to the covenant with Yahweh.[61]

In this context, Moses' sermons present Israel with a vision of society brought together under the authority of the Lord alone, a people bound to God by his covenant with them. This covenant is now renewed.

In his first sermon (Deuteronomy 1:6–4:40), Moses reviews the recent history of the Israelites, the forty years since they left Sinai, and reminds the present generation of Israelites of the important lessons to be learned from their parents' experience. The people's future well-being in the land will depend on their loving and serving God from the heart. Moses' second sermon revisits in detail the law that is central to the covenant and expands it in relation to the Israelites' future life in the land. Moses reminds the Israelites of the Ten Words and then issues a powerful exhortation to love God by obeying these laws and making them absolutely central to their lives and their children's lives:

> Hear O Israel: The Lord our God, the Lord is one. Love the Lord your God with all your heart and with all your soul and with all your strength. These commandments that I give you today are to be upon your hearts. Impress them on your children. Talk about them when you sit at home and when you walk along the road, when you lie down and when you get up. Tie them as symbols on your hands and bind them on your foreheads. Write them on the doorframes of your houses and on your gates. (6:4–8)

The Lord intends that he should instruct Israel in every area of life. Only then will Israel truly become a light to the nations. "There is not a square inch of life of which he does not say, '*That is mine!*'"[62] Religion is no merely *private* affair: the Lord wants his law (*torah*, "instruction") to permeate every part of his people's experience. His words should frame the personal life of each individual (being present in the mind and the heart, whether one is waking or lying down).[63] They should shape the thoughts and actions of all his people, each day of their lives (being present on both the "forehead" and the "hand").[64] The torah claims both family life and public life. Upon leaving the house one sees God's words of instruction written on the gate. Upon returning, one sees them again, written on the door of the house.

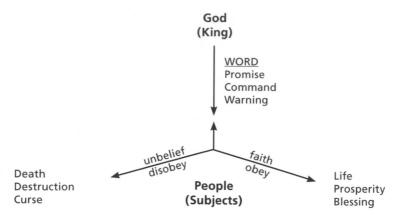

**Figure 12** *Covenant Structure*

The detailed laws that follow in Deuteronomy all relate to how to make this vision a reality. "In this covenant, religion and politics are one. Israel fulfils its political obligations by virtue of its loyalty to Yahweh, which has an integral social dimension. There is not only a theology of the gift of the land, but a vision, sketched in the laws, of how the land should be held. The laws bring the concept of the rule of Yahweh down to particular instances."[65]

Modern readers of the Bible often find the instruction to drive out the other nations from the land difficult to stomach (Numbers 33:50–54; Deuteronomy 7). We should note, however, that this part of the biblical story does show sensitivity to the potential injustice inherent in the Israelites' conquest of lands that has been the home of other people. According to Genesis 15:16, God does not take the land away from its first inhabitants until their sin has reached such depths that they have in effect forfeited their right to it. They *will* be disinherited, but this decision is just. In fact, the behavior of the Canaanites reaches such deep depravity that judgment, when it does come at the hands of the Israelites, is long overdue. Because the Israelites must be fully committed to the LORD, the presence of other cultures with other gods alongside the people of Israel would present a constant temptation to idolatry, undermining Israel's identity as God's covenant people. This is why in Deuteronomy (as in 7:5; cf. Numbers 33:52) the instruction to displace the former inhabitants of the land is part of the exposition of the first commandment: "You shall have no other gods."[66]

Moses thus has reminded the Israelites of the covenant and its implications for the whole of their life in the land. He sets before them two options for their future: judgment or blessing (Deuteronomy 27–28). If they respond to God's word in faith and obedience, they will experience life, prosperity, and blessing. If they respond in unbelief and disobedience, then they will face death, destruction, and curse (30:11–20). Moses urges the people to choose life and blessing by pursuing obedience to the LORD, then renews the covenant with them and appoints Joshua as his successor. God allows Moses to see the land of promise, though not to enter it. The book of Deuteronomy ends with Moses' death on the border of Canaan.

## Scene 2: A Land for His People

### *Joshua: The Gift of the Land*

The book of Joshua tells the story of the Israelites' conquest of Canaan under Joshua's leadership. Taking possession of their own land is a huge step forward in the story of the nation of slaves who left Egypt: "At this moment Israel does indeed become a new creation, a slave becomes an heir, a helpless child becomes a mature inheritor."[67] Although the conquest is achieved by means of several battles, the narrative stresses throughout that the Israelites are entirely dependent upon the LORD for their success. Indeed, the land is a gift from the LORD and a fulfillment of his promises to Abraham, Isaac, Jacob, and Moses. The LORD himself commands Joshua to prepare the Israelites to cross the Jordan River and enter the land he is about to give to them (Joshua 1:2–3). Joshua is exhorted to be strong and courageous because the LORD is going to give the land to the Israelites, thereby fulfilling his promise to their forefathers (1:6).

Joshua prepares for the conquest by sending spies to survey the land. When these men return with their report, it does not have the tone of fear that dominated the report of the spies whom Moses forty years earlier sent into Canaan (Joshua 2; cf. Numbers 13). The spies are given refuge in the house of a prostitute named Rahab, who hides them from the king of Jericho. She tells them how the LORD's reputation has spread even here in Canaan, creating fear among the inhabitants of the land. Rahab secures a promise from the spies that she and her family will be treated kindly when the Israelites come in force to conquer the land. Back on the east side of the Jordan, the Israelites receive their spies' favorable report. Thus encouraged, they set out for their new homeland. They are led across the Jordan by the ark of the covenant, which holds back the waters and enables them to cross. Twelve stones are taken from the riverbed and set up as a memorial just within the boundary of Canaan, to remind them that it is the LORD who enables the Israelites to cross this river and take possession of the land.

This conquest is the LORD's work, as illustrated vividly just west of the river near Jericho: an angel appears to Joshua with a sword in his hand. When Joshua asks him whose side he is on, the angel replies, "Neither, but as commander of the army of the LORD I have now come" (5:13–15). In words reminiscent of God's command to Moses at the burning bush, the angel tells Joshua to take off his sandals, for he stands on holy ground. Clearly, it is not Joshua but the LORD himself who is the general in charge of this campaign: the LORD is the one who will grant success to the Israelites.

The details of the conquest of Jericho repeatedly reinforce this concept. Under the LORD's instruction, the Israelites march around Jericho for seven days, with the ark (representing the presence of the LORD) leading the way. On the seventh day the walls of Jericho collapse when the trumpet is sounded and the people shout. The Israelites attack the city and destroy every living thing in it, in obedience to the LORD's command (Joshua 6:21). They spare only Rahab and her family.

Several aspects of this "holy war" are hard for us to understand. Was it really necessary, was it just, to kill all the citizens of Jericho and their animals? We will discuss this further below, but suffice it here to note that God is quite clear in his instructions to the Israelites. They *must* fight in this way. Indeed, when they first attempt (just after their defeat of Jericho) to conquer the town of Ai, they are defeated precisely because just one man among them, Achan, of the tribe of Judah, has disobeyed God. He has kept back some of the plunder from Jericho for himself (Joshua 7). This disobedience is taken very seriously, and Achan is stoned to death. After this, they successfully conquer Ai (Joshua 8), but this time the Israelites are allowed to carry off the livestock and other goods from the city—as the LORD has instructed Joshua. The earlier problem at Ai caused by Achan's sin is a reminder that Israel will be successful in the land only if the people remain obedient to the LORD and keep the terms of his covenant.

After Ai, Joshua fulfills Moses' commands in Deuteronomy 27:1–8 by renewing the covenant between the LORD and the Israelites at Mount Ebal (Joshua 8:30–35). The Israelites assemble on both sides of the ark of the covenant, half of them in front of Mount Gerizim and half in front of Mount Ebal. Joshua has copied all the words of the law onto stones, and in the ceremony he reads them to the Israelites so that they clearly understand the options of blessings or curses that lie before them. God is giving the land to the Israelites so that they can live in it as his people and thus be a light to the nations. But (as they will learn to their cost)

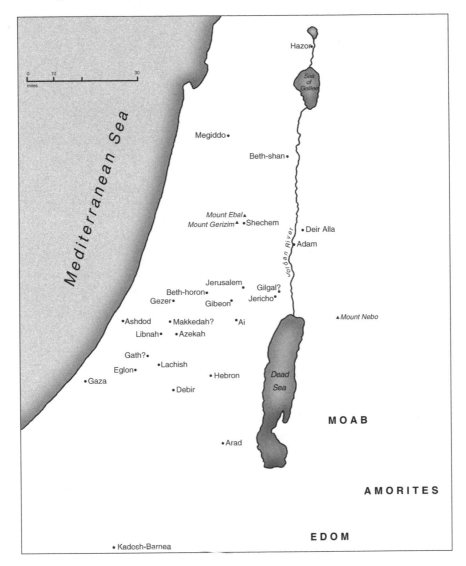

**Figure 13** *Conquest of the Land*

he will not tolerate a lifestyle among them that is radically at odds with his own character.

Joshua 9–12 tells the stories of the campaigns by which Joshua and the Israelites conquer the entire land. The Gibeonites trick the Israelites into establishing a treaty with them (Joshua 9), but this is the only group with whom they make a treaty. Leaders and peoples of other Canaanite

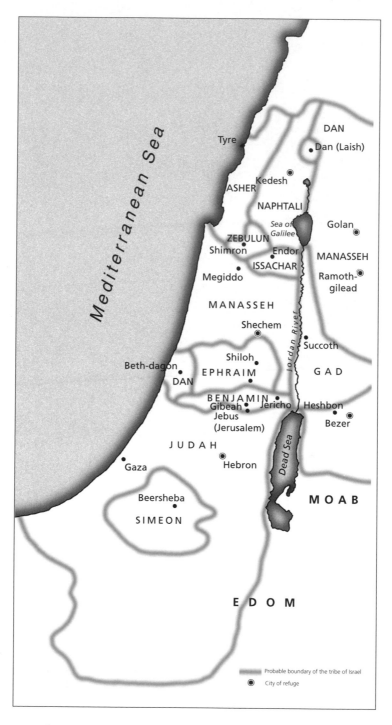

**Figure 14** *Land Distribution among the Twelve Tribes*

groups are put to death as the Israelite conquest moves across the land. At the end of this phase of conquest, a summary is given: "Joshua took the entire land, just as the LORD had directed Moses, and he gave it as an inheritance to Israel according to their tribal divisions. Then the land had rest from war" (11:23). Joshua 13–19 tells how the land was allocated to each of the tribes of Israel. The inheritance of each tribe is assigned by lot (14:2–3): nine and a half tribes receive inheritances west of the Jordan, and two and a half tribes are given land east of the Jordan. Cities of refuge are set up in the land (Joshua 20) to ensure justice for those who kill someone accidentally. Towns are assigned for the Levites (Joshua 21), who do not have a separate area for themselves because of their priestly role. But since two tribes (Ephraim and Manasseh) come from Joseph, there are still twelve tribes inheriting land (14:4).

The book of Joshua ends with the Israelites established in the land. This represents a major stage in the fulfillment of God's promises to Abraham, even though the road to this point has not been easy. The promised land for Abraham's descendants has now become a reality in the life of Israel. The stage is set for Israel to live as a light to the nations. God's response to mutiny in his good creation has been to elect one man, Abraham, and then to recover part of the earth and to place Abraham's descendants there.[68] Israel in the land is meant to be a taste of what God intends for the whole of his creation.

Once more we are reminded of God's concern for the whole of life as he has made it. Brueggemann rightly states: "This concern for a material, physical promise gives credibility to Christianity as a religion of materialism. When Christianity went spiritual and denied its proper focus on land it rightly earned the strictures of Marxism."[69] This particular place on God's earth is a gift to the Israelites; Joshua describes it as "this good land" (23:15; cf. Deuteronomy 6:10–11):

It is a good land, the work of the good word. . . . The land matches the word that gave it. It fulfils every anticipation of the wilderness: water—brooks, fountains, springs; food—wheat, barley, vines, fig trees, pomegranates, olives, honey; plenty—without scarcity . . . without lack . . . minerals—iron, copper. . . . Such a land makes possible the living of a less exposed, less vulnerable life, the kind it had yearned for both in slavery and in sojourn.[70]

The land is like a second Eden. And as for Adam and Eve in the garden, Israel is not free to exploit the land at will. Israel always lives in the land with the LORD, and his laws contain many instructions about how to manage the land properly. In particular, the law of the Sabbath is a powerful reminder that the LORD is the one who sustains the creation and that there is more to life than consumerism.[71]

Will Israel live up to this challenge? Great and wonderful possibilities are set before her. Joshua claims that the land is to be the place of rest for the Israelites, but it is also a place of testing, of temptation. By no means are all of the Canaanites out of the land.[72] The Israelites have too often shown their disposition to rebel against the LORD. During Joshua's life the people do keep the covenant (Joshua 24:31), but their future in the land now given them will depend on how they choose to live after Joshua's death. In his farewell speech to the leaders of Israel, Joshua reminds them that the land is a gift from the LORD and that their future well-being depends on how they love and obey him. Joshua assembles the tribes at Shechem, where he reviews their history and exhorts them to decide whom to serve, the gods of the Amorites or the LORD (24:15). The Israelites respond by committing themselves to serving the LORD, and Joshua renews the covenant with them.

The book of Joshua is clearly an essential part of the biblical story. Without it, Israel would not be established as a nation in a land, and God's plan for it would run aground. But as mentioned earlier, Joshua presents difficulties for the modern reader. Indeed, how we decide to approach the book of Joshua will have important implications for how we tell the whole story of the Bible. Even among Christians who do read the Bible as a story, some see Jesus' teachings as standing in radical contradiction to certain concepts illustrated in the "holy war" of the book of Joshua. Many modern readers find the wholesale destruction of Canaanites particularly hard to accept, counting it as too much at odds with our contemporary morality. One cannot resolve this difficulty entirely, but there are several clues within the story line of the Bible that may help us to understand God's instructions to his people in the time of Joshua.[73]

We have already recognized that God patiently waits until the evil in the land of Canaan has grown to a point at which he is compelled to judge its people (Genesis 15:16). In Deuteronomy 20:16–18 the command to destroy the inhabitants of the land is motivated further by the danger that the Israelites might succumb to idolatry.[74] Above all else, Israel is to be characterized by the worship of the LORD alone (the first commandment). And if the Israelites live among Canaanites, they are in danger of being lured into the worship of other "gods." "It is thus in the context of the whole struggle with heathenism that we are to see this terrible call to drive out the heathen nations. [The book of Joshua] is the story of a group of people, few in number and almost unbelievably weak and fickle in their spiritual loyalties, battling against mighty forces which were degrading, seductive and ruthless."[75] Today it is hard for us to take idolatry and its dangers this seriously. But a key to understanding the command to clear Canaan of the Canaanites is to recall

God's holiness and to be reminded of just how much is at stake in the Israelites' remaining faithful to the LORD.

### Judges: Failure to Be a Light to the Nations

Unlike Moses, Joshua is not replaced as leader of the Israelites. The expectation appears to be that the Israelites will live directly under the LORD's reign with some help from elders whom Moses and Joshua have appointed. Government is decentralized. But Israel does not flourish under such a tribal system. The book of Judges tells of what happens once Joshua and his generation have died—and the news is not good.

In recent years, the tradition of foxhunting by red-coated riders following a pack of hounds has become a controversial issue in England, with strong views for and against it. When the British parliament discussed the issue, supporters and opponents demonstrated outside Westminster. The opponents of foxhunting had a most effective, rhythmic, chilling chant: "It's evil, it's evil." There is something like this refrain in the book of Judges: time and again the Israelites do what is evil in the eyes of the LORD, so that the LORD hands them over to their enemies. "Israel is chosen by God but too weak to live up to its calling. This conflict between choice and weakness creates the dramatic tension of the unfolding narrative."[76] Judges tells the story of a spiral down into rebellion and disaster at every level in the nation of Israel.

The book of Judges begins by noting that Israel has not expelled all the Canaanites from the land (Judges 1). Judges 2:1–5 describes a covenant court case. The LORD comes to judge his people for their refusal to wage war against pagan idolatry. Judgment is pronounced: God will not drive out the remaining pagan nations, and their gods will be a snare to Israel. The temptation to the Israelites to follow the old "gods" of Canaan remains. And the Israelites regularly succumb to the temptation, serving "the Baals" (2:11–13). Baal is a fertility god, and the plural ("Baals") indicates not a plurality of gods but several local manifestations of one god. The Israelites, unlike the Canaanites, are new to agriculture. The seductive attraction of Canaanite religion for the newcomers is that it promises fertility of the land and thus economic success. Furthermore, the worship of Baal offers immediate physical gratification:

> It was not only great business to worship Baal but great fun! The Baal cult operated on the principle of sympathetic magic, so in order to ensure fertility of people, animals, and crops, a person would engage in sexual intercourse with a cult prostitute—male or female—at the local Baal shrine. The purpose was to inspire Baal to act likewise on the person's behalf and thus to ensure fertility in all areas of life.[77]

There thus was a certain perverse logic to Israelite idolatry, but the LORD was not impressed. In anger God judges his people.

God's judgment is carried out in cycles that characterize Israel's life and the book of Judges: (1) The Israelites sin by worshipping the Baals and the Ashtoreths. (2) This violates the covenant and provokes the LORD to anger. (3) The LORD therefore hands the Israelites over to their enemies. (4) Because of distress under oppression by their enemies, the Israelites cry out to the LORD for deliverance. Finally, (5) the LORD raises up a military deliverer (a "judge") to deliver them from their oppression (2:11–19).[78] This pattern would run its course. All would be well for a while, and then (as the judge died and the Israelites forgot the lesson, they once more slid into idolatry) the whole sorry cycle would repeat itself.

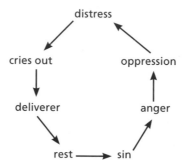

**Figure 15** *Cycles of Judgment*

The first "judge" mentioned is Othniel, the younger brother of Caleb (who has been Joshua's right-hand man). Because of Israel's apostasy, the LORD has "sold" them into the hands of Cushan-Rishathaim, king of Aram Naharaim (3:7–11). The Israelites are subject to this king for eight years, then they cry out to the LORD, and he raises up Othniel as the judge to rescue them. The Spirit of the LORD comes upon Othniel, and he delivers Israel from the grip of King Cushan. Then Israel enjoys peace for forty years until, "Once again . . ."

The cycle of disobedience continues throughout the book, but the level of sin worsens until the circular pattern of disobedience-oppression-repentance-deliverance becomes a downward spiral into chaos. The successive judges become more and more flawed; the Israelites embrace debauchery, rape, and murder (Judges 19). At last the nation is divided by civil war. The last of the judges is Samson, an image of what Israel herself has become (Judges 13–16).

Samson is a Nazirite, an Israelite who has made "a vow of separation" to the LORD to abstain from certain things (such as wine) for a specified period. The three areas of life prohibited to the Nazirite are fertility (symbolized by grape products), sympathetic magic, and the cult of the dead. These are the main religious practices the Israelites are tempted to adopt from the Canaanites.[79] Thus, the separation of a Nazirite symbolizes for all Israelites how they should live holy lives, not contaminating themselves with these pagan practices.

Separation and holiness should be hallmarks of a man like Samson, who is a Nazirite for life (13:4–7).[80] And Samson indeed achieves great things for God, delivering the Israelites from the Philistines through many superhuman feats of strength. But his own life is a mess. He marries one Philistine woman, consorts with prostitutes, and then becomes fatally attracted to yet another Philistine woman, Delilah (Judges 16). Through Delilah the Philistines discover the secret of Samson's strength—his hair! Samson tells Delilah, "No razor has ever been used on my head, because I have been a Nazirite set apart to God since birth. If my head were shaved, my strength would leave me, and I would become as weak as any other man" (16:17). While he is sleeping, Delilah has his hair cut off; when he awakens, his strength is gone. The Philistines gouge his eyes out and throw him into prison.

But the LORD allows Samson his revenge against the Philistines. At a special feast, the Philistine rulers celebrate their god Dagon's power over the Israelites (and over the Israelites' God). For some entertainment they have Samson brought before them. However, by now his hair has grown, and his strength has returned. Samson pulls down the pagan temple on top of the crowd gathered for the celebration. The story of Samson concludes, "Thus [Samson] killed many more when he died than while he lived" (16:30). This is a strange epitaph, and Samson's complex life symbolizes what Israel itself has become:

> Samson's awareness of his separation to God, and yet his disregard for it, his fatal attraction to foreign women, his wilfulness and his presumption all hold up the mirror to the behavior of Israel itself. So too does his fate. . . . Samson dies, Israel does not, but neither is it delivered . . . and Samson's tragic fate makes us wonder to what straits Yahweh will have to reduce Israel before it, too, is reconciled to its separateness.[81]

The book of Judges begins and ends with war. At its beginning the nation is engaged in a holy war; by the end of the book, the Israelites are fighting one another. Throughout Judges we see the tendency of the Israelites to do "what was right in their own eyes" (17:6; 21:25 NRSV). By the time of the last judge, Samson, even Israel's ruler habitually obeys no higher authority than his own corrupt will. The perfect standard of God's law has been all but forgotten in Israel.

### Samuel: Israel Transformed into a Kingdom

#### THE NEED FOR A KING

One reason given in the book of Judges for Israel's rapid descent into chaos is that "in those days Israel had no king; everyone did as he saw fit" (Judges 21:25). This raises an important question: What leadership does Israel need if it is to live effectively as God's covenant people?[82] Does Israel *need* a king? Of course, in one important sense Israel already does have a king: its king is the LORD! But what kind of human leadership is appropriate to ensure that Israel remains faithful to the LORD?

The books of 1 and 2 Samuel start with the story of a barren woman and a barren nation. The woman is Hannah. Like the Israelites, who at this time are being oppressed by their enemies, Hannah cries out to the LORD to take away the stigma of her infertility (1 Samuel 1). The nation too is barren in the sense that it is not producing the fruits of obedience to God's covenant. Even the formal worship of God in Israel has become corrupt and lost its sense of God's holiness. The sons of Eli the priest are completely self-serving and without any "regard for the LORD" (2:12). The seriousness of the situation is well captured in the name given to one of Eli's grandsons: "Ichabod," meaning "the glory has departed" (4:21). The true glory of the nation, God's presence among the Israelites, literally departs from them when the Philistines capture the ark of the covenant.

This "ark" is a highly decorated wooden box containing a copy of the Ten Words and thus symbolizing the living presence of God among his people. The Israelites have begun to treat it as if it were a magical charm, a way to bring God in on their side when they are threatened by enemies. When Israel suffers one defeat in battle against the Philistines, the ark is fetched to the next skirmish in an effort to guarantee a victory. But instead of achieving victory, the Israelites are crushed, thirty thousand of them slaughtered, and the ark itself captured by the Philistines. In this rout, both of Eli's sons are killed. Eli himself dies of shock and grief when he hears the dreadful news.

#### GOD'S KIND OF KING

Israel is indeed barren. Though the nation has not actually been taken out of the land, God has departed from it and is living amid its enemy! Once again, Israel's only hope is that God will bring new life out of its barrenness and return to his people. And return he does: the ark's presence among the Philistines causes such havoc that they are desperately glad to let it return to Israel (1 Samuel 5–6). God also answers Hannah's prayer, delivering her from her barrenness and, at the same time, delivering Israel from its lack of spiritual integrity. God gives Hannah a son, Samuel, who is also the last and greatest of the "judges." Like Samson, Samuel is a Nazirite (1:11, 24–28). But *unlike* Samson, Samuel is the genuine article. He is a charismatic leader who courageously delivers Israel from its enemies and wisely settles disputes among the Israelites themselves: "Samuel continued as judge over Israel all the days of his life. From year to year he went on a circuit from Bethel to Gilgal to Mizpah, judging Israel in all those places" (7:15). Samuel is both judge and priest, and he is also honored as a prophet because of the reliability of his words (3:19–20) and his integrity in life (12:3–4).

Samuel also bears some similarity to Moses in that he too admonishes the Israelites to turn away from idols and serve the LORD from their hearts (1 Samuel 12). But perhaps his great role is as God-appointed kingmaker. Though his own sons Joel and Abijah are appointed to be judges in Samuel's old age, they turn out to be more like Eli's sons than like their own father, Samuel. Thus it comes about that the leaders of the tribes of Israel come to Samuel and instead request a king "such as all the other nations have" (8:1–5).

These few words generate a heated debate among Samuel, God, and the elders of Israel, for the question of who is to lead the people is central to the very identity of Israel (1 Samuel 8). If Israel is to be a light to the nations and bring blessing to them, then it must be different from them. But in asking for a king, it seems to want to be like the other nations. Samuel complains to the LORD, and the LORD has him warn the Israelites about the dangers of monarchy (8:11–18; cf. Deuteronomy 17:14–20). But the Israelites are adamant: they want a king to lead them and to provide military success. They do *not* express any desire to live more obediently as God's covenant people. At last the LORD tells Samuel to listen to the Israelites and to give them a king. But God will make the choice, and he instructs Samuel to anoint Saul as king over Israel.

Although the details are not spelled out, we are told that Samuel explains to the Israelites the "regulations for the kingship," which he writes down and places in the tabernacle before the LORD (1 Sam. 10:25; cf. Deuteronomy 17:18–20). Because Samuel's prophetic messages from God to the Israelites provide a check on their monarchical ambitions, kingship in Israel (by design) remains compatible with the covenant. In relation to the emerging kingship in Israel, Samuel's prophetic role is clearly designed to provide a system of checks and balances. Thereby kingship, with all its dangers of independent action, is not to put the covenant at risk. The struggle between prophecy and kingship, between spiritual goals and political aims, characterizes the subsequent history of Israel until the exile.

Lest Israel lose its distinctive nature, an important aspect of the monarchy in Israel is the establishment of a clear theology of kingship. With Saul and his successor David, the LORD is the one who chooses the king, has him anointed by Samuel, and endows him with the Spirit. Only then is the king publicly attested before Israel. Thus, the mortal king is firmly established as an under-king of the great King, the LORD. When Samuel the prophet anoints the king of Israel, that mortal king becomes the LORD's messiah ("anointed one"; 1 Samuel 2:10; 10:1; 16:13).

From this imagery the future hope of a messiah will be constructed. As Dumbrell rightly notes, "Old Testament eschatology invariably projects content drawn from past history of salvation as the shape of future expectation."[83] Because this connection exists between the Old Testament kings and the coming Messiah, the question of the extent to which the institution of the monarchy in Israel is a positive development is important. Some scholars, such as Goldingay, read the books of Samuel as expressing a negative attitude toward kingship: "The story makes quite explicit that the trappings of state are at best ambivalent in significance, that the dynamic of God's dealings with Israel during this period resides in the prophets, not in the official institutions of state, and that the exile constitutes an eventual negative judgment on the period of being a state like other states."[84] But in our view this is in danger of confusing the healthy *structure* of kingship (which Deuteronomy 17:14–20 mentions as a legitimate possibility) with an unhealthy use or *misdirection* of that structure. One of God's original promises to Israel was that it would become a great nation, and strong political leadership is an important part of coming to nationhood.

## SAUL RULES UNFAITHFULLY

In the beginning of Saul's reign, Israel is not used to having a king, and initially Saul's role is much like that of a judge. Only after he raises the siege of Jabesh and rescues its people (1 Samuel 11) does all Israel start to accept him as king (11:14–15). Under Saul's leadership Israel achieves significant military success against the Philistines. Despite his youthful promise, however, almost from the start Saul's disobedience to God compromises his career. Early in his reign, preparing to attack the Philistines, Saul grows impatient of waiting for Samuel to come and assure him of God's blessing (1 Samuel 13). So he takes upon himself Samuel's priestly role. When Samuel arrives, he rebukes Saul and prophesies that the kingdom will be taken away from him. Later,

Saul attacks the Amalekites as God commands him to do. But then, in defiance of God's specific instructions, he plunders the enemy camp, carrying off its animals to make an extravagant sacrifice to God. Once more, Samuel confronts King Saul and reminds him that God wants obedience, not sacrifice: "For rebellion is like the sin of divination, and arrogance like the evil of idolatry. Because you have rejected the word of the LORD, he has rejected you as king" (15:23). In attempting to force God's blessing, Saul actually forfeits it.

For a time Saul remains king, but Samuel immediately seeks out the future king and anoints David, a young man from Bethlehem. From this time onward, Saul becomes more and more unhinged; David rises to prominence as Saul declines. The Spirit comes upon David, but departs from Saul (16:13–14). As a skilled musician David provides comfort for Saul in the king's periods of mental turmoil, but later becomes a target of the older man's vicious, manic anger. David's military success in defeating Goliath and the Philistines draws him to Saul's attention, and Saul's son Jonathan becomes David's devoted friend. David marries Saul's daughter Michal. But David's growing reputation as a military leader arouses Saul's jealousy. Hearing the Israelite women chanting, "Saul has slain his thousands, and David his tens of thousands," is too much for Saul, and he tries to kill David (18:7–11). The younger man is forced to flee and becomes a fugitive with a band of outlaws. However, God blesses David and he prospers, with a string of military successes. Though during this period David has several opportunities to kill Saul, he refuses to lift up a hand against "the LORD's anointed" (as in 24:6).

Saul's forty-year reign ends after several unsuccessful attempts to have his appointed successor murdered. Desperate because God himself is silent, Saul even consults a spirit medium for advice about how to deal with the threat from the Philistines (1 Samuel 28). At the end, facing the defeat of his own army at the hands of the Philistines, Saul takes his own life (1 Samuel 31).

This is not an auspicious start for the monarchy in Israel. The grim history of Saul points out how the institution of the human monarch is dangerous for Israel. According to Nelson, "Much about God's relationship with [Saul] remains unfathomable, and God's motives remain largely hidden from the reader just as they are from Saul."[85] But one thing is clear: God wants an under-king who enhances and facilitates his own sovereign rule over Israel, a king who will enable the Israelites to live up to their covenant calling. This is why God must deal so decisively with the disobedience of Israel's first human king.

The story of Saul's death told in 1 Samuel is also narrated at the start of the narrative section of 1 Chronicles (chapter 10). In fact, the story of the rise and decline of kingship is told in *three* Old Testament double books (Samuel, Kings, and Chronicles). From the story of Saul's death onward, Chronicles covers the same ground as Samuel and Kings. It is widely accepted that Samuel and Kings are intended as a single, progressive narrative and that Chronicles is a distinctly separate work, though it does cover much of the same ground. It is as though, at this point in the story of the Old Testament, we have two points of view on this period of history. This is not unique in the Bible: in the Gospels we have *four* accounts of Jesus' life and work. We should not find this disconcerting. All history-telling is selective, depending on what the presenter is trying to do. First Kings, for example, looks back on the rise and decline of the monarchy, seeking to explain to exiled Israelites just how their exile to Babylon came about. The book of Chronicles was written perhaps as much as a hundred years after Kings, around the time of the building of the second temple. Its story's historical focus is upon the *first* temple and the worship of God in those earlier days. Chronicles ends with Cyrus's command to go and build the second temple (and in this respect is more forward looking than Kings). Chronicles also looks *further back*, establishing through its nine chapters of genealogies that Israel is connected to Adam and thus to God's purposes for his entire creation. In the Hebrew Bible, Chronicles is the *last* book. Perhaps it begins its story with Adam so as to remind us of the *first* book in the Bible: "The Chronicler is keen to assert that the purposes of God in creation are realized through Israel in the Old Testament."[86]

## David Rules Faithfully

After the deaths of Saul and Jonathan, war breaks out between the houses of David and Saul, but David's faction grows steadily stronger. Judah (the southern part of Israel) first chooses David as king (2 Samuel 2:1–7), and then all Israel agrees with this choice (5:1–4). David enjoys further military victory against the Philistines and begins to consolidate his rule. He brings the ark of the covenant of God to Jerusalem, which is to be both David's own city and the fixed place where God himself will dwell among his people. David raises his palace in Jerusalem and then wants to build a home for the LORD, too. But Nathan the prophet tells him that David's son and successor will do this, not David. The LORD does confirm David as king and promises to establish David and his heirs in dynastic reign over Israel.

In his covenant with David, God promises (1) to make David's name great, (2) to provide for his people Israel a place where God will "plant" them so they are secure, (3) to give them rest from their enemies, (4) to establish David's dynasty, and (5) to enable David's son to build God's permanent "house" (2 Samuel 7). The first three elements of the Davidic

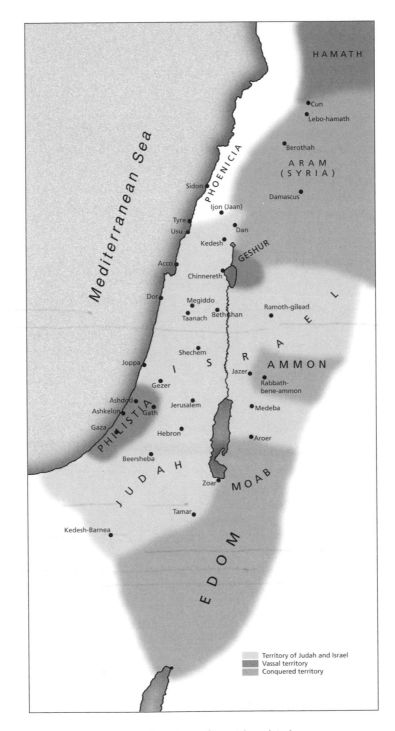

**Figure 16** *Empires of David and Solomon*

covenant deliberately evoke the Abrahamic covenant. Responding to God with thanksgiving and worship, David places God's promises to himself clearly in relation to the promises made long ago to Abraham (7:18–29). The new element in the covenant with David is that kingship is grafted onto the Sinai covenant. Israel is now officially constituted as a kingdom; Israel will now fulfill its calling to be a light to the nations as a kingdom. Israel's human king will lead the people to be a holy nation and priestly kingdom. He will do so as he removes idolatry from the land and gives Israel rest and shalom.

At first, with David on the throne, there *is* rest and peace for Israel. David is fabulously successful in military matters and soon secures Israel's borders. He reigns "over all Israel, doing what [is] just and right for all his people" (8:15). He is generous in victory. He searches out Saul's relatives, but not (as might have been expected) to kill them. Instead, he shows them kindness, as when he gives to Jonathan's crippled son Mephibosheth the property of his grandfather Saul and welcomes him into his own family.

However, David is no sinless paragon, and the remainder of 2 Samuel records a catalogue of sins and errors in judgment. David commits adultery with Bathsheba, then conspires to have her husband murdered. But Nathan the prophet comes to know of these things and confronts David with a parable, which has a real sting in the tail (2 Samuel 11–12). He tells David of a rich man, the owner of many flocks, and a poor man who owns just one ewe lamb, a family pet. When the rich man needs a special meal for a visiting guest, he arrogantly slaughters the poor man's lamb (instead of one of his own). This tale of greed and injustice so angers King David that he vows to visit terrible punishments on the "rich man." Suddenly Nathan turns on the king and declares that David himself is the "rich man" figure in the parable. He has acted out of arrogance and greed in taking another man's wife. The story convicts David of his sin. He weeps for his guilt before God, repents, and is forgiven (cf. Psalm 51). But his actions bear tragic consequences. The child conceived in David's adulterous union with Bathsheba dies. Rape, murder, and rebellion erupt in David's own extended family. At last God's judgment on David reaches its climax with the death of David's beloved son Absalom, who has tried to take the throne of Israel for himself.

The book of 2 Samuel ends with God giving a positive answer to David's plea for an end to famine. This is a sure sign of reconciliation between the king and the LORD. Indeed, on the whole King David is regarded quite positively in the Bible. In the short evaluative notes given in 1 and 2 Kings concerning each of the kings who come after Solomon, David is invariably the standard by which each king's reign is measured. For example, the text says that King Abijah's "heart was not fully devoted to the LORD his God, as the heart of David his forefather had been" (1 Kings

15:3). The primary interest is to show how each of the kings relates to the LORD; the author cares little for other kingly accomplishments, such as building projects. Though we know from extrabiblical sources that King Omri achieves great things in architecture and nation-building, in the book of Kings he is dismissed (in a few verses) as a king who displeases the LORD. David, by contrast, is depicted as genuinely devout. Throughout the Old Testament his name is closely associated with the Psalms, many of which he may have written. They reveal a profound spirituality in this surprisingly complicated man and king.

As we have seen, nothing about Israel's experiment with monarchy is straightforward. Every step seems fraught with difficulties, and this is true also of the matter of King David's succession. God promises to establish David's line forever, but this does little to prevent power struggles among his heirs. After David's son Absalom builds up a military force, he seizes the throne and forces David to flee for his life (2 Samuel 15), but in the course of the ensuing battle, Absalom himself is killed. At Bathsheba's request, David finally declares his son Solomon to be the heir to the throne and thereby establishes his dynasty (1 Kings 1).

### Kings: Covenant Failure

#### SOLOMON BEGINS HIS RULE WISELY

If David is best known for his trust of the LORD and his profound spirituality, Solomon is renowned for his wisdom. When he offers a thousand burnt offerings to the LORD at Gibeon, the LORD responds by offering this young princeling whatever he asks for. Solomon declares himself inadequate for the task of being king and requests "a discerning heart to govern [God's] people and to distinguish between right and wrong" (1 Kings 3:9). The LORD is pleased with this request, gives Solomon the wisdom he asks for, and promises him riches and honor as well. Solomon's wisdom becomes legendary. Its most famous example is in the story of how he settles the difficult legal case of two prostitutes and one live baby, which each woman claims to be her own child (3:16–28). Solomon commands that the child be cut in half and divided between them. This "judgment" causes the real mother to cry out that the child should go to the other woman alive rather than be slaughtered. Solomon thus discerns who the *real* mother is, and she is reunited with her baby. Solomon was also an expert in proverbial wisdom and had extensive knowledge of plants, animals, reptiles, and fish (4:29–34). He is also credited with establishing a developed structure of government for Israel (4:1–19).

In the Old Testament are several books of "wisdom": Proverbs, Ecclesiastes, and Job. Both Proverbs and Ecclesiastes are associated with

Solomon, and much of their material may originate with him. The association of this kind of writing with Solomon indicates the sort of thinking that he particularly initiated in the cultural and religious life of Israel. In these books "wisdom" is all about knowing how to live effectively, how to express God's glory in a good though fallen world. "Wisdom" begins with "the fear of the LORD"—that is, in a profound reverence for the LORD as God the Creator and Redeemer (Proverbs 1:7). This is precisely the sort of attitude Solomon manifests when God offers him whatever he wants. Solomon recognizes himself to be a fallible, limited human creature, utterly dependent upon God. God rewards this humility by giving him great wisdom.

"The fear of the LORD" is also the starting point for a journey of exploration that may extend throughout the whole creation. The theological presupposition of wisdom is that the LORD is the LORD God, the Creator: the very fabric of creation comes from him. Wise service of the LORD will therefore take seriously the whole of creation in all its magnificent variety, and this is precisely what Solomon does. To study the nature of plants, reptiles, animals, and fish, and to study how to use language in proverbs that sum up insight in short, pithy aphorisms—these are ways in which Solomon's wisdom shows itself. In the book of Proverbs there is no area of life that wisdom does not reflect upon, including family life, sexuality, politics, economics, business, and law. Indeed, Proverbs ends with a powerful portrait of wisdom incarnate in the "virtuous woman," who manifests her fear of the LORD in a truly extraordinary variety of activities (Proverbs 31).

## SOLOMON ESTABLISHES THE TEMPLE IN ZION

Solomon's greatest achievement is that he builds God's temple. He uses only the best materials and spares no cost in the construction of the temple in Jerusalem. The walls of the temple are painted with cherubim, palm trees, and flowers, deliberately invoking the idea of Eden within the temple itself. "Yahweh's presence in the temple established it in Zion as the centre of the universe. . . . The Exodus traditions are transferred to this sacred mount which then became representative for all Israel. Zion is now the cosmic centre, the point of contact between heaven and earth."[87] The ark is brought into the temple to mark the fulfillment of the Israelites' journey out of bondage in Egypt. The LORD and Israel are now at rest in the land. When the ark is deposited in the temple, the exodus cloud fills the temple, showing that the glory of the LORD is present in Jerusalem (1 Kings 8:11). God now has an address on earth among his people.

In the huge dedication ceremony, Solomon specifically relates the founding of the temple to the fulfillment of God's ancient promises to Israel. Before this, the LORD has not settled in one place in Israel, but now he has chosen Jerusalem as his city, "for his Name to dwell there" (8:19–21; cf. Deuteronomy 12:5). Some have suggested that the reference to the "Name" of God implies a symbolic presence rather than a real presence, because the LORD is the transcendent God and cannot be limited to one single place. In his prayer of dedication, Solomon acknowledges that the very heavens themselves can never contain God, much less can a building made by human hands. However, as the cloud descending to the inner sanctuary of the temple alerts us, the God of glory and transcendence *is* truly present amid his people. Solomon offers pleas to God that the temple may be a place where the Israelites can pray and be heard by God. This demonstrates that God's "presence" there signifies his closeness in his relationship to his people, rather than his mere physical proximity.

Solomon's time is thus one of great fulfillment of promises. Israel is now a great nation, which has claimed its homeland as promised, and the LORD is at rest in its midst. Religiously and politically, Israel is established as a cohesive nation, and for these things Solomon gives thanks: "Praise be to the LORD, who has given rest to his people Israel just as he promised. Not one word has failed of all the good promises he gave through his servant Moses" (1 Kings 8:56). Jerusalem is established as the capital of Israel, with the temple and the King's residence within its walls. This marks a new chapter in the story of Israel.

Jerusalem (or "Zion," as it is also known) fires the imagination of the prophets and leaders of Israel in the time of Solomon and after. The city with God's temple in it is celebrated in much of Israel's poetry:

> Great is the LORD, and most worthy of praise,
> In the city of our God, his holy mountain.
> It is beautiful in its loftiness,
> The joy of the whole earth.
> Like the utmost heights of Zaphon is Mount Zion,
> The city of the Great King.
> God is in her citadels;
> He has shown himself to be her fortress. . . .
> Great is the LORD in Zion; he is exalted over all the nations. (Psalm
>     48:1–3; 99:2)

Jerusalem is now the center for Israel's formal worship, and Israelites will make regular pilgrimages to it, pilgrimages that are to inspire the psalms of ascent (120–134). As we read these poems, we need to imagine pilgrims approaching Jerusalem—the LORD's own dwelling place—reciting, "I lift up my eyes to the hills—where does my help come from? My help comes from the LORD, the Maker of heaven and earth" (121:1–2). As they approach Jerusalem, the pilgrims lift up their eyes to the hills of Jerusalem and reflect on the source of their help. These pilgrims know quite well that the LORD, who has a local "address" in this city and is their constant helper, is also the Creator of the whole world. He is therefore able and willing to help.

To bring their messages to Israel, the prophets too would use the imagery of Zion again and again. Unfortunately, as we will see, this was often because things in Jerusalem were not going well as the prophets fulfilled their calling. But in Solomon's great day at the dedication of the temple, it must seem as though Eden itself has been recovered. Shalom and great blessing lie before Israel. The monarchy appears to have brought peace and prosperity in a measure that Samuel and other critics of the institution of kingship could never dream of. Now perhaps Israel can draw the nations to God.

## THE KINGDOM IS RENT IN TWO

Sadly, however, the seeds of civil strife and apostasy are already present in Solomon's day, and these seeds soon bring a deadly harvest. Solomon, alas, is not opposed to the worship of God taking place at the "high places," where the Baals have been worshiped, despite the danger of syncretism that comes with such a practice. Moreover, he also begins to use forced labor to fulfill his ambitious building plans. Third, he takes many foreign wives. The first and last of these decisions leave the kingdom vulnerable to idolatry, and such idolatry starts to pollute Israel as Solomon grows older. His use of conscripted labor begins to alienate the populace; at the time of Solomon's death the resentment of the people has become intense. More important, the LORD himself becomes angered by Solomon's idolatry (1 Kings 11:33), which has violated the heart of the covenant. God therefore tells Solomon that he will tear much of the kingdom from Solomon's heirs, leaving only one tribe to be ruled by his successor (11:13, 36).

True to God's word, after Solomon's death Israel splits into a northern kingdom (Israel) under King Jeroboam and a southern kingdom (Judah) under King Rehoboam. The rebellion of the northern tribes against Solomon's heir is their explicit response to Solomon's policy of using forced labor. When Rehoboam rejects the northern tribes' request that he lighten the burden of forced labor, the kingdoms separate. The political consequences of this schism are immense (1 Kings 12). The nation of Israel is now divided against itself, and both kingdoms are far more vulnerable to their enemies. Soon each begins to regard *the other* as an enemy. And how, after the northern kingdom separates, can

**Figure 17** *Divided Kingdom*

it remain true to the LORD, who "lives" in the south, in Jerusalem? Jeroboam (the northern king) is caught on the horns of a real dilemma: if he lets his people go south to worship at Jerusalem, he may lose control of his kingdom. Instead of this, Jeroboam embraces idolatry. Tragically, he repeats the sin of the Israelites at Sinai (Exodus 32): he has two golden calves made and set up in sanctuaries at Dan and Bethel (1 Kings 12:26–33). This is an ominous beginning for the northern kingdom, and their subsequent history will have apostasy written all over it. Through the prophet Ahijah, God declares his rejection of Jeroboam, principally because of the idolatry of the northern kingdom (1 Kings 14).

### ELIJAH AND ELISHA CONFRONT AN UNFAITHFUL ISRAEL

At this point in Israel's story, the prophets begin to play an increasingly important role in the biblical story. Throughout Israel's history, God's word plays a key role, whether it comes through Moses, Samuel, or another prophet. However, as the office of king becomes firmly established in Israel, the office of prophet becomes more clearly delineated from other public roles. All the prophetic books in the Old Testament come from the time of the monarchy or after its demise. The prophetic office thus appears in Israel as a counterbalance to the powerful office of kingship. There is no dynasty of prophets; God calls each of them for the purpose of bringing his word to Israel and especially to its leaders at a specific moment in the nation's history. Israel is a theocracy, and God's word is to have final authority, not the word of the king. Hence, we often find a prophet in bitter confrontation with the king of his day. For example, when Jeroboam's son is ill, he sends his wife to consult Ahijah. This prophet then has the unenviable task of telling King Jeroboam's wife that her son will die as soon as she steps back into her city. In addition, this death will be preferable to what is about to happen to the rest of Jeroboam's house. The LORD will "uproot Israel from this good land that he gave to their forefathers and scatter them beyond the [Euphrates] River, because they provoked the LORD to anger by making Asherah poles" (14:15).

But God is patient and longsuffering, and he does not quickly cast the northern kingdom into exile. Sadly, the kings that follow Jeroboam in the northern kingdom are too much like him in their sin. Events in the north reach their nadir when Ahab takes the throne of Israel. Ahab marries Jezebel, a foreigner who brings Baal worship with her into the marriage and into the northern kingdom. King and queen together actively promote the worship of Baal in Israel. Their rebellion against God is utterly brazen.

In this context of radical apostasy, Elijah the prophet comes onto the stage as the one who must confront Ahab in the name of the LORD. Underlying the struggle between Elijah and Ahab is the more fundamental conflict between Baal and the LORD: to which will the north give its allegiance? There is a great public contest between Baal and the LORD on the top of Mount Carmel. Elijah assembles the people and appeals to them not to waver between Baal and the LORD: "If the LORD is God, follow him; but if Baal is God, follow him" (18:21). The people remain quiet, and so Elijah has two bulls sacrificed and declares that the true God will send fire from heaven to consume one of the sacrifices. The prophets of Baal cry out to their god all day, but there is no answer. Elijah taunts them: Perhaps Baal cannot hear them because he is asleep or perhaps he is traveling. Elijah then builds an altar with twelve stones (to represent the twelve tribes of Israel). Wood and the sacrificial bull are put on the altar, and water is poured over it all. At the time of the evening sacrifice, Elijah prays to the "LORD, God of Abraham, Isaac and Israel," and the LORD sends fire, which consumes the sacrifice and the altar. The people fall on their faces and cry out, "The LORD, he is God" (18:39).

We need to understand Elijah's ministry, and that of his disciple Elisha who follows after him, in the context of this life-and-death clash between Baal and the LORD. Through Elijah and Elisha the LORD overcomes drought (18:41–46), hunger (17:8–16), thirst (2 Kings 2:19–22), debt (4:1–7), infertility (4:11–17), disease (5:1–19), and death (1 Kings 17:17–24; 2 Kings 4:18–37). Baal worshippers think these areas of life are under Baal's control.[88] What Elijah and Elisha show is that the LORD is lord of his people, of *every* aspect of their lives, and of the whole creation.

The blessings that come from the LORD through his prophets are not limited to Israel. When Naaman, a commander in the army of Aram (Syria), suffers from leprosy and comes in desperation to Elisha for healing, God answers his prayer (2 Kings 5). Naaman then takes away with him as much earth from Israel as two mules can carry, so that he can worship the LORD on "the land" in his own country of Aram. Here we have a wonderful example of Israel's bringing blessing to the nations. But sadly, Israel itself is all this while becoming more and more like the surrounding pagan nations because the people refuse to serve the LORD alone.

## ISRAEL'S STEADY SLIDE TOWARD DISASTER AND EXILE

In much of 2 Kings the histories of the northern and southern kingdoms are told through a "split-screen presentation of both kingdoms. The reader encounters parallel stories about mirror-image reforms and their results."[89] In the north, Jehu is called by God and anointed by Elisha, with the specific instruction to wipe out Ahab's house (2 Kings 9). This he does, but he also maintains the worship of the golden calves and the traditions of Jeroboam. Israel thus continues to slide steadily toward disaster. Assyria is the great Middle Eastern empire of the day,

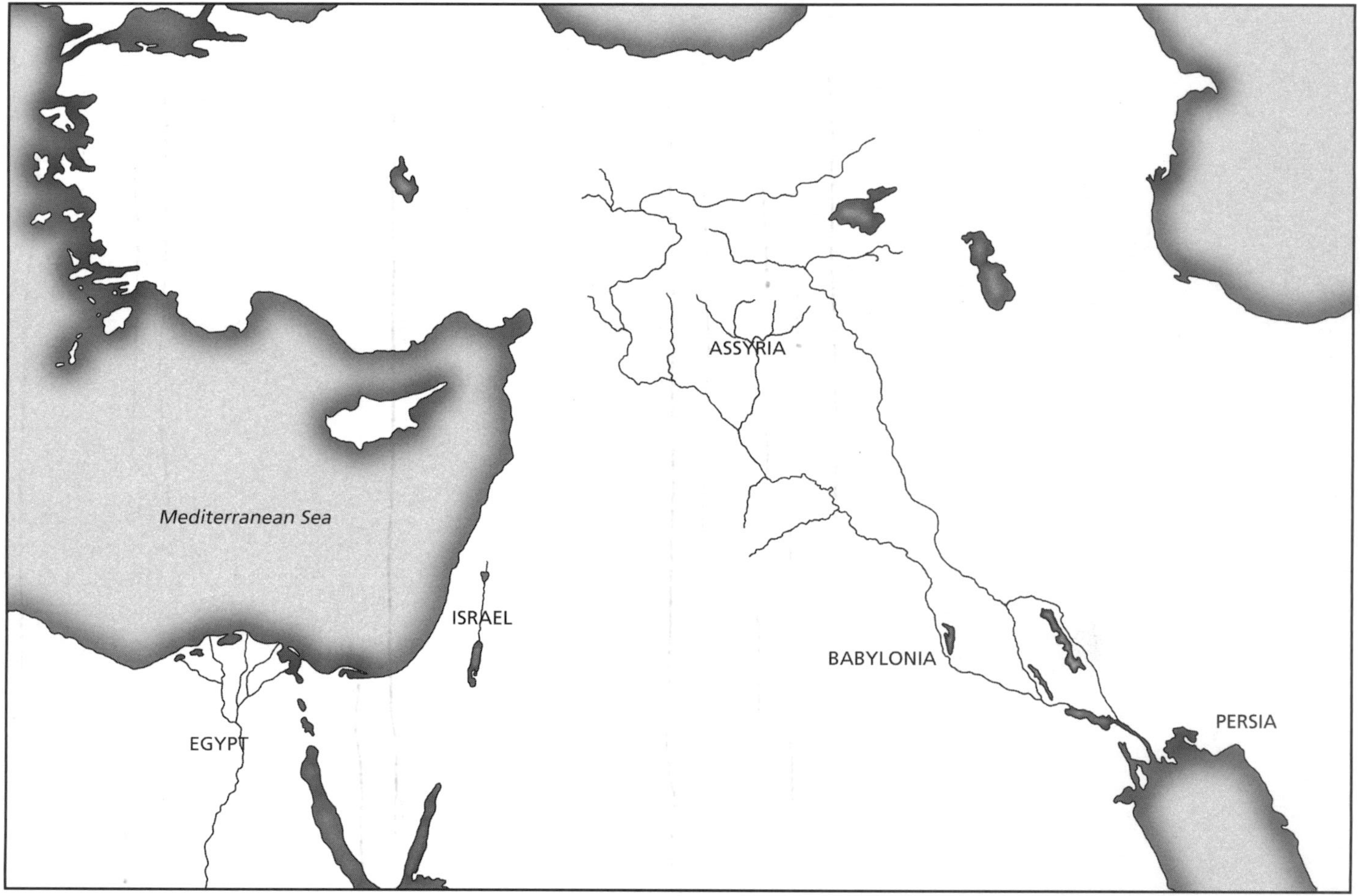

**Figure 18** *World Empires*

and its shadow falls increasingly on the northern kingdom. During the reign of Israel's King Hoshea, Assyria invades the northern kingdom, lays siege to its capital Samaria for three years, and then deports the Israelites to Assyria in 722 BC (2 Kings 17). This marks the end of the northern kingdom of Israel.

In 2 Kings the narrator pauses at this point for a lengthy reflection on why such a thing has happened to Israel. Its exile raises the most fundamental questions in the minds of faithful Israelites. Wasn't the land a gift from the LORD himself? How then could he have allowed his people to be taken from it? Where are God's promises? What will happen now to the southern kingdom, Judah? Has God really abandoned his vows to Abraham, Moses, and David?

The answers to these questions come in 17:7–23. The narrator makes it clear that the LORD has punished the northern kingdom in this way because of their own disobedience to the covenant. Though God has repeatedly warned the people (through his prophets) of the consequences of idolatry, they have persisted in their sin and rebellion. So "the LORD . . . removed them from his presence" (17:18). They are exiled *not* because of Assyria's power, but because the LORD cannot stomach them anymore. In reflection, the narrator turns to the subject of Jeroboam, first of the northern kings, and again tells how Jeroboam established a pattern of apostasy and rebellion that plagues the northern kingdom from its beginning to its end.

Ominously, the narrator notes that the southern kingdom, Judah, has not been much different (17:19). The tendency in the south is to follow the terrible example of the north. However, Judah continues unconquered, and the monarchy there undoubtedly fares much better than it ever has in the north. In the years following 722 BC, there are two outstanding kings in Judah, Hezekiah and Josiah, who do seek to honor the LORD. Since in Judah the Davidic line rules, is there still hope for the south? Hezekiah's reign parallels Hoshea's in the north. But when Assyria also threatens Hezekiah, he (unlike Hoshea) casts himself upon the LORD. By God's aid, mediated through the prophet Isaiah, Hezekiah holds firm, and Judah is miraculously delivered from the Assyrian threat (2 Kings 18–19; cf. Isaiah 8:6–10).

But signs of serious trouble appear even in Hezekiah's reign. As Assyria wanes, Babylon emerges as the new international power. When Hezekiah foolishly shows Babylonian envoys around his storehouses, this folly evokes an oracle of judgment from the prophet Isaiah: the southern kingdom too will go into exile; Babylon will conquer Judah (2 Kings 20:12–19).

Many of Isaiah's prophecies in Isaiah 1–39 chronicle the ambiguity of the times in which he lives, in which Judah is, on the whole, a sinful nation heading for judgment. King Manasseh (Hezekiah's successor) promotes idolatry and syncretism and is renowned for perpetuating injustice in his kingdom. Judah's doom seems inevitable.

But Manasseh's grandson Josiah suddenly becomes king—at only eight years of age! While still a young man, Josiah hears a newly discovered law book being read aloud in the temple and is greatly moved by what he hears. Josiah then leads the people of Judah in public repentance, renews God's covenant with them, and embarks on a major reform of worship. Josiah pleases the LORD in this respect and is commended for his reign. But even Josiah's exemplary life and rule are too little, too late for Judah. From the prophet Jeremiah we know that the reforms instituted by Josiah probably are not widely embraced in the kingdom. The people's tendency toward apostasy remains. Babylon's shadow is felt more and more strongly in Judah. During Zedekiah's reign, Babylon conquers the southern kingdom and sets fire to the temple and the king's palace. Jerusalem is reduced to ruins, and most of Judah's people are exiled to Babylon in 587/6 BC (2 Kings 25).

As we follow the biblical story of Israel, at this point we might well be tempted to write "THE END" (cf. Ezekiel 7:1–2). For the Israelites being marched off as slaves to Babylon, it certainly must seem like the end. What has come of God's great promises to Abraham, of his covenant with Israel at Sinai, of his vow that David's house would go on forever? The house of the LORD himself has been destroyed! Where was the LORD while Babylon triumphed over Israel? Have God's purposes for his people finally run into the sand? Worse, have God's purposes to redeem the creation through Israel failed?

Only from the LORD himself can Israel hope for answers to such perplexing questions. This is what makes the voices of the prophets so important in the biblical story and in our understanding of Israel's shifting fortunes. As a result of the Israelites' disobedience, they are defeated and crushed—but Yahweh is still the LORD, and his purposes endure. In the centuries leading up to Israel's expulsion from the land, its history has been punctuated and regularly interpreted by the voices of God's prophets. And these voices do not become silent with the exile. By no means is the LORD confined to the land. Though he has graciously lived there among his people, *their* apparent end as a nation is not *his* ending.

The double book of Kings concludes on a tentative note of hope: King Jehoiachin of Judah is released from prison in Babylon and eats at the table of the king of Babylon (2 Kings 25:27–30). Perhaps the story of Israel is not quite finished? But Israel's surest hope for a future lies not in the chronicles of its history, but in the writings of its prophets.

### The Voices of the Prophets

We have already looked briefly at the ministries of Elijah and Elisha in the ninth century BC. Hosea too (in the eighth century) prophesies to the northern kingdom in powerful and moving ways. He compares Israel to a wife who has become a prostitute—and yet her husband cannot give her up. He agonizes over her and longs for her to return to him and to be a faithful spouse. In this way the horror of adultery becomes a metaphor for what Israel is committing against the LORD. Hosea's children are given names that evoke the miserable state of Israel: *Jezreel* ("God sows"), *Lo-Ruhamah* ("Not loved"), and *Lo-Ammi* ("Not my people"). God is sowing punishment for his unfaithful people. The evocative names of the prophet's children are a startling rebuke to Israel.

Amos is another prophet of the ninth and eighth centuries before Christ, a shepherd called by the LORD to become a prophet to both the northern and southern kingdoms.[90] Amos's preaching is highly creative and his message altogether devastating. He portrays the LORD as a lion about to pounce on his prey (Amos 1:2). In an extraordinary sermon (1:3–2:16), Amos denounces Israel's neighbors one by one. You can almost hear a loud "Amen!" from Israel as Damascus, Gaza, Tyre, Edom, Ammon, and Moab are condemned in turn. Then comes the twist: Amos moves on to Judah and Israel, denouncing them because they have rejected the LORD's instruction and are full of idolatry and injustice. They too will suffer terrible judgment. (The "amens" likely cease here.)

Jeremiah and Ezekiel prophesy to Judah during its expulsion from the land. Jeremiah begins his ministry in King Josiah's reign, warning the people of Judah against trusting in mere symbols of God's presence, such as the temple. The LORD tells Jeremiah to stand at the entrance of the temple, to warn them against a false trust in ritual:

> This is what the LORD Almighty, the God of Israel, says: Reform your ways and your actions, and I will let you live in this place. Do not trust in deceptive words and say, "This is the temple of the LORD, the temple of the LORD, the temple of the LORD!" If you really change your ways and your actions and deal with each other justly, if you do not oppress the alien, the fatherless or the widow and do not shed innocent blood in this place, and if you do not follow other gods to your harm, then I will let you live in this place, in the land I gave to your forefathers for ever and ever. But look, you are trusting in deceptive words that are worthless. (Jeremiah 7:2–8)

Such sermons are not popular. Jeremiah suffers terrible opposition, even as he agonizes over his message to the southern kingdom. The extent of his agony and struggle is evident in his prayers scattered throughout his writings.[91] In Jeremiah 12, for example, the prophet cries out to God, asking why the wicked prosper and the faithless live at ease. God responds by asking Jeremiah, "If you have raced with men on foot and they have worn you out, how can you compete with horses?" Though Jeremiah is crying out *now* in his sense of injustice and injury, he should expect his circumstances to get worse instead of better! In chapter 15, Jeremiah tells of how he once "ate" God's words with joy and delight, but now his pain is unending and his wound grievous and incurable (15:16, 18). It is certainly no easy thing to be God's prophet.

The message of all these prophets is that unless God's people repent, return to him, and obey him, judgment will come. The prophets begin to speak ominously of the Day of the LORD. No longer is it anticipated as a day of blessing and judgment on Israel's enemies; instead, it is to be a day of judgment for Israel itself. As we saw above, that "day" did come, first for the northern kingdom (in 722 BC), and then (in 587/6 BC) for the southern kingdom.

Ezekiel ministers among the exiles *in Babylon* itself. He depicts the glory of the LORD departing from Jerusalem (Ezekiel 10) and interprets for the Israelites what has happened in the exile. To be plucked out of the land is a catastrophe for Israel, and yet . . .

Prophets such as Ezekiel insist that the exile is not "THE END." The LORD's purposes remain, as do his promises to Abraham, to Moses, and to David. The judgment oracles of the prophets are mercifully interspersed with oracles of hope and of a future for God's people. Thus, Jeremiah promises that the nation will return from exile and once again occupy the land of promise. He looks forward to a time when, as God says,

> I will make a new covenant
> with the house of Israel
> and with the house of Judah. . . .
> I will put my law in their minds
> and write it on their hearts.
> I will be their God,
> and they will be my people. . . .
> They will all know me. (Jeremiah 31:31–34)

## The Catastrophe of Exile in Babylon

Because the land and the temple were such important symbols to Israel of its nationhood and of its identity as the people beloved of God, exile was a catastrophic experience for the Israelites. The instruments of exile were the great powers of the day: first Assyria, then Babylon. After the fall of Assyria (in 612 BC), Babylon gained control of the Near East.

Nebuchadnezzar, king of Babylon (605–562), defeated the Egyptians at Carchemish in 605, and he and his successors maintained their dominance until Cyrus of Persia defeated the Babylonians (in 539). After the battle of Carchemish, the southern kingdom of Judah became subject to Babylon, but some years later, King Jehoiakim of Judah rebelled against his Babylonian overlords (2 Kings 24). Nebuchadnezzar then besieged Jerusalem and took Jehoiakim's successor Jehoiachin off to Babylon as a prisoner. Ten years later, Zedekiah (the puppet-king of Judah whom Nebuchadnezzar had appointed) also rebelled against Babylon. Once more Nebuchadnezzar returned to Jerusalem, but this time his army destroyed the city and the temple and took most of Jerusalem's citizens to Babylon (587/6 BC; 2 Kings 25). Thus the LORD used the ungodly empires of Assyria and Babylon as instruments of his judgment upon his people Israel.

We should not think that the LORD has been quick to cast his people out of the land. On the contrary, God is portrayed throughout the Old Testament as moving slowly and regretfully toward this judgment. Hosea forcefully conveys the agony God experiences in coming to the decision to eject Israel from the land. God's pain is evident when he cries out through the prophet, "How can I give you up, Ephraim? How can I hand you over, Israel?" (Hosea 11:8). The Old Testament prophets bear ample witness to God's patience with his people and to the repeated efforts he makes to call them back to faithfulness within the covenant.

Habakkuk prophesies to the southern kingdom as Babylon's influence is overshadowing its life. When the prophet asks how God can stand by and allow injustice and violence to prosper in Judah, he gets a most surprising answer: God is going to use the Babylonians to punish Israel! In the rest of his oracles, Habakkuk wrestles with God, struggling to come to terms with what God is going to do. Finally, though God's ways remain mysterious to him, the prophet does arrive at a place of trust:

> I heard and my heart pounded,
> my lips quivered at the sound;
> decay crept into my bones,
> and my legs trembled.
> Yet I will wait patiently for the day of calamity
> to come on the nation invading us.
> Though the fig tree does not bud
> and there are no grapes on the vines,
> though the olive crop fails
> and the fields produce no food,
> though there are no sheep in the pen
> and no cattle in the stalls,
> yet I will rejoice in the LORD,
> I will be joyful in God my Savior. (Habakkuk 3:16–18)

Just how catastrophic the exile was for the Israelites is clear from the psalms of this period and from the book of Lamentations. Psalm 80 cries out to God about Jerusalem: "Why have you broken down its walls so that all who pass by pick its grapes? Boars from the forest ravage it and the creatures of the field feed on it" (Psalm 80:12–13). The book of Lamentations is a series of carefully structured laments that give ordered expression to the profound grief experienced by the exiles as they are forced to leave the land. As the book of Job struggles with the issue of individual suffering, so Lamentations wrestles with the suffering of an entire nation. Job is innocent, but Israel is guilty. Lamentations articulates Israel's grief, acknowledges the LORD's justice in judgment, and appeals to him to bring restoration and a future to his people Israel. There is heart-wrenching material in these poems: "The roads to Zion mourn, for no one comes to her appointed feasts. All her gateways are desolate, her priests groan, her maidens grieve, and she is in bitter anguish" (Lamentations 1:4).

Paradoxically, perhaps, these writings offer a glimmer of hope to the Israelites in exile. Lamentations gives shape to their grief and, with its focus on the LORD, holds out the possibility of renewal and restoration. This kind of literature was crucial to Israel's survival as a nation. Without hearing God's voice through the prophets, the Israelites would not have maintained their sense of God's claim upon them as his own people. It is true that the temple had been razed. But in exile, Israel was to learn that its God was far more than his house, far greater than the nation itself. He is truly the LORD of the nations, the LORD of all creation. Though his people may suffer exile in Babylon, God is not conquered.

Though some of the exiles hoped for a quick return from Babylon to their own land, the prophets had to dash this hope. Once Jerusalem fell (in 587/6 BC), prophets like Jeremiah and Ezekiel concentrated on comforting the Israelites. Jeremiah insists that there can be no quick return. He exhorts the exiles to "seek the peace and prosperity of the city to which [God has] carried you into exile" (Jeremiah 29:7). God's people have lived before as a minority amid other nations, and for the present they must do so again.

We do not know a great deal about the life of the Israelites while they were in exile. Certainly their situation in Babylon must have been far from pleasant—but there were worse conquerors than the Babylonians. The Israelites were at least able to be part of the Babylonian Empire while remaining in their own communities and holding on to some of their cultural and religious distinctiveness. Nevertheless, two Old Testament narratives, the books of Daniel and Esther, deal with the conflicts of loyalty that could arise for committed Israelites while in exile.

The book of Daniel tells of the experiences of Daniel and three young Israelites who have been taken off to Babylon about fifteen years before the mass exile of 587/6 BC. Daniel's own story is an amazing account of an Israelite rising to political heights in exile while refusing to compromise the key distinctives of his faith. (In this he is strongly reminiscent of Joseph in Egypt.) The four young men refuse to compromise their dietary laws, and yet they flourish in a place where much more lavish food is customary. Daniel's three friends refuse to worship the image Nebuchadnezzar sets up (Daniel 3). They survive their punishment of being thrown alive into a furnace—and afterward they are promoted within the government of Babylon. Daniel also resists idolatry. He will not pray to the image of Nebuchadnezzar, and he too survives his punishment in the lions' den (Daniel 6). With God's help, Daniel (unlike Babylon's own wise men) is able to interpret Nebuchadnezzar's dreams (Daniel 2 and 4).

The second half of the book of Daniel contains Daniel's own symbol-filled visions, which give insight as to how history will unfold. Empires will rise and fall in turn, but their rising and falling will come within the context of the reign of the LORD (2:44; 4:3, 34; 6:26). Indeed, one of the great messages of Daniel is that God is sovereign and honors his servants as they put him first in their lives. In the vision of 7:1–14, there is "one like a son of man" who comes to the Ancient of Days and is given authority and sovereignty over all nations. In the Gospels Jesus refers to himself as "the Son of Man." His implicit claim is to the authority promised this figure in Daniel's prophetic vision.

### Ezra and Nehemiah: Israel Returns to the Land

In 539 BC, the Persian king Cyrus defeated Babylon and allowed the Israelites to return to their land if they so wished. Many did return, but by no means all. The book of Esther is set in the reign of the later Persian king Xerxes (486–465 BC) and is another fascinating story about Israelites in exile.

Esther, an Israelite, is chosen to replace Vashti as King Xerxes' queen. Around this time a noble called Haman is elevated to a high political position. All the royal officials kneel and pay honor to him, but Esther's cousin (and foster father) Mordecai will not do so, presumably because this is too close to idolatry. Haman is furious and obtains Xerxes' permission to have all the Israelites in the empire killed. Mordecai sends news of this threat to Esther and suggests, "Who knows but that you have come to royal position for such a time as this?" (Esther 4:14). To save the Jews, Esther intervenes with Xerxes by exposing Haman's plot, and Haman is hanged. Mordecai, like Joseph and Daniel, rises to great political heights. It is intriguing that the name of God is never used in the book of Esther, though she does call the people to fast—presumably including prayer to God (4:16). Yet the story exudes a powerful sense of God's providence in the experience of the Israelites who remain in exile. The festival of *Purim* celebrates this deliverance (9:18–32).

The books of the Chronicles end on exactly the same note with which the book of Ezra begins: Cyrus, king of Persia, proclaims a decree that the temple shall be rebuilt in Jerusalem (538 BC). This is a note of great hope, for it is the LORD who has moved Cyrus's heart to do this (Ezra 1:1; cf. Isaiah 44:28–45:1, 13). Cyrus releases any of the exiles who desire to return in order to rebuild the temple at Jerusalem. Ezra 2 presents a list of exiles who return: many choose to do so, but not all. We can only imagine their feelings as they make their way back to the land fifty years after the temple was destroyed. Once they have settled into their towns, they gather in Jerusalem and under the leadership of Jeshua and Zerubbabel begin to rebuild the altar of the God of Israel. This is an act of great courage because other peoples have settled in these areas while the Israelites were away, and the Israelites do not know how these people will react.

As soon as the altar is rebuilt, the Israelites celebrate the Feast of Tabernacles, a reminder of the time when the Israelites lived in tents in the desert wilderness on their way to the promised land from Egypt. Since the nation is now, once again, gathering in the promised land, this great feast must be a deeply moving time within the small community of Israelites. The altar and the worship of God are potent symbols of God's presence among his people in the land. Even though the temple is not yet rebuilt, the Israelites' worship provides a great sign of hope. Once they have the rituals of worship in operation, they get on with rebuilding the temple. The project to rebuild the Jerusalem temple suffers from local and even international opposition, but eventually the builders prevail. With strong encouragement from the preaching of the prophets Haggai and Zechariah (Ezra 6:14), and some twenty years after their return from exile in Babylon, the courageous Israelite builders complete the temple and dedicate it to the LORD (516 BC).

The reader who has been following Israel's story up to this point might be pardoned for wondering whether the Israelites will, this time, do any better than they have done in previous attempts to serve God. The rest of the books of Ezra and Nehemiah tell of the two leaders (for whom these books are named) who come in later years to Jerusalem and play major roles in keeping the returned exiles on track. Ezra is a priest and a scribe who returns to Jerusalem some sixty years after the temple is dedicated. By this time the Israelites have begun to allow intermarriage between their own people and foreigners and thus have again opened the door to idolatry through syncretism. Ezra confesses this sin, reminding the people of God's grace in allowing his people to return to the land, and he dissolves such marriages.

Nehemiah is a cupbearer in the royal court of Artaxerxes in Babylon. When he hears of the desolate state of the walls of Jerusalem, Nehemiah requests and receives permission to return to Jerusalem (around 445/4 BC). In the face of violent opposition, Nehemiah heads up the rebuilding of the walls of the city (Nehemiah 1–7). Ezra gathers the Israelites and reads to them from the book of the Law of Moses, and the Levites instruct the Israelites in the Law (Nehemiah 8). The people weep from a deep sense of their sin as they hear the Law. Later the Levites lead them in liturgical prayer as they review their relationship with God, from creation through the call of Abraham and on to the present. They pray fervently to God and renew the covenant between the LORD and the nation of Israel (9:38–10:39).

At the end of the Old Testament, the future of Israel remains uncertain. Israelites are back in the land but—even with the temple rebuilt—its existence as a nation is tenuous: the temple has nothing like its former glory (cf. Haggai 2:3). If we focus just on Israel's political situation at this point in its history, we might have real doubts about its future. But the prophets give us a much stronger assurance about the future of Israel and about the triumph of God's purposes for his people. Much of the preaching of the prophets relates directly to the contemporary situation of Israel. But the prophets—before, during, and after the exile—also look toward the future and speak of what is to come. To do this they make use of imagery culled from the history of Israel, speaking of the future of the "son of David," of "Mount Zion," of Israel as God's servant, and of the temple. They craft for the Israelites a vision of what is to come.

To a great extent the message of the prophets deals with the fact that God is going to judge his people because of their continued disobedience. God's glory and renown among the nations is at stake in Israel's life, and thus God cannot tolerate Israel's rebellion forever. This observation naturally raises questions concerning God's purposes for the future, for Israel, and for the whole creation. Even as the prophets pronounce present judgment on Israel, they also look to the future and declare that, because God reigns, his purposes must triumph. Jeremiah (31) speaks of a "new covenant," and Ezekiel (40–48) of a "new temple." Isaiah (49:6; 52:13–53:12) prophesies the advent of a suffering servant who will truly be a light to the nations. These images together craft a vision of a time when God will act decisively to establish his purposes in his creation and to establish his people as truly *his* people. The Messiah, the anointed one, will come, and Israel will be genuinely converted, the hearts of the people turned to God at last (as in Micah 5). This will be a time in which the nations and all those who have opposed the LORD will endure his judgment. However, it will also be a time of salvation for the nations:

> The prophets do not tire of witnessing to this. Again and again in the midst of their prophetic judgments of Babylon, Assyria, and Egypt, they sometimes suddenly break out in joy over the salvation that shall come. They always set forth the fact that after all the flaming judgments of the Messiah upon Israel itself, and upon the nations, a new and glorious Israel will become the gathering point to which the peoples of the earth shall assemble.[92]

God has not forgotten his promise. God will renew Israel and then draw all nations to himself as he promised Abraham. In that process the whole of the creation is to be renewed. God's kingdom will be established over the whole earth. With this hope the Old Testament ends.

## Interlude

# A Kingdom Story Waiting for an Ending

## The Intertestamental Period

As the Old Testament story draws to a close, the people of Israel are living on "the land" in relative peace under the rule of the Persians, who have allowed Israel to return. But as the New Testament story begins, its context is quite different. The Persian Empire has crumbled long since, and Israel now suffers under the brutal mastery of imperial Rome. Only a fraction of the people of Israel actually live in Palestine—the majority are scattered throughout the Roman Empire and even beyond its borders, where they too are subject to pagan masters. Among the Jews, whether in Palestine or elsewhere, there is a fervent longing for God to act, to bring liberation to his people. The captive nation seethes with anger and dreams of one day throwing off the yoke of oppression and driving the Romans out of the land for good. In our journey through the biblical story, we must therefore pause to consider *the intertestamental period*: four hundred years of Israel's history between Malachi and Matthew. During this time the Jewish people strain to reconcile their faith in God's promises of blessing with the ugly experience of life under a succession of increasingly malignant pagan rulers.[1]

## The Jewish Community in Palestine and the Diaspora

Though the Persian conquerors permitted the Jews to return to their own land from exile in Babylon, in fact only a minority of them did so. Those who did return to Palestine managed to reestablish a thriving Jewish community there, and it is this community that we often read about in the pages of the Gospels. But most Jewish people remained outside their homeland. By the first century AD, Jewish communities were in almost every city of the then-civilized world.[2] These Jews, living not in Palestine but among the nations, are normally referred to as the Diaspora, "the scattered" (from two Greek words meaning "among/ throughout" and "seeds," as of a farmer scattering seeds across his field). These diasporic Jews continued to believe that Israel *as a whole* remained in exile, and so they were particularly zealous to maintain their distinctive covenant identity and the religious observances that reinforce it. The Torah in particular remained foundational for their lives. Some of these Jewish communities outside Palestine were more successful than others in remaining faithful to the Torah and resisting accommodation to the surrounding pagan cultures. But neither the Jews' distinctive hope in God nor their sense of identity as his own people was ever eradicated.

In an effort to maintain their cultural and religious distinctiveness, the Jews (both those in Palestine and the Diaspora) created synagogues for Sabbath worship, prayer, and study of the Scriptures. This institution provided an educational, judicial, social, economic, and political center for the Jewish community in the midst of an alien culture. On the Sabbath, Jews would meet in synagogues for worship and prayer and to hear the Scriptures expounded, but for most of them the synagogue could never entirely replace the temple. Jews everywhere continued to revere the temple and hope for its future glory. They paid temple taxes and on important festivals would often make pilgrimages to Jerusalem. As we trace Israel's story between the testaments, we must remember that there was a substantial Jewish population outside of Palestine who also participated in these events.

## Israel's Faith

Five fundamental beliefs, the product of Israel's two-thousand-year journey with God from the time of Abraham, shaped Jews' life during the intertestamental period. The first of these was *monotheism*: Israel believed in one God, the Creator of the world and Ruler of history. The second belief was *election*: God had chosen Israel for a special purpose:

through this nation and no other he would work to rid his creation of the evil that had marred and thwarted it since the sin of Adam. In his covenant with Abraham, God had promised not only that Abraham's descendants would become a great nation, but also that through this nation all peoples would ultimately receive God's blessing. The third belief concerned the Law, or *Torah:* God had given Israel the Law to direct its way of life as God's holy people and promised that the Israelites would be blessed if they continued in steadfast faithfulness to this Law. The fourth belief concerned the *land* to which God had brought his people through Moses and Joshua, and the *temple* that had been built there. For Israel, the *land* was much more than merely a neutral piece of real estate, more even than the home they lived in and the garden that sustained them. The land was *holy* because it was here that God dwelt with Israel (Zechariah 2:12). Nowhere else could the nation enjoy the same rich communion with him. God had himself chosen this home for his people and chosen more particularly the Jerusalem temple as the place where he might meet with them. This fact constituted the defining center of their lives.

Thus, the Jews believed themselves to have been chosen by the one true God to serve and worship him in his temple at Jerusalem and to experience his blessing as they lived under the direction of his word. As a faithful priestly kingdom, they were to share these blessings with the surrounding nations. This, they knew, was what God intended for his people. But sin—their own unfaithfulness to God—had kept them from receiving what he had promised. For generations Israel had followed practices of nearby pagan nations; idolatry had taken the place of the worship of the LORD. And yet—the prophets promised Israel again and again—*and yet*, in spite of Israel's faithlessness, its LORD would remain faithful to his people. He would fulfill what he had promised in and through his chosen nation. Though Israel would be judged and punished for its sin, God would yet restore to Israel the glory he had always intended for the nation; he would complete his redemptive work. Thus Israel's *hope for a future redemptive act of God* was the fifth belief that ruled its life as a nation during the intertestamental period.

## Growing Tension: From Persia to Rome

Yet these beliefs were severely tested by Israel's actual experience during the four hundred years between the testaments. Though the people had in part returned to the land promised them by God, even those now in Palestine remained under the domination of one foreign power after another, almost as if their exile had never ended. Foreigners dictated their political life, which was bad enough. Far worse was the relentless pressure to conform to pagan culture. This threatened to undermine the nation's very existence and purpose as the chosen of God, through whom he would bring blessing to the world. As the people of Israel endured these centuries of testing and waiting, they wondered why God did not intervene to deliver them and vindicate his name among the pagans. As they were ruled at the whim of one foreign colonial government after another, they must have asked many times what had become of the promises of the prophets.

### Life within the Persian Empire

When the Persian king Cyrus had ordered, as long ago as the sixth century BC, that the Jews should be allowed to return to their homeland, there had been a tremendous sense of elation among them. Surely this was God's deliverance! Surely this was the fulfillment of the promises of Scripture, as in Deuteronomy 30:5–9:

> He will bring you to the land that belonged to your fathers, and you will take possession of it. He will make you more prosperous and numerous than your fathers. The LORD your God will circumcise your hearts and the hearts of your descendants, so that you may love him with all your heart and with all your soul, and live. The LORD your God will put all these curses on your enemies who hate and persecute you. You will again obey the LORD and follow all his commands I am giving you today. Then the LORD your God will make you most prosperous in all the work of your hands and in the fruit of your womb, the young of your livestock and the crops of your land. The LORD will again delight in you and make you prosperous, just as he delighted in your fathers.

These were the first of the Torah's promises of blessing upon postexilic Israel and were reiterated again and again by the prophets of the exile, such as Isaiah, Jeremiah, and Ezekiel. But elation soon gave way to perplexity and frustration. The experience of the returning exiles did not measure up to what they had expected, which had been no less than a cosmic revolution of God's work in and through themselves, his chosen ones. First, not all of Israel returned to the land: many remained where they had settled in Babylon or Egypt. It was true that the temple had been rebuilt, but the new temple seemed to them a shabby thing compared to the glorious temple of Solomon's day, which had been destroyed (Haggai 2:3). Though the people of Israel could once again settle in Palestine, which God himself had given to Abraham, they had come and remained there now only at the pleasure of their foreign—and thus *pagan*—rulers.

The dream of a life on their own land and without foreign masters led many in Israel to look again at the Scripture's promised blessings, to which they had been clinging all these years. What they found there stirred them with fresh zeal for the Torah:

> The LORD will again delight in you and make you prosperous, just as he delighted in your fathers, if you obey the LORD your God and keep his commands and decrees that are written in this Book of the Law and turn to the LORD your God with all your heart and with all your soul. Now what I am commanding you today is not too difficult for you or beyond your reach. . . . For I command you today to love the LORD your God, to walk in his ways, and to keep his commands, decrees and laws; then you will live and increase, and the LORD your God will bless you in the land you are entering to possess. (Deuteronomy 30:9–11, 16)

This seemed to provide the answer to their frustration. If the nation, though physically restored to their land, was still politically and religiously a nation in exile, it must be so because God had not yet finished his judgment on the people for violating his covenant. Thus, they could expect a full and final deliverance only when they had demonstrated a sufficient measure of faithfulness to the Torah, had begun indeed "to walk in his ways, and to keep his commands, decrees and laws." As a result an oral tradition of teaching sprang up, in which scholars sought to apply the ancient laws of the Torah to the new situations in which the people found themselves. In addition, they established synagogues in which God's law could be taught to the common people.

### The Greek Empire under Alexander the Great

When (in 331 BC) Alexander's armies conquered the Persians, the control of Palestine and the governance of the people of Israel fell to the Greeks. Yet the more serious threat to Israel's existence was neither military nor political, but cultural. Alexander's vision was to consolidate his new empire by imposing *Hellenistic* (a word derived from the name *Hellen*, a legendary tribal chieftain from Thessaly in ancient Greece, hence "Greek") culture, including the Greek language.

Alexander did not force the Jews to conform to Hellenistic culture. However, Greek ideas and practices beginning to saturate Israel's culture and the pervasive Greek language itself (so influential that scholars of the Torah translated their sacred Scriptures into Greek: the *Septuagint*) all began to undermine Israel's own cultural and religious integrity as

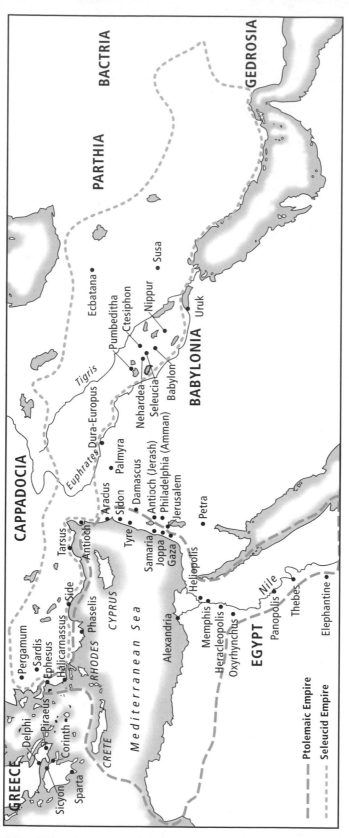

**Figure 19** *Ptolemaic and Seleucid Empires, c. 240 BC*

the singular people of God. How could the nation be faithful when everything that made it distinctive was called into question by the beliefs and practices of those who ruled its life? This pressure to conform to pagan, Hellenistic cultural patterns would only intensify in the years to come.

## The Greek Empire after Alexander

When Alexander died at the age of only thirty-three (in 323 BC), he left no heir, and a struggle ensued among his generals for his massive empire. Two dynasties—the Ptolemies in Egypt and the Seleucids in Syria—ruled their respective fragments of the former Alexandrine Empire and fought each other's armies for overall mastery of the area around Palestine. Israel stood between these two bitter rivals and was ruled first by the Ptolemaic faction (311–198 BC) and then by the Seleucids (198–164 BC). In the latter period, the tension between Israel's faith in God's promises and its experience of life in the midst of an alien culture came to a dramatic crisis. This was especially true during the reign of the Seleucid king Antiochus IV Epiphanes, who was lauded in life as a "[god] manifest," but whose death made "the power of God manifest" (2 Maccabees 9:8–12 NRSV).

Antiochus IV faced two grave threats to his empire, one external and one internal: (1) Rome, which had already begun to assume the dimensions of a world power, was demanding large amounts of money from Antiochus as "tribute," a bribe to keep the Romans from attacking Greek-controlled territories. (2) The ethnic diversity of the Greek Empire itself threatened to tear it apart from within; fighting erupted among various tribal and national factions. Antiochus answered these threats by (1) invading various client states (like Israel) and looting them to pay his debts, and (2) forcing subject peoples (again, like Israel) to adopt Hellenistic culture wholesale. He wanted to homogenize the entire empire and thus (he hoped) put an end to civil wars within it.

Both of these policies—looting and hellenizing—were perceived by many in Israel as direct assaults on the nation's life as the covenant people of God. Antiochus dared even to plunder God's temple in Jerusalem, removing everything of value:

> He arrogantly entered the sanctuary and took the golden altar, the lampstand for the light, and all its utensils. He took also the table for the bread of the Presence, the cups for drink offerings, the bowls, the golden censers, the curtain, the crowns, and the gold decoration on the front of the temple; he stripped it all off. He took the silver and the gold, and the costly vessels; he took also the hidden treasures that he found. (1 Maccabees 1:21–23 NRSV)

To this pragmatic Greek, indeed, *nothing* in Israel was sacred. In his ruthless attempt to hellenize the Jews, Antiochus passed strict laws against all of the religious practices that marked Israel out as God's own people. He forbade circumcision, the observance of the Sabbath, and temple sacrifices, and those who dared to disobey Antiochus were put to death by cruel means. Copies of the Torah were burned. Jews were ordered to offer unclean sacrifices to pagan gods. Finally, on the 25th of December in 167 BC, Antiochus deliberately polluted the temple to desecrate it, setting up an altar within it to Zeus, the preeminent god of the Greek pantheon, and offering up a pig—the most unclean animal in Jewish law—as a sacrifice. Outraged and grieving Jews referred to this act in the language of Daniel (11:31) as "the abomination of desolation," "the abomination that desecrates" or "causes desolation."

But Antiochus had not reckoned with the Jews' tenacious faith in God and commitment to God. Israel believed that the LORD would act to vindicate his name and to reclaim for himself the temple, the land, and the people. They also believed that they themselves must act to carry out God's vengeance on the pagans. Accordingly, the Jews rose up against their Seleucid overlords.

### The Maccabean Revolt (167 BC) and Hasmonean Dynasty (to 63 BC)

It began with an elderly priest, Mattathias ben Johanan, who had been ordered to offer up an unclean sacrifice to one of the pagan gods. Mattathias refused to do this. Instead, he killed both the compromising Jew who *did* offer the sacrifice and the Greek soldier who was there to see that his government's law was carried out. After this brave and dangerous act of defiance, Mattathias fled to the desert with his five sons and there organized a band of rebels. When in the next year the old priest died, his third son Judah assumed leadership of these guerrilla warriors. Judah was nicknamed *Maccabee*, "the hammer," for hammering at the enemy, and so the rebels loyal to him came to be called *Maccabeans*.

Though hopelessly outnumbered by the opposing Seleucid army, the Maccabeans achieved many remarkable victories. On the 25th of December, 164 BC, three years to the day from Antiochus's desecration of the temple, Judah Maccabee (also known—especially from Handel's oratorio about him—by the Latinate form of his name, *Judas Maccabaeus*) rode into Jerusalem to shouts of "hosanna" and the waving of palm branches. He cleansed the temple, removing from it the images of Greek gods, the foreign altars, and the other despised trappings of pagan worship, and rededicated the whole of the temple to the LORD. A new feast, *Hanukkah*, was established to memorialize this remarkable deliverance of the Jews from their pagan overlords (1 Maccabees 4:41–61). Yet it was not until just over twenty years later that Seleucid rule was completely removed from Israel (142 BC). This ushered in a period of Jewish independence and self-rule, during which the descendants of Judah Maccabee's older brother Simon (the *Hasmoneans*) governed for eighty years.

It is important for us to know about these events—the Seleucid oppression of the Jewish people under Antiochus and the subsequent Maccabean revolt against the occupying pagan rulers—if we are to understand the ongoing story of Israel. This event, like the exodus, became for the Jews a defining moment in their history: God had acted to deliver his people, to restore his temple, and to vindicate his law. And since God had visited his people once in this dramatic act of redemption, *surely* he would do so again. Surely the time of the Jews' oppression under pagan rulers was at an end, and God would restore his kingdom in Israel as the prophets had promised for so long.

But it was not to be—not yet. The rebel leaders Mattathias ben Johanan and his famous son Judah Maccabee had been committed to God's rule and God's law for Israel. Yet the Hasmonean kings that followed were deeply compromised by their affection for pagan, Hellenistic culture and by their concern to maintain the political power they had inherited.

### Israel within the Fist of Rome

Rome had been rising steadily in wealth and power since Seleucus I and Ptolemy I assumed rule over parts of the Greek Empire two hundred years earlier (in 323 BC, when Alexander the Great died). In the early years of the first century BC, Rome had become the dominant military and political force in its part of the world. In 63 BC Pompey the Great at the head of his army marched into Jerusalem to bring Israel also within the Roman Empire, beginning a Roman presence there that was to last nearly five hundred years. Rome chose to rule Israel indirectly, through cooperative (and thus compromising) puppet kings and governors: the last of the Hasmoneans, Herod the Great and his descendants, and finally a series of Roman-appointed procurators, or prefects, including Pontius Pilate. The Roman government (not the Jews!) also made the appointment of the temple's high priest to his important position.

The frustration and anger that Israel had always felt for its pagan masters now found a new target in Rome, the most powerful and brutal of them all. Many who looked to the Torah for understanding now identified Rome with the prophet Daniel's vision of the last and worst of four "beasts" rising out of the sea: "There before me was a fourth beast—terrifying and frightening and very powerful. It had large iron teeth; it crushed and devoured its victims and trampled underfoot whatever was left. It was different from all the former beasts" (Daniel 7:7). This truly fit Rome's way of doing business in its empire. The Romans ruled by force, fear, and intimidation, trampling on the cultural sensitivities of their conquered peoples, taxing them into penury, forcing their own brand of Hellenistic culture down stubborn Jewish throats, and meting out savage punishments for any who opposed their will.

Under this oppressive regime, racial hatred of Gentiles increased in Israel. It spilled over to include hatred of any of those among the Jews who would collaborate with Rome, including many of the priests and tax collectors, as well as the Roman-appointed king Herod and his cronies. Stronger and stronger grew the common people's urgent longing for God to return to them and to rule the world from Jerusalem. From time to time this zeal for a new kingdom to be ruled by God broke out into local acts of rebellion against the hated Roman usurpers. These were swiftly and violently put down, ending with mass crucifixions of the would-be rebels, a grisly exhibition of the price to be paid for opposing Rome. Still, Israel remained a stubborn and intransigent province of the empire for almost a century before the birth of Jesus and for a century after. During this period about ten or twelve revolutionary movements arose around a messianic or quasi-messianic figure.[3]

Thus, the Israel to which Jesus came was a nation in which both hopes and fears were intense, even feverish. The people were weary of subjection to pagan masters, full of longing for the coming of God's kingdom, and ready to *act* to help usher it in.

## Israel's Hope for the Kingdom

The people of Israel thought of history as being comprised of two very distinct periods: *the present age* and *the age to come*. In *the present age*, which had begun with Adam's rebellion against God's rule, the whole of creation had been stained by sin. Inevitably, therefore, evil would continue to flourish in the world throughout the present age, even among God's own people of Israel, who had been called out to provide the solution to that evil. But in *the age to come*, God would intervene to cleanse and renew his creation. This renewal would begin with Israel, many of whom were still in exile among the pagans and/or estranged from God because of its sin. Thus, before this great act of liberation could occur, God would need to deal with Israel's sin.[4] Many among the Jews believed that the night of exile would grow darker until God brought his final judgment on his people. This judgment would be like the darkest hour of the night before sunrise or like the birth pangs before the birth. Then the day of God's renewal would dawn, a new world would be born, and Israel would be a forgiven, cleansed, and renewed people.

Through *this* nation, newly prepared for its task, God would then extend the blessings of redemption and restoration even to the surrounding Gentile nations. Then redemption would reach further, until God had reclaimed for himself the whole world, including the nonhuman creation. All of this would take place in the last days of history: God's Spirit would be poured out upon his people to make all these things possible, and the present evil age would draw to a close. God himself would set things right. He would act in power to restore the whole of creation and the whole of humankind to live again under his gracious rule. He would save his creation from the ravages of sin, Satan, pain, and death.

This division of history into two eras was rooted in the writings of the Old Testament prophets. From the prophets the people of Israel learned that God would not abandon either his original purposes for the creation or his covenants with his servants. In the last days of history God would visit the earth to restore his cosmic rule. He would bring about a comprehensive salvation from evil, in which the knowledge of God, justice, and peace would fill the earth. This salvation would begin with Israel, and then all the nations would be gathered to Israel.

Some among the Jews believed that the Gentile nations would, at such a time, finally acknowledge Israel's God as their own king and joyfully live under his rule (Isaiah 49:6). Many more, however, inclined to a different prophetic theme in Scripture. They held that Israel was destined to become the ruler of those who had formerly lorded it over the Jews: Israel would conquer and subjugate the Gentiles, and they would either willingly serve Israel or be destroyed in God's judgment (Isaiah 60:12, 14). Israel's long years of humiliation had bred such hatred for the pagan oppressors that the dominant note sounded in Israel was not that the nations would flock to Zion to learn the way of God (Isaiah 2:3). Instead, Israelites looked for the nations to be dashed into pieces like a potter's vessel (Psalm 2:9). In that day, those who still refused to acknowledge God's rule would face his unsheathed wrath. In vengeance God would destroy the oppressors who had so long sought to keep Israel from serving him according to his covenant. And so God would deliver his people.

This mighty act of deliverance would be accomplished by a *messiah* (a Hebrew word meaning "anointed," translated by the Greek word "Christ"). The divine agent of redemption was to be an anointed king who would usher in God's renewed kingdom. Perhaps the deliverer would be descended from David's own royal line and liberate the nation by leading his people out against the Romans on the battlefield. Perhaps he would be a priestly figure who would first restore Israel to pure worship. And some believed that God's redemptive work would be accomplished by more than one messiah.[5] There were many conflicting notions of what the nation should expect to see when God at last sent his messenger to deliver them. But any notion of a *suffering* messiah was almost absent (Isaiah 53:3; cf. Luke 24:25).

The image that best captured Israel's expectation was "the kingdom of God." Israel looked to a day when there would be "no king but God." The holy land, trampled and polluted by pagans, would be cleansed so that Israel could again live in communion with the LORD. He would return to the temple that he had abandoned and would once again dwell among his people (Malachi 3:1). The nation would be liberated from its bondage to pagan oppressors, just as it had been delivered from Egypt and Babylon. The rule of Caesar in Rome and of his puppet kings and priests in Israel would be swept away, and the rule of God would set things right. The coming kingdom would mean liberation from foreign cultural dictates and an endorsement of Israel's status as the elect people of God. It would mean the reformation of the people in obedience and faithfulness toward God as he poured out his Spirit upon them and "circumcised their hearts" (Deuteronomy 30:6) so that they could obey the Torah. Jews of past generations who had remained faithful to God throughout Israel's many years of exile and bondage would be raised from the dead to experience—together with the living remnant—the coming of God's kingdom (Daniel 12:2). Until that day, the faithful in Israel lived in hope: they prayed, studied the Scriptures, celebrated the festivals to keep hope alive,[6] remained faithful to the Torah, and continued to be ready for military action. On these, most agreed. But on the matters of *how, when,* and *through whom* God would accomplish these things, and on *how they were to live* until that day, there was much division among the Jews.

## Differing Expressions of Israel's Hope

### The Pharisees

By taking a position of compromise toward pagan Hellenistic culture, the later Hasmonean kings had largely betrayed the original spirit of the Maccabean revolt. For many people in Israel, such compromises among their own Jewish leaders served to intensify an already profound hatred of all Gentile usurpers. Though the Maccabeans had driven their former Greek overlords from Palestine, the Greeks had managed to leave behind their pernicious and seductive pagan culture. That culture tempted the people and their leaders toward apostasy. Such things should not be in Israel! Hope began to grow that the revolution begun in the days of old Mattathias and his son Judah might be taken up again and that all vestiges of pagan thought and practice might finally be purged from Israel along with the last of the Gentiles. One such group of Jewish nationalists, the Pharisees, began to rise in prominence about this time. The Pharisees were prominent in the synagogues as teachers of the law and an oral tradition that purportedly stemmed from Moses. They were inspired with an urgent sense of the need for two things: (1) revolutionary change in the nation, to separate Israel completely from the ideas and practices of the pagans; and (2) radical obedience to the Torah among God's faithful ones.

To the Pharisees, separation and obedience were two sides of one essential truth. They thus came to emphasize aspects of Torah law that marked the Jewish people as unique. Circumcision, food laws, and observing the Sabbath all assumed new significance as boundary markers, dividing faithful Jews from faithless pagans. Many among the Pharisees were ready to advance this godly revolution with political activism and even with violence. The Pharisees were successful because they gave voice to some of the deepest desires of the people of Israel: their longing for liberation, their loyalty to the Torah, and their long-held hope for a renewed kingdom in which God himself would reign over his people.

## The Essenes

This group also arose during the Maccabean revolt and was driven by the desire to reverse the assimilation and compromise with Hellenistic culture that yet plagued Israel. However, they were not content to work within the system as were the Pharisees. The Essenes chose the path of withdrawal. Since they believed that the corruption of Hellenism had become so deeply rooted in Israel, reaching even into the temple and the priesthood (whose members were appointed by the Romans), the Essenes turned their backs on all of it. They believed that they alone were the *true* Israel, heirs of the scriptural promises and the vanguard of God's liberating army. Many withdrew to form an alternative community at Qumran outside Jerusalem, where they studied the Scriptures, prayed, and enforced careful adherence to the Torah.

Again, the Essenes must be understood in the context of their hope for liberation and for the coming of the kingdom. They believed that their faithfulness to the Torah would bring God back to restore the fortunes of Israel. The Essenes did not participate in revolution because they believed that God would come back in his own time, sending a priestly and kingly messiah to lead them in a war against Gentiles and compromising Jews—the "sons of darkness." That time, they believed, was very close. When it came they would be ready to rise up and slay the pagan enemies of God. But until that time they took the quietist path of withdrawal, ritual purity, and prayer.

### The Sadducees and Priests

These were the official teachers of the Law and the recognized representatives of mainline Jewish religion. Along with the Pharisees they were members of the ruling council, the *Sanhedrin*. Because they depended on the favor of the Romans to get and to keep their influential positions in society, the priests and Sadducees certainly did not have the revolutionary spirit of the Pharisees or the Essenes. They also lacked the longing for change held by most Jews (cf. John 11:48). Their own power had been established precisely because they collaborated with the Romans, and so they had every reason to maintain the status quo.

### The Zealots

This last group is not as easy to define. They were not so much an organization as a subculture within the nation, representing a cross section of people with differing interests and including many among the Pharisees who were zealous for Israel and willing to take up arms in violent revolution. The Zealots took their inspiration from the account of the old priest Mattathias, the initiator of the Maccabean revolt. He "burned with *zeal* for the law" and rallied men to him by crying out, "Let every one who is *zealous* for the law and supports the covenant come out with me!" (1 Maccabees 2:26–27 NRSV; cf. Numbers 25:6–15). The Zealots carried on this tradition: they were loyal to the Torah, fiercely resisted compromise with pagan culture, embraced the use of violence to achieve their ends, and were willing to be martyred for the cause if that should be necessary.

By the time of Jesus there were many groups of Zealots in Israel, eager to participate in armed revolt so as to liberate their people and cleanse the land and temple of pagan pollution. The members of one such group were called the *Sicarii*, "dagger-men," because they concealed knives beneath their robes with which to murder compromising Jewish leaders. Often these bands of revolutionaries would be led by one who claimed to be the messiah. Inevitably, the Roman authorities would crush such a band, crucify the "messiah," and savagely punish his followers. This was the fate of Judas of Galilee and his group in AD 6 and of others from time to time (Mark 13:22; Acts 5:36–37). One of Jesus' own apostles is identified in Scripture as Simon *the Zealot* (Luke 6:15).

### The Common People

Most of the Jews of this period were not members of *any* party.[7] About a half million lived in Israel, with perhaps three million others scattered across the Roman Empire. Most looked for a day when God would return to redeem his people from their pagan oppressors. They would then be free to obey the Torah and to worship God in a cleansed temple on a cleansed land. The promised Messiah was the focus of their longing: until his coming, they would seek to be faithful so that God would speed the day. They would attempt to learn about the Torah at the synagogue and obey it as best they could. They would celebrate the festivals in their own towns and perhaps sometimes in Jerusalem. They would pray, keep the food laws and the Sabbath, and circumcise their baby boys. And they would wait in hope.

In the context of this fervent expectation, a young man from Nazareth, the son of a carpenter, would announce that the kingdom of God had come to Israel *and was even now present in him*.

# Act 4

## The Coming of the King
### Redemption Accomplished

We cannot grasp the meaning of the story of Jesus until we begin to see that it is in fact the climactic episode of the great story of the Bible, the chronicle of God's work in human history. When his good creation was fouled by human rebellion, God immediately set out on a salvage mission. He had created it, and it thus belonged to him by right. Now he would *redeem* it, buy it back for himself, so that it might be restored to what he had always intended it to be. The Old Testament tells of God's moving among the people of Israel to make progress toward this goal, of his first acts of redemption and restoration, and of his repeated promises that one day he will complete for the whole of creation what he has begun within this one small nation. In God's purpose, at last the very heavens and earth themselves are to be renewed and restored. In Jesus Christ, that renewal and restoration is revealed in its final shape as the *kingdom of God*.

In his life, Jesus shows us what salvation looks like: the power of God to heal and to make new is vividly present in all his words and actions. In his death, Jesus accomplishes that salvation: at the cross he wages war against the powers of evil and defeats them. In his resurrection, Jesus opens the door to the new creation—and then *holds that door open* and invites us to join him. *Gospel* (from the Old English *gōdspel*, "good tale") means "good news," and this is the best news there can be: in Jesus, the kingdom of God has come!

The good news was initially spread by word of mouth after Jesus was raised from the dead and the Spirit had come to his followers at Pentecost. Many stories about the life, death, and resurrection of Jesus were told and passed along as those followers (the early church) attempted to bring good news to their neighbors and those they met in their travels. Soon many of these stories were written down and began to be collected into more complete narratives of Jesus' life. At least four authors took up this challenge, writing the books we call Matthew, Mark, Luke, and John. We call these volumes "Gospels"[1] because their primary purpose is to tell the good news about Jesus: in him, God's new day has dawned at last.

The Gospels are not like modern biographies; they do not try to give a precise chronological record of the events of Jesus' life. Rather, each of the Gospel authors shines the light of the good news on a particular historical situation, selecting events from the eyewitness stories of what Jesus said and did. Each evangelist interprets those events in light of the needs of his own moment in history, arranging the events to convey a particular theme. The Gospels thus vary according to the writers' differing situations and purposes. The Holy Spirit certainly moved these human authors to give a reliable account of, and compelling witness to, God's work in Jesus. Yet we can also detect in what they wrote both the normal processes of history writing and the particular, personal concerns of the writers.

Since the arrangement of the Gospels is not simply chronological but more episodic and thematic, and since each Gospel differs from the others in many ways, it is difficult simply to narrate the story of Jesus. Yet its basic structure is clear. Following his early years in Nazareth (about which we are told little), Jesus begins an itinerant ministry in Galilee. In his words and actions he reveals the coming kingdom of God. As more people come to hear of this revolutionary prophet from Nazareth, his following grows ever larger, and he increasingly draws the attention of the (mostly hostile) Jewish leaders. He determines to go to Jerusalem itself, the center of both the nation and the most bitter opposition to what he has been saying and doing. In Jerusalem, Jesus is arrested, brought to trial, and—though his judge pronounces him innocent of any crime—crucified. *He then is raised from the dead.* Jesus' death and resurrection form the climax of his ministry, demonstrating that, though all the powers of evil have sought to destroy him and defeat his purposes, he has instead defeated *them*: his victory over sin and death ushers in the kingdom of God.

The remainder of act 4 will tell this story of Jesus. It is usually as-sumed that Mark was the first Gospel written. Hence, to tell the good news, we will use his basic structure, with appropriate references to the other Gospels.

## In His Life Jesus Makes Known the Kingdom of God

### Jewish Expectation for God's Kingdom

Jesus' entire mission turns on the central theme of *the kingdom of God*.[2] He proclaims this in his first words in Mark's Gospel: "The time has come. The kingdom of God is near. Repent and believe the good news!" (Mark 1:15). But then Jesus goes further: not only has God's kingdom come at last to Israel, it has come *in himself*, he claims (Luke 4:18, 21). He, Jesus of Nazareth, has been sent by the Father for one purpose alone: to make known the good news of the kingdom (4:43).

It is surprising that two thousand years after this startling announce-ment, many Christians who sincerely want to follow Jesus know so little of the "kingdom" that was at the heart of his ministry. Living as we do in modern Western democracies, the whole notion of kingdom is alien to our everyday experience. But if we are truly to understand the astonishing announcement that Jesus makes to explain his own life's purpose, we must at least try to walk in the sandals of the first-century Jews who first hear these words and enter into their experience. Only then can we grasp what they think and feel, what longings stir in them when Jesus suddenly announces the arrival of the kingdom of God.

Jesus does not stop to define or explain the phrase "the kingdom of God." Those to whom he is speaking are quite familiar with such lan-guage. After all, there is a widespread expectation among the Jews of first-century Palestine and of the Diaspora that God is about to act—soon, suddenly, in love and wrath and great power—to renew his creation and restore his reign over the whole world. But until God acts, how should one live in anticipation of that day? How can the coming of the kingdom be hastened and the hated Romans driven out? What does God require of his people?

In the previous chapter we surveyed four well-known answers to these questions: the Zealots espoused revolution, the Sadducees promoted compromise with the Roman authorities, the Pharisees taught strict cultural and religious separation, and the Essenes advocated complete withdrawal. Four different approaches—and yet they are bound by a common loathing for the Gentiles, a deep-seated hatred or at least wariness for all those outside the covenant. And then comes Jesus, who refuses to walk in any of these paths. His way is startlingly different: it is the way of love and of suffering, "love of enemies instead of their destruction; unconditional forgiveness instead of retaliation; readiness to suffer instead of using force; blessing for peacemakers instead of hymns of hate and revenge."[3]

### Jesus Prepares for His Kingdom Mission: His Early Years, Baptism, and Temptation

Each of the Gospel writers is concerned to show us that the stories he tells about Jesus' life are to be understood as episodes taking place in the context of a much larger story. Mark thus begins the story of Jesus with John the Baptizer's (or *Baptist's*) ministry, to remind us of the Old Testament prophecies of the forerunner who is to prepare the path for the coming Messiah. Matthew's Gospel looks back further, rooting Jesus' ministry in the story of Israel begun in Abraham: for Matthew, Jesus enters history in order to complete Israel's story. Luke reaches back even further—all the way to Adam—to show that the good news about Jesus has significance for all humankind. And John takes us back to a time *before creation*: Jesus is the eternal, uncreated Word, present with God from the beginning.

The birth of Jesus is the incarnation of God in human history. His birth is miraculous: he is begotten not by his (legal) earthly father (Joseph), but by the Holy Spirit's power in the womb of the virgin Mary (Matthew 1:18–23; Luke 1:26–35). Jesus is born in the line of David and even shares the same birthplace: Bethlehem. His birth announcement is made to outcast[4] shepherds: "I bring you good news of great joy! This is good news for all people! Today a Savior-King has been born. He is the long-awaited Messiah, the Lord!" (Luke 2:10–11 authors' paraphrase). As a Jew he is circumcised when eight days old, a sign of entry into the covenant community. At his circumcision Anna and Simeon—part of the godly remnant of Israel waiting in hope—witness that this baby is the fulfillment of Isaiah's prophecies promising salvation to Jew and Gentile (Luke 2:29–32, 38). Jesus grows up in Nazareth with his brothers and sisters, the son and apprentice of a carpenter. Little is known of these years, the time between his birth and the launch of his public mission, except that his awareness of his sonship to God and his mission is already beginning to develop. When he is twelve years old, his parents accidentally leave him behind in Jerusalem after the annual celebration of the Passover. They find him in the temple. When his mother gently rebukes him, he answers: "Didn't you know I had to be in my Father's house?" (Luke 2:49).

Jesus' public mission begins in connection with his cousin John the Baptizer (Mark 1:1–8), who has appeared in Palestine as a prophet with a message from God: The kingdom is about to come. God is about to act, to return to his people, to rule them just as the Old Testament prophets promised. His kingdom will be inaugurated by the "Coming One" who brings salvation and judgment. The kingdom of God is so close, John says, that the winnowing fork separating (godly) wheat from (ungodly) chaff is *already* in the hand of the Messiah (Luke 3:9, 17). John's own task is (just as Isaiah promised) to prepare the way for the coming king, to prepare the *people* to receive him (Isaiah 40:3–5; cf. Malachi 3:1; 4:5–6).

John's message is that God's subjects must repent—turn from sin to God, seeking his promised salvation—and be baptized in water. *Where* this happens is important, since for the Jews geography is drenched with symbolic meaning. John baptizes in the Jordan River because it was here that, more than a thousand years earlier, Israel entered the promised land to become God's light to the nations. John's return to this place signals a new beginning for Israel, a new summons from God to carry out that original (long-neglected) task. Baptism is a vivid symbol of this new beginning, suggesting cleansing from sin. The people of God are (symbolically) crossing the Jordan once more, entering into the land, cleansed and ready to take up their task again.

One day, among the crowds who have come to John to be baptized, Jesus also comes (Mark 1:9–11). Though he (unlike the others) does not need to be cleansed from sin, he identifies himself with the nation, taking on himself their mission to become the channel of God's salvation to the nations (Matthew 3:14–15). While he is being baptized in water, the Spirit visibly comes upon him to equip him for his task. The Father himself confirms Jesus' calling: "You are my beloved Son" (Mark 1:11 NLT). These words of the Father affirm that Jesus is Israel's anointed king, here to inaugurate the kingdom of God. The Spirit will empower him to carry out God's work of salvation.

Before this work begins, the Spirit leads Jesus into the wilderness to encounter Satan (Matthew 4:1–11; Mark 1:12–13). This is a story of spiritual battle, but *not* about an individual soul seeking personal holiness. As we read the story, we must remember the differing points of view in first-century Israel concerning how God's kingdom should come, for *this* is what Jesus' temptation is all about.

Satan shows Jesus three different paths he might take as the Messiah: we can refer to them as (1) the way of the populist, (2) the way of the wonder-worker, and (3) the way of the violent revolutionary. By traveling the first path, turning stones into bread, Jesus could use his power to become a populist messiah. He could give the people what they want, gratifying their urgent need for simple food, putting himself forward as the leader of a popular revolution. The people would surely demand that such a provider should be their king. Alternatively, Jesus could become a messianic wonder-worker, throwing himself from the temple wall and forcing God to act in a spectacular way to save him. The people would be completely dazzled and follow Jesus in whatever he does or says thereafter, compelled by their sheer sense of wonder. Or again, Jesus could become a political messiah in the mold of the Zealots, using violence and coercion in a militarist shortcut to the throne. But to do this would be to agree with Satan, to adopt his own program of domination, to bow before Satan.

Jesus sees that all such paths in fact begin with Satan, and he refuses to twist his own mission to conform to popular expectations of what a messiah of God should or should not be. Instead, he chooses the hard road into the kingdom: the road of humble service, self-giving love, and sacrificial suffering. The way of Jesus is the way of the cross. Empowered and led by the Holy Spirit, and resolute in his sense of calling as the Messiah, Jesus is ready to begin his mission given to him by the Father.

## Jesus Launches His Kingdom Mission in Galilee

Jesus' mission begins humbly. He moves from place to place in the northern Palestine province of Galilee, often near the city of Capernaum. In his words and actions he makes known the kingdom of God and begins to gather a following, the nucleus of a kingdom community. Jesus' teaching and actions come with such authority that soon a large crowd begins to gather and to follow him in his travels. But not all who come to Jesus like what they hear: opposition mounts against him among the Jewish leaders; even some of his own followers abandon him (John 6:66). [5]

### JESUS ANNOUNCES THE ARRIVAL OF THE KINGDOM

While John the Baptizer emphasized God's judgment against sin and the need for the people to repent in preparation for the coming of the kingdom, Jesus announces *good news*: *the kingdom of God has arrived* (Mark 1:14–15). The Greek word here for "good news" (*euangelion*, from which comes the word "evangel" in its many forms) is the word commonly used in that culture for the kind of announcement that brings great joy. It might be news of a wedding, the birth of a son, a military victory, or an enthronement introducing a new era of peace.[6] Jesus announces the good news that God's power to save his creation has arrived. God has entered human history in love and power to liberate, to heal, and to

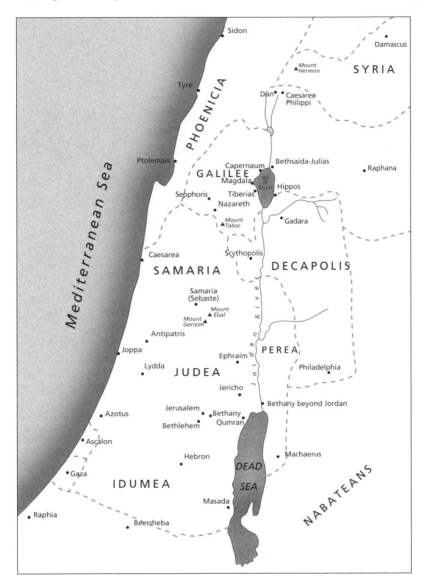

**Figure 20** *Palestine in the Time of Jesus*

renew the whole world.[7] This is not the sort of announcement that would be tucked away in the religion section of *Time* or *Macleans;* this is front-page stuff! *"God is now acting in love and power through Jesus and by his Spirit to restore all of creation and all of human life to again live under the benevolent reign of God himself."* God is becoming king again![8]

There is an image in the book of Isaiah (52:7–12) that has become so precious to the beleaguered Jews of first-century Palestine that they recognize it instantly. The prophet Isaiah was writing (almost six hundred years before Jesus' day) to his people trapped in miserable exile from their homes, held captive in pagan Babylon. He describes a day to come when Israel will once again be free and return in thousands from the land of oppression to their beloved Palestine and to the holy city of Jerusalem. All those who had stayed behind in that city while the rest were driven into exile now stand on tiptoe, watching from Jerusalem's walls and towers. They look for the herald who will run ahead of the crowd to proclaim the long-hoped-for news of the end of the exile and the beginning of God's renewed reign. The people see this messenger while he is still a long way off, running now across the mountains that guard the approach to the city. Soon they can even hear his voice, faintly at first, gradually louder, finally shouting the message: "God is King! He brings salvation and peace. God is victorious. He is returning to Zion to rule over the whole world!" At this, those who watch from the city's walls and towers lift up their voices, too, calling to the herald, to each other, and to the returning exiles, weeping and shouting for joy, taking up the cry of victory: "God returns to Zion! The LORD our King brings salvation and peace!"

And now, many hundreds of years since the Babylonian exile has ended, the words locked up in an old scroll of the prophet are again ringing in Jewish ears, for Isaiah's herald *has* come. Though he voices familiar words from the scroll, he does not speak like a man remembering an old story. His name is Jesus, and he announces in his own voice, boldly and with authority: "God is returning to rule!"

Some messages can be received merely for information. Others, like "there is a fire in the building," demand an immediate response from anyone who hears—anything less is ludicrous. One cannot remain impassive once one has truly heard the news that God is at last acting to usher in his universal kingdom. This is a message to be heard by all people, and it demands a response. Jesus calls those who hear him first to "repent and believe" and then says simply, "Follow me" (Mark 1:15–17).

Jesus' call to repent and believe might be paraphrased thus: "Turn from your false views of the world and embrace the reality and presence of the coming kingdom of God in me. You may not *see* the power of God's healing kingdom breaking into history, but you can *believe* that in me God's liberating power is now present. Give up your old way of life, and trust me for a new one." Jesus then calls those who have repented and believed to "follow" him. Similarly, in Jesus' day a disciple would give up his own plans in life to follow and live with a rabbi, learning the *Torah* and all the rabbi's ways. In choosing these words, Jesus gives an invitation that is familiar to his Jewish hearers: "Come. Be with me. Learn from me. Give up your own way of life. Do what I do. Learn to live as I do." However, though these words in one way are quite familiar to the first-century Jews who hear them, in another way they are strange.[9] For Jesus is much more than a rabbi: he is Lord and Christ. The lives of those who choose to hear and follow Jesus are not to center in the Torah, but in Jesus himself. His disciples are to give full allegiance and devotion *to him*. Few images express more vividly the total commitment and absolute loyalty Jesus demands: loyalty to God's kingdom is expressed in loyalty to Jesus.

Simon and Andrew, followed by James and John, are the first to respond to Jesus' startling call on their lives. With these few, a kingdom community begins to form (Mark 1:16–20).

## JESUS REVEALS THE KINGDOM THROUGH HIS MIGHTY WORKS

Jesus' claim to be the Messiah of God's kingdom is soon validated by some amazing acts that reveal the saving power of God at work in him. People witness miracles of healing, demons driven out, the powers of nature subdued to Jesus' will, death itself unraveling and giving back life (Mark 1:21–34, 40–45). While miracle-workers and exorcists are not unknown in Jesus' day, the sheer scope and power of his deeds proclaim that something fresh, a new power, is irrupting into history. When the disciples of John the Baptizer come to Jesus inquiring whether or not he really *is* the Messiah, Jesus sends back a gentle answer. He points to what he has done. "Go back and report to John what you have seen and heard: The blind receive their sight, the lame walk, those who have leprosy are cured, the deaf hear, the dead are raised, and the good news is preached to the poor" (Luke 7:22). This is clear evidence that the healing power of God's kingdom has come upon the earth, confirming Jesus' own role as God's anointed king. Thus, when the Pharisees later accuse Jesus of doing these things by the power of *Satan*, Jesus gives a searing rebuke: "If I drive out demons by the finger of God, then the kingdom of God has come to you" (Luke 11:20). It is not surprising that the first miracle recorded in Mark is expelling an evil spirit (Mark 1:21–28), for Jesus has come to destroy the devil's work (1 John 3:8).

All of Jesus' "deeds of power" (Mark 6:2, 5 NRSV) indeed are unmistakable evidences of God's liberating power at work through him. When Jesus heals the blind (Luke 18:35–43), the lame (Mark 2:1–12), the mute and deaf (7:31–36), and the leper (with some skin disorder; Luke 17:11–19), people see God's healing and renewing power flowing into human history to end the reign of sickness and pain. When Jesus calms the sea (Mark 4:35–41), feeds the hungry (8:1–10), and prepares an extraordinary catch of fish for weary fishermen (Luke 5:1–11), he demonstrates the power of God to renew and restore a cursed creation. When Jesus raises Lazarus (John 11), the widow's son (Luke 7:11–17), and Jairus's daughter (Mark 5:21–43), people see the power of God conquering even death. Not only does Jesus display God's power to liberate humankind from the ravages of evil, suffering, and death; he also shows God at work to heal the entire creation. These miracles are like windows through which we catch glimpses of a renewed cosmos, from which Satan and his demons have been cast out. Sickness and pain are to be no more, death itself gone forever, and the creation restored to its original beauty and harmony. No trace of sin or sin's effects will deface or defile God's new creation.

## THE SOURCES OF JESUS' POWER ARE THE HOLY SPIRIT AND PRAYER

Following an exhausting day of healing people and driving out demons, very early the next morning Jesus finds a solitary place to pray (Mark 1:35). Luke tells us that Jesus "often" withdraws to pray, and on occasions he prays all night (Luke 5:16; 6:12).[10] These reports of prayer take us to the heart of Jesus' ministry and the secret of his power: an intensely intimate relationship with God, as of a son with his father, and the working of the Spirit in and through Jesus.

Jesus carries out his mission in intimate communion with God, addressing him as *Abba*, "Father" (Mark 14:36; John 17:1–3). *Abba* is an Aramaic term, a *family* word used to express the special intimacy that can exist between close family members. "Father" was only one of the many titles by which Israel knew God, and it was most unusual for Jews to address him in such intimate terms. Their deep reverence did not ordinarily permit such familiarity with the LORD, the Maker of heaven and earth, the Lord of the hosts of heaven, Israel's divine King. So it is particularly striking that when Jesus relates to God, this most intimate language, such as would be used between a cherished father and his beloved son, becomes the primary term of address.

The Father responds to his dearly loved Son by the powerful working of his Spirit. Indeed, the kingdom comes as the Spirit works in response to prayer. In the mission of Jesus, prayer is "the means by which men become subject to the Spirit's power and influence."[11] The Spirit is at work in and through Jesus from the very beginning of his life. He is conceived in the womb of Mary by the Spirit's power. At Jesus' baptism, the Spirit is poured out on him, and he soon announces in the synagogue at Nazareth that the Spirit is on him to empower him for his mission (Luke 4:18–19). Jesus carries out his mission in the power of the Spirit (Acts 10:38). He counters the Pharisees' suspicion that the power at work in him might be demonic: "If I drive out demons by the Spirit of God, then the kingdom of God has come upon you" (Matthew 12:28). Where the Spirit of God is at work, *there* the kingdom of God has come. James Dunn makes the remarkable statement that "it is not so much the case of where Jesus is there is the kingdom, as where the Spirit is there is the kingdom."[12] Jesus maintains intimate communion with the Father in prayer, and this unleashes the Spirit's power to heal and renew.

### JESUS AROUSES OPPOSITION TO HIS KINGDOM MISSION

When Jesus returns to Capernaum, among the crowd that gathers there to hear him are some of the Jewish leaders, Pharisees and teachers of the law, come from as far away as Jerusalem to check out the orthodoxy of this new "kingdom" movement (Mark 2:1–12; Luke 5:17–26). And what these men see and hear mightily disturbs them. In a series of episodes, Mark narrates the developing clash between Jesus and these skeptical leaders concerning various traditional Jewish practices. In each encounter, Jesus challenges the status quo, announcing and embodying a radically new and different view of the kingdom of God than that held by the reigning guardians of Jewish culture and religion. The story he tells is unlike anything they have heard.

Jesus' story explains the coming of God's kingdom in a way that the Pharisees cannot swallow. *They* are looking for a kingdom in which Israel will be suddenly, forcibly delivered from the control of pagan Rome. They are separatists, self-appointed guardians of Jewish identity, which they believe is under attack, threatened by the people's assimilation to the surrounding pagan culture. Careful attention to food laws, tithing, Sabbath keeping, and the choice of "acceptable" mealtime companions—these all are parts of the Pharisees' strategy to keep themselves pure. They have established a rigid boundary between the pure Jews and the despised pagans or Romans—or even between the pure, orthodox Jew and the Jew who has become soiled by cultural and religious compromise, the one who has failed to measure up to the Pharisaic standard of separation. Jesus boldly challenges the Pharisees' rigid views on the Sabbath and food laws. He deliberately eats and drinks with all those the Pharisees would exclude. But it is important for us to understand that Jesus' challenge is not simply a matter of his rejecting Jewish cultural symbols. What he does reject is what these things have come to represent in his own day: separation, hatred, and a thirst for vengeance. These things have no place within God's call for the Israelites to *love* their neighbors, to be the channel of God's *blessing* to the nations, to be a *light* to the world. Against the Pharisees' deeply held misunderstanding of Israel's identity and vocation, Jesus holds up Israel's missionary calling. His refusal to abide by their rules and see things their way incenses the religious leaders because *his story of what Israel was always meant to be* shows their story to be a lie.

In a series of narratives, Mark highlights this conflict and the opposition to Jesus' mission that grows among the Jewish leaders and those who listen to them (Mark 2:1–3:6; cf. Luke 5:17–6:11). Jesus offers forgiveness of sins to a paralytic and then heals the paralyzed man to validate his authority (Mark 2:1–12). What so angers the Pharisees here is not simply that Jesus offers to forgive the man, but that he does so "outside the official structures, to all the wrong people, and on his own authority."[13] In their view of things, the *Jerusalem temple* is the only place designated by God where one might find forgiveness. Yet Jesus acts on his own authority to offer this kingdom gift, thus bypassing the temple. It is, says Wright, as if someone were to offer drivers' licenses on his own authority.[14] Naturally, since (in the Pharisees' view) Jesus' gift of forgiveness competes with God's own forgiveness, this draws their charge of blasphemy.

The Pharisees also are offended that Jesus associates with all the "wrong" people. They demand of him, "Why do you eat and drink with tax collectors and 'sinners'?" (Mark 2:16). Since the time of the Maccabees (when many Jews became deeply compromised by paganism), the Pharisees have exhorted all those zealous for God's rule in Israel to renew their holiness by applying in their *homes* the purity laws regarding food that had been prescribed for the *temple*. Thus, everything concerning food—not merely what one ate but also how it was prepared, how people washed themselves before eating, and who was welcome at your table—all these are for the Pharisees marks of personal holiness. They have become rituals meant to keep distance between the "holy" Jew and the "unholy" outsider (whether Jewish or Gentile; cf. Mark 7:2–4). Jesus challenges these separatist traditions, scandalizing the Pharisees by extending his fellowship to the very people they despise, welcoming those they consider "unclean."

Fasting also becomes a contentious issue between Jesus and the Pharisees (Mark 2:18–22), for the Pharisees ritually abstain from certain foods at certain times, while Jesus' followers do not. For the Pharisees, fasting signifies Israel's present condition: God's people remain in exile, under God's judgment, awaiting the coming of God's Messiah to liberate them from oppression and bring in his kingdom.[15] Jesus simply explains that he and his disciples are not fasting *because the kingdom has already come*. While the bridegroom is away, it is appropriate to abstain from the banquet; but when he is present, it is wrong to fast.

The final two conflicts concern the Sabbath, a central symbol in the Pharisees' understanding of the coming kingdom (Mark 2:23–3:6).[16] For them, keeping the Sabbath is an important part of the obedience to God's Torah. The Sabbath helps to distinguish Israel from its pagan neighbors and prepares Israel for God's return. The Pharisees watch closely to see if this man Jesus, who claims that the kingdom *is* coming, will at least affirm their Sabbath laws. But again, his response is disappointing: he challenges their separatist understanding of the Sabbath.

Among the common people, Jesus is (at least for a time) greatly popular. His words and deeds capture the attention of the people in Galilee, and soon a large crowd follows him (Mark 1:33; 2:12; 3:7). However, their understanding of Jesus' mission is generally superficial. As it becomes more clear what Jesus is all about, this popular support begins to dwindle (John 6:60–69).

### Jesus Gathers a Community

Early in his Galilean ministry, Jesus begins to gather a community around him (Mark 1:16–20; 2:13–14). Matthew's Gospel, written to the Jews, especially highlights the fact that Jesus' early efforts to form a community take place primarily within Israel.[17] When a (Gentile) Canaanite woman comes seeking relief for her demon-possessed daughter, Jesus first tells her, "I was sent only to the lost sheep of Israel" (Matthew 15:24). After the woman's persistence and witty challenge, he does then cast the demon out (15:25–28). To the disciples gathered to share in his mission in its early days, he says, "Do not go among the Gentiles or enter any town of the Samaritans. Go rather to the lost sheep of Israel" (10:5–6). At first Jesus' meaning is hard to understand, especially for readers who happen to be Gentiles. But when what he says here is heard within the context of Israel's prophetic hope in the first century, it becomes much clearer.

The people of Israel have been chosen to live as a nation under the rule of God, but they have failed to live up to their calling, and God has scattered them in judgment. The prophets promised that Israel would one day be restored, its scattered people brought together once more under God's reign. Ezekiel speaks to Israel when the nation has been judged by God and is in exile, promising that in the end time God will regather his people and give them new life (Ezekiel 37; 39:23–29). God will appoint his servant David as a shepherd to gather the flock of Israel, which has been scattered among the nations in God's judgment (36:23–24). Thus, when Jesus says he is sent to *the lost sheep of Israel,* this is what he has in mind: the end-time gathering of Israel has begun.[18] The gathering is not (contrary to what many believe) a gathering of the diasporic Jews to Palestine. The people *will* gather, not to the land, but *to Jesus himself.* With *him* they through the Spirit will share in the life of the kingdom.

According to the prophets, this end-time salvation will not be limited to Israel, though it will start with the chosen people. In prophetic literature, Israel is first to be renewed, and *then* the (Gentile) nations will be gathered to it, to share in its salvation. Once Israel is gathered to the land, says Ezekiel, "the nations . . . will know that I am the LORD . . ." (39:27–28; cf. 37:28). Isaiah employs two memorable images to describe the same event. In the first, all peoples come to Israel to share in a great feast (Isaiah 25:6–9; 55:1, 2). In the second, Israel becomes a beacon for the lost, to which all the nations of the world are drawn. But this light will shine out only when Israel has truly become the people of God (2:2–5; 60:2–3). For Isaiah, this is God's purpose in Israel's long season of misery at the hands of Gentile overlords. The chosen people have been exiled because they were not fulfilling their calling to be "a light to the nations" (42:6; 49:6 NRSV).

Now Jesus announces the dawning of just such a day, the beginning of a renewal for Israel that eventually will draw all nations to God. This prophetic hope lies behind the words he speaks to his newly gathered disciples: "You are the light of the world. A city on a hill cannot be hidden. Neither do people light a lamp and put it under a bowl. Instead they put it on its stand, and it gives light to everyone in the house. In the same way, let your light shine before men, that they may see your good deeds and praise your Father in heaven" (Matthew 5:14–16).[19] This newly gathered kingdom community of disciples to which Jesus speaks is to be the beginning of a restored Israel. Isaiah's prophecy is being fulfilled: Israel is being renewed!

This community begins to form as Jesus announces the good news of the kingdom and calls for individuals to respond with repentance and faith (Mark 1:14–15). Some who hear Jesus' claims are (like Mary, Martha, and Lazarus) called to be loyal to him while remaining in their homes and villages, living out the life of God's kingdom there. Such followers of Jesus are "by their adoption of his praxis, his way of being Israel, . . . distinctive within their local communities."[20] Others are called to leave everything behind and travel full-time with Jesus. From among this latter group, Jesus appoints twelve who spend their lives with him, and he designates them *apostles* (from the Greek for "one who is sent"; Mark 3:13–19; Luke 6:12–16). These Twelve, whose number represents the twelve tribes of Israel, are to become the nucleus of the renewed nation (Luke 22:30; Revelation 21:12–14). Jesus' choosing of them is thus "a symbolic prophetic action" by which he portrays the end-time gathering of the twelve tribes of Israel to share the salvation of the kingdom.[21]

The Twelve are appointed for a twofold purpose: (1) "that they might be with him [Jesus]," and (2) "that he might send them out to preach and to have authority to drive out demons" (Mark 3:14). To "be with" Jesus means to watch him and come to know his way of life, to listen to him and be instructed about life in the kingdom. It means to learn of Jesus' intimate communion with the Father and to model their own lives on his life empowered by the Spirit. They hear him proclaim the good news with his words and demonstrate it in his actions. They see a life of love (John 15:9–13), obedience (17:4), joy (15:11), peace (14:27), justice (Luke 4:18), compassion (Matthew 9:36), gentleness and humility (11:29), and deep compassion for the needy (Mark 2:15–17). Hence, they would learn to build these things into their own way of life. Much of the Gospels' text is taken up with Jesus teaching his disciples what it means to live as citizens of the kingdom he is bringing. The Sermon on the Mount is our clearest example of Jesus' instruction to his disciples about life in the kingdom of God (Matthew 5–7; cf. Luke 6:17–49). The Twelve are also called to follow Jesus so that they can participate in his mission by their own actions. He soon sends them out to pursue the same kingdom mission that he himself is involved in (Mark 6:7–13; Luke 9:1–9). For the disciple community, to be in communion with Jesus means to take active part in his mission.

### Jesus Welcomes Sinners and Outcasts

Within his kingdom community, Jesus includes the poor, the sick, and the lost—all those who are marginalized within Israel.[22] He does not entirely ignore the Pharisees and religious leaders (they are welcome if they choose to come), who often characterize him as a "friend of tax collectors and 'sinners'" (Matthew 11:19; cf. Luke 7:36; 14:1–24). Likening himself to a doctor (who treats the sick and not the healthy), Jesus explains why his ministry is directed primarily toward sinners and not the "righteous." He has come "to seek and to save what was lost" (Luke 19:10; cf. Mark 2:17; Luke 15). In the parable of the Great Banquet, the master directs his servants to bring in the poor, crippled, blind, and lame (Luke 14:21). Those shunned by Jewish society receive from Jesus a warm welcome into the kingdom of God.

Though this dimension of Jesus' mission is clear in Mark's Gospel, Luke gives it particular emphasis. There are four specific groups that Luke shows as the special objects of Jesus' attention: (1) "sinners," (2) tax collectors, (3) prostitutes, and (4) the poor and sick.[23] By "sinners," Luke means "persons in despised occupations, or people with immoral lifestyles, such as adulterers, prostitutes, murderers, robbers, defrauders."[24] When this word comes from the lips of Pharisees, a factional rivalry may also shape the term. "Sinners" may mean those who don't follow the Pharisees' program. Jesus' welcome to tax collectors is equally offensive. Jewish society ostracizes tax collectors because many cheat and over-charge the citizenry. Even if they do not cheat and extort, all of them are considered traitors to their own people because they collect taxes for the hated Romans. Jesus also welcomes prostitutes and women of question-able character, scandalizing the Pharisees by allowing such a woman to anoint his feet with perfume (Luke 7:37–50) and forgiving another woman caught in adultery (John 8:1–11). He says to the leaders of the Jewish people, "I tell you the truth, the tax collectors and the prostitutes are entering the kingdom of God ahead of you" (Matthew 21:31). Jesus may well have welcomed prostitutes into table fellowship.[25]

Jesus also welcomes into the kingdom of God the poor, the beggars, the sick, and the physically handicapped. In Jewish thought of the time, poverty and sickness are often interpreted as signs of God's judgment against an individual's sin. Jesus angrily denounces the traditional "wis-dom." Once his disciples ask concerning a blind man, "Rabbi, who sinned, this man or his parents, that he was born blind?" Jesus responds, "Neither this man nor his parents sinned." He tells his disciples *not* to see his affliction as God's punishment for some misdeed but as an op-portunity for God's work to "be displayed in his life" (John 9:1–3; cf. Luke 13:1–5).

His teaching makes it clear that those on the margins of Jewish society are welcome in the kingdom of God. In two kinds of actions he most forcefully illustrates the point. As signs of the coming kingdom, Jesus enjoys table fellowship with these "outcasts," and he heals them. "Jesus practised a radically inclusive table fellowship as a central strategy in his announcement and redefinition of the in-breaking rule of God."[26] Meals are not casual matters in Jesus' time. They are "highly complex events in which social values, boundaries, statuses and hierarchies were reinforced."[27] A meal is richly symbolic of a warm welcome into one's social group. The Pharisees believe that many kinds of "sinners," the sick, and the poor should be excluded from fellowship within the com-munity because they stand under the judgment of God (cf. John 9:2). Jesus' practice thus is an affront to the Pharisees' sense of what is right and good. In eating with these folks, Jesus makes a positive statement about the kingdom: sinners, tax collectors, prostitutes, the poor and sick, though religious outcasts to some, are not barred from the Messiah's kingdom banquet. Jesus welcomes them and symbolically demonstrates that welcome in his table fellowship with them from day to day.

Jesus' miracles of healing also demonstrate how he accepts into the kingdom of God those who live on the margins of Jewish society. A writ-ten fragment from an Essene community around Jesus' time shows how these strict Jews exclude many from the kingdom: "Neither the blind, nor the lame, nor the deaf, nor the dumb, nor the lepers, nor those whose flesh is blemished shall be admitted to the council of the community."[28] The Pharisees, rather like the Essenes, believe that they alone are the true Israel of God, and their list of excluded people is similar. When Jesus touches the blind, the deaf, the leprous, and the lame, he not only heals their bodies and liberates them from oppression but also restores them to full membership in the kingdom.[29]

### JESUS EXPLAINS THE KINGDOM WITH HIS PARABLES

Jesus announces the arrival of the kingdom of God, demonstrates it in his actions, and gathers a kingdom community. However, this kingdom does not look at all like what the Jews expected. Jesus himself does not look like the Messiah of Old Testament prophecy as popularly understood. The world itself does not seem much changed by what this prophet from Galilee is doing and saying. Jewish expectations seem doomed to disappointment yet again. For anyone in first-century Israel who takes the claims of Jesus seriously, perplexity and bewilderment reign.

We glimpse this confusion in John the Baptizer when he is in Herod's jail. John has preached that the kingdom of God is near, the final judgment about to fall. The ax is already in the hand of the Messiah, John says, and he is about to chop down any tree that does not produce good fruit (Luke 3:9). John fully expects this prophetic message to be fulfilled. He explicitly identifies Jesus as the one sent by God to set these things in motion (John 1:29–34). Then Jesus announces the arrival of the kingdom—and apparently nothing major happens. John expects the Messiah to bring down the wicked rulers of the earth and to release their righteous prisoners (Isaiah 40:23; 61:1). Yet John himself remains rotting in prison while Herod continues his unjust rule and immoral lifestyle. Pagan Roman soldiers infest the holy streets of Jerusalem. Idolatrous Rome rules the world with impunity; oppression, injustice, and unrighteousness reign. Have not the prophets promised that the kingdom of God will come with justice, peace, and the knowledge of God? John wonders if he misunderstood everything. He calls his disciples and sends them to Jesus with a question: "Are you the one who was to come, or should we expect someone else?" (Luke 7:19). Jesus answers by pointing to his miracles and his message of good news for the poor as signs that God's redeeming power is present. Then he sends John's disciples back with a promise: "Blessed is the man who does not fall away on account of me" (Luke 7:23). No doubt John holds on to his belief that Jesus is the Messiah. But until Salome[30] has his head cut off for her mother's sake, John is probably still confused about the kingdom and about his own role in announcing its coming (Matthew 14:1–12; Mark 6:16–29).

It is just this kind of confusion that Jesus addresses in the parables. His disciples struggle to understand how the promises of the prophets are being fulfilled in Jesus. It certainly doesn't look like what they expect. Throughout the Gospels it is clear that the disciples just "don't get it." Jesus' parables are told to explain the "secret" of this kingdom that has appeared among them in such an utterly unexpected way (Matthew 13:11). The parables help those who receive Jesus' word in faith to understand the nature of the kingdom as it appears in Jesus. At the same time the parables veil the truth from those who refuse to believe (13:12–17; cf. Isaiah 6:9–10; Acts 28:26–27).

Mark 4 and Matthew 13 offer an important selection of these stories. They are introduced with Mark's phrase "The kingdom of God is like . . ." and Matthew's "The kingdom of heaven is like . . ." (meaning the same; Matthew, writing to Jews reticent about using the name Yahweh, refers to God indirectly by naming the *place* from which he rules). In this series of parables, we learn the secret of the kingdom.

1. *The kingdom does not come all at once.* Though the Jews have expected the kingdom to arrive in fullness immediately, or at least very soon after the Messiah appears, this does not happen. Sometimes as Jesus talks about the kingdom, he speaks of it as if it is present already; at other times he suggests that it is coming in the future. Many of his parables help to explain this seeming contradiction. The parable of the sower and weeds teaches that in the *present* the kingdom comes by the "sowing" of the gospel. In the *future* the weeds will be separated from the wheat (Matthew 13:24–30, 36–43). The parables of the mustard seed and the yeast suggest that though the kingdom at *present* is small and seems insignificant, it will in the *future* be glorious and impossible to ignore (13:31–33; Mark 4:30–32). The parable of the net teaches that in the *present* all sorts of fish are gathered in to the kingdom, but in the future there will be a great separation (Matthew 13:47–50).

Thus, the kingdom Jesus describes is both present and future: *already begun here*, *not yet here* in fullness. But this is not a contradiction, and Jesus is not mistaken. How then can something as important as God's kingdom have these two apparently opposite qualities? How does it stand in tension between "already" and "not yet"?

In the parables Jesus offers his bewildered followers a resolution of this "already–not yet" quality of the kingdom. With the coming of the kingdom, the Jews expect the present evil age to pass away quickly. The parable of the weeds teaches them that the power of evil continues alongside the new healing power that has come into the world in Jesus. The age to come *overlaps* with the old age; the powers of both are present.

2. *In the present, the kingdom does not come with irresistible power.* The Jews have expected that when God's kingdom arrives, no enemy would be able to resist it. They remember Nebuchadnezzar's dream in which a rock not cut by human hands (representing the kingdom of God) strikes a great statue (representing the world kingdoms of Babylon, Media, Persia, Greece, and in later interpretation Rome) and shatters it (Daniel 2). Daniel says: "The God of heaven will set up a kingdom that will never be destroyed. . . . It will crush all those kingdoms and bring them to an end, but it will itself endure forever" (2:44). Surely God will sweep his enemies away. Who can stand against the power of God?

But Jesus says: "Listen! A farmer went out to sow his seed" (Mark 4:3). And what a different picture emerges in the parable of the sower (4:1–20; Matthew 13:1–23). The Messiah does not come as a military conqueror but as a humble farmer. The kingdom does not arrive in irresistible power and force but by the message of the kingdom. The seed falls on the footpath, in rocky places, and among thorns—producing no fruit. In other words, listeners can reject the call of the kingdom and may well seem to be none the worse for it. Certainly no great rock hurtles from the sky to destroy those who refuse Jesus. The kingdom is hidden in a humble form and makes its way in the world in apparent weakness. In his ministry Jesus announces the message of the kingdom—the gospel—through his words, demonstrates it by his deeds, and embodies it in his life. The gospel is a seed, given to produce the fruit of the kingdom in the soil of receptive and believing hearts. Later Paul speaks of the gospel as the "power of God" (Romans 1:16), yet that power does not trample down or root out all resistance by force. The parable of the weeds gives us a picture of how this works (Matthew 13:24–30, 36–43). Jesus says: "The kingdom of heaven is like a man who sowed good seed in his field. But while everyone was sleeping, his enemy came and sowed weeds among the wheat." The wheat and weeds appear together. When the servants want to root out the weeds, the farmer forbids this, explaining that at the harvest he will separate the good plants from the weeds. Some people receive the word, and God's power brings about the fruit of the kingdom, but others reject that message—and *seem* to suffer no harm.

3. *The final judgment of the kingdom is reserved for the future.* Jesus' hearers expect God's judgment to fall swiftly on the ungodly. The prophets spoke of a day when God would bring his kingdom in by judging his enemies in his wrath (Isaiah 63:1–6). Redemption and wrath are two sides of one reality: God saves his creation by judging the enemies that have ruined it (61:2; 63:4). But the parable of the weeds (Matthew 13:24–30, 36–43) shows the Jews that the judgment they expect does not fall immediately. The workers in the field want to root out weeds

immediately (13:28), but the owner instructs his servants to allow both wheat and weeds to grow together. At the end of the age the judgment will indeed fall; until then the powers of God's kingdom and of evil must continue together.

Many other parables similarly illustrate a judgment postponed: good fish will be sorted from bad (13:47–50) and sheep from goats (25:31–46). The master who has entrusted money to his servants will return to settle accounts (25:14–30). Five maidens keep oil for their lamps and are ready for the return of the bridegroom (25:1–13). Two men invest their master's money wisely and are commended for it; another who merely buries his money is condemned as a "wicked, lazy servant" and thrown into outer darkness (25:14–30). Jesus' true followers are those whose lives imitate his: they feed the hungry, clothe the naked, offer drink to the thirsty, and visit the prisoner. These faithful ones are invited into the kingdom of the Father. But another group whose lives show nothing of Jesus' own life are sent away at last to eternal punishment (25:31–46). When Jesus speaks of the final coming of the kingdom in his parables, he stresses readiness and faithfulness in the present. One is to respond to the message of the kingdom and live a life centered in Jesus until the last day.

4. *The full revelation of the kingdom is postponed, to allow* many *to enter it during the present age.* Since the coming of the kingdom has already begun in Jesus, why does God not complete his work? Why does he delay the final judgment? Why hide his kingdom's glory and power? When we find an answer to these questions, we can begin to understand our own place and calling in the biblical story, between Jesus' inauguration of the kingdom and its final revelation. One of Luke's parables offers such an answer (Luke 14:15–24). A banquet is being made ready: the table is set and laden with food and drink. But there the host pauses; the guests must wait yet a little while. The enjoyment of the banquet is suspended—but the host has a very good reason for the delay. It is so that the lost can also be brought in to share at the banquet table. All—and *especially* the poor, the lost, the forgotten ones—are invited and welcomed to share in the banquet that is God's kingdom. "This gospel of the kingdom will be preached in the whole world as a testimony to all nations, and then the end will come" (Matthew 24:14). When the Pharisees mutter that Jesus is welcoming all the wrong people, he tells them three parables: of a lost sheep (Luke 15:3–7), a lost coin (15:8–10), and a lost son (15:11–32). When the lost son (who has for a time wandered from his home and family) repents and turns back, the Father welcomes him with joy and favor.

Jesus tells many parables—at least forty—and we have looked at only a sampling. Yet in these few, the main themes of Jesus' teaching are evident: the parables reveal what the kingdom is *really* like, in contrast to the misunderstandings of Jesus' hearers.

## Jesus Journeys outside Galilee

The first part of Jesus' kingdom mission (many of the miracles and his teaching in parables) have taken place in the Galilean region surrounding Capernaum. Now, after some two years, misunderstanding of his mission and growing hostility toward him move Jesus to travel further. He increasingly concentrates his attention on teaching his disciples. During these later journeys outside of Galilee, two pivotal events take place: Peter confesses that Jesus is the Messiah, and Jesus reveals his divine glory to his closest disciples in the transfiguration.

### JESUS SOJOURNS IN GENTILE TERRITORY

While Jesus' kingdom mission in Galilee begins in relative obscurity, his power and authority soon attract a large following. The Jewish leaders oppose Jesus because his "kingdom" movement does not correspond to their expectations. Herod also perceives Jesus as a threat. Jesus faces two problems with the crowds. Some, in misguided enthusiasm, want to put Jesus forward as a political messiah. Others (and there are more and more of these as time goes on) become disillusioned and join the opposition to Jesus. This combination of opposition and misunderstanding leads Jesus to move into Gentile areas north of Galilee. There his mission continues. But Jesus increasingly turns his attention to instructing his closest disciples, giving them the teaching and direction they need to carry on his work.

As Mark begins to narrate the story of Jesus' leaving Galilee, he includes an episode in which Jesus discusses with some of the Pharisees the matter of "clean" and "unclean" foods. Especially since the end of Israel's exile in Babylon, these distinctions are part of the dietary laws so precious to the Pharisees as a means of deciding who is a pious Jew and who is not. Separation is *everything* to the Pharisees. Yet here is Jesus, deliberately standing against their separatist and revolutionary agenda. The Pharisees even consider the *land* occupied by Gentiles to be polluted. They taught that, to be righteous, a Jew must cleanse himself ritually after passing through Gentile territory (John 11:55; cf. Luke 9:5). But Jesus defies the oral traditions that have grown up around the laws of the Torah and restores these purity laws to their true context and significance. So this discussion in Mark's Gospel of what is "clean" and "unclean" prepares the way for the story of Jesus' departure to the "unclean" Gentile lands, where he will cast out demons, heal those who are blind and mute and deaf, and feed four thousand people (Mark 7:24–9:27).

### Who Is Jesus?

Jesus has been carrying on his kingdom mission for some time, and there are many opinions about him among the people. The crucial question is, *"Who is* Jesus?" In several stories Luke clearly shows this question. After Jesus calms the storm, the disciples ask one another in fear and amazement, *"Who is this*? He commands even the winds and the water, and they obey him" (Luke 8:25, italics added). When Herod, who has put John to death, hears of the commotion caused by Jesus' healing ministry, he asks, *"Who . . . is this* I hear such things about?" (9:9, italics added). Pausing in his travels at Caesarea Philippi, Jesus now confronts his disciples with the same question: "Who do people say I am?" They reply: "Some say John the Baptist; others say Elijah; and still others, one of the prophets." Then Jesus makes it personal: "But what about you? Who do you say I am?" On behalf of all of them, Peter answers: "You are the Christ" (Mark 8:27–29). This—the identity of Jesus—is the heart of the matter. Peter's confession is a turning point in the gospel that we must understand.

The Greek word *christos* ("Christ") translates the Hebrew *messiah*, "anointed one."[31] In Old Testament days, certain people were anointed with oil to take up some special office, such as that of priest (Aaron) or king (David) or prophet (Elisha). The anointing signified that this person was specially chosen and prepared by God to carry out the appointed task. During the intertestamental period, the term "messiah" or "Christ" was used prophetically as the title of the figure(s) whom God would appoint to restore his rule and usher in his kingdom. The title often took on political and military connotations. Jesus accepts the confession of Peter: indeed, Jesus *is* the Messiah. But the popular understandings of what the "anointed one" is, and of what God calls him to do, are not adequate. Therefore, Jesus warns the disciples not to tell anyone who he is (Mark 8:30). The people's expectations must be adjusted to fit the reality of Jesus. Thus, though most Jews expect that the Christ will be God's agent to usher in the kingdom of God, they have no notion of his having to suffer the humiliation of crucifixion (cf. 8:31). They anticipate the coming of a man from the royal line of David (cf. 12:35–37). But Jesus is much more: he is the transcendent and glorious Lord, the Son of God. So Jesus breaks the mold of expectation. He *is* God's chosen one, appointed to usher in God's kingdom—but he is also the crucified victim and the divine Son.

Peter and the disciples, however, do not yet understand this, and their misunderstanding becomes clear in the next verses. When Jesus tells them plainly that he will soon be crucified, Peter begins to argue with him, saying that he must be mistaken—the Christ cannot die such a shameful death (8:32). Jesus silences Peter, rebuking him sternly, for he and the rest of the disciples have not yet grasped the truth and cannot understand the necessity of the cross: Jesus *must* die (8:33). Not until much later do the disciples come to realize the full significance of Peter's confession. Only when they have experienced the resurrected glory of Jesus will they see what it means for Jesus to be the Christ.

To Mark's account of Peter's confession, "You are the Christ," Matthew adds an important phrase: "the Son of the Living God" (Matthew 16:16).[32] Behind these words there also is a rich Old Testament tradition.[33] All the people of Israel, and particularly Israel's kings (as the nation's representatives before the LORD) were designated *God's sons* (Exodus 4:22–23). The title suggests a special *relationship* to God and a special *task* to fulfill in obedience to God. The Jews of Jesus' time looked for a messiah who would be indeed a "son of God" like the Old Testament kings (2 Samuel 7:14; Psalm 2).[34] Jesus does come to them as one who stands in just such a special relationship to God and with just such a divine task, to inaugurate God's rule. However, Jesus is more than these things, important as they are. His intimacy with the Father and his messianic task are unique and exclusive. He indeed is the "Son of God" in a sense that never has applied and never could apply to any one but himself. He is the long-awaited One of the Old Testament prophecies. Thus, though Jesus *does* stand within a long tradition of "God's sons," he is in another sense absolutely unique, God's *"one and only* Son" (John 3:16).

The next verses in Mark give us one more important title that underscores Peter's confession. Jesus begins to teach his disciples that the "Son of Man" must suffer, die, and rise again. But who is the Son of Man?[35] The title comes from the book of Daniel (7:13–14), a text very popular in Jesus' time because of its promise of a golden future for Israel after a long history of oppression. In Daniel's vision, four beasts (representing four successive pagan world empires) rise out of the sea. But in the midst of this pagan rule, "thrones [are] set in place" and God, "the Ancient of Days," takes his seat. The fourth beast is slain. Then one "like a son of man" approaches the Ancient of Days and is led into his presence. This "son of man" is given authority, glory, and power; all peoples and nations worship him. His dominion and kingdom are to last forever. In Jesus' time, many Jews see the figure from Daniel of "one like a son of man" to be a prophetic vision of Israel's Messiah—with glory, authority, and power—vindicating Israel in the victory over pagan kingdoms and sharing the throne of God, ruling an everlasting kingdom. Jesus claims to be this "Son of Man."[36]

Jesus' identity is confirmed in an event that takes place about a week after Peter's confession, when Jesus takes Peter, James, and John to a high mountain (perhaps Mount Hermon, just northeast of Caesarea Philippi). There Jesus' appearance changes as the other men watch (Mark 9:2–8; Luke 9:28–36). His face and clothing take on an unearthly brilliance: his face shines like the sun, and his clothing becomes dazzling. For a moment the disciples see the unveiled glory and majesty of the Son of Man—the Son of God (cf. 2 Peter 1:16–18). Moses and Elijah (Old Testament figures carrying weighty authority among the Jews and representing the Law and the Prophets) appear and stand with Jesus. *God himself* appears, in the form of a cloud, and speaks to the quivering disciples: "This is my Son, whom I love. Listen to him" (Mark 9:7). When the disciples look again, only Jesus is standing there. But no greater confirmation of his identity can be imagined. In his glorious transfiguration and in God's own confirmation of his Son's status—higher even than that of Moses or Elijah—Jesus is revealed to the disciples as the chosen one of God (Luke 9:35). For the disciples, shaken by growing hostility among the people, and especially by Jesus' odd words about crucifixion, the way forward is clear: Listen to Jesus.

### Jesus Journeys to Jerusalem

Jesus' brief visits to Gentile territory climax in Peter's confession and the transfiguration. Peter and the other disciples still do not fully understand that Jesus must go to the cross. Nevertheless, Jesus sets out with them toward Jerusalem for the final confrontation between the kingdom of God and the powers of darkness, which lie behind Jewish opposition to the kingdom.[37] As Jesus continues to teach his disciples, two themes now dominate: (1) the necessity of suffering and (2) the cost of being a disciple.

#### THE WAY OF THE CROSS

As Jesus begins his last journey toward Jerusalem, he instructs the disciples that he must suffer and be rejected, betrayed, and killed (Luke 9:22, 44). But the disciples do not yet understand (9:45). He explains that he must undergo another "baptism" and is distressed until it is completed (12:49). Responding to Herod's threat to kill him, he answers: "Go tell that fox, 'I will drive out demons and heal people today and tomorrow, and on the third day I will reach my goal. . . . For surely no prophet can die outside Jerusalem!'" (13:32–33). During this journey

Jesus discusses the coming of God's kingdom in relation to what lies immediately before them: "First he [the Son of Man] must suffer many things and be rejected by this generation. . . . He will be handed over to the Gentiles. They will mock him, insult him, spit on him, flog him, and kill him. On the third day he will rise again" (17:25; 18:31–33). And still the disciples do not understand. The meaning of Jesus' plain words is hidden; they do not know what he is talking about (18:34).

Jerusalem is to be the scene of the final battle between the kingdom of God and the powers of evil. Many in Israel do expect a climactic military battle between God's army of pious Jews and the pagan Gentiles, who oppose God's will. But this is not the battle for which Jesus is preparing. Instead, he is about to take the full force of cosmic evil upon himself, and so to exhaust its power. For Jesus, the battle will be won not by killing the enemy, but in allowing himself to be killed, to give up his life on the cross.

### DISCIPLESHIP IN THE WAY OF THE CROSS

The disciples do not yet understand Jesus' mission of love and suffering. Like many of their generation, they still want to see God's fiery judgment fall on those who reject his kingship. And even now, after all this time with Jesus, they still do not understand. Time is short; there is an urgent need for "intensive training in discipleship."[38] The disciples must truly learn what it means to follow Jesus so they can continue what he has begun after he is taken from them.

This instruction on discipleship is closely tied to the theme of Jesus' last journey: he describes discipleship as a "way" to be followed, a journey to be taken. The disciples are—quite literally—on *the way* to Jerusalem, but at the same time they are being taught *the way* of discipleship.[39] Yet each "way" has, as its destination, suffering love and rejection.

> Because the journey narrative is punctuated with these reminders of what awaits Jesus in Jerusalem, the journey itself is cast in the dark hues of the passion. It becomes difficult, then, to read the demands of discipleship or of the hostility Jesus encounters without reference to the significance attached to them by their location on the journey toward death. The journey thus . . . has a pedagogical side, for it urges Jesus' followers to come to terms with the nexus of rejection and divine mission.[40]

This last journey itself teaches the disciples that to follow Jesus means to walk the way of the cross.

Jesus speaks sharply to halting, half-hearted followers. The way of discipleship is costly: it demands total commitment, complete devotion and allegiance to Jesus and the kingdom of God (Luke 9:57–62). "If anyone would come after me," Jesus says, "he must deny himself and take up his cross daily and follow me" (9:23; cf. 14:27). The decision to follow entails significant consequences: "For whoever wants to save his life will lose it, but whoever loses his life for me will save it" (9:24).[41]

Discipleship training continues on the road to Jerusalem. To follow him means to *participate in his mission* (Luke 10:1–24). The disciples are likened to farmhands, sent out to help Jesus gather in the harvest. Their mission, like Jesus' own, is to engage the powers of darkness by their words and actions: "Heal the sick . . . and tell them, 'The kingdom of God is near you'"(10:8). His disciples must also *love* God with their whole being, and love their neighbors as they love themselves (10:25–37). In the context of the widespread loathing within Israel for compromising Jews, Samaritans, and Gentiles, Jesus tells the story of a (Jewish) man beaten, robbed, and left for dead on the road from Jerusalem to Jericho. The leaders of the Jewish people—represented in Jesus' story by a priest and a Levite—do not help the man in his need. But a hated Samaritan takes pity on him and cares for him. The "righteous" Jew thus discovers that the "ungodly" Samaritan is his neighbor, *the one whom God has commanded him to love*. Jesus tells this story in response to a lawyer's question, "What must I do to have a share in the age to come?" and this is the answer: "Follow Jesus in finding a new and radicalized version of Torah-observance. Loving Israel's covenant God [means] loving him as creator of all, and discovering as neighbours those who [are] beyond the borders of the chosen people."[42]

### Jesus Concludes His Kingdom Mission in Jerusalem

At last Jesus arrives in Jerusalem, where his final days are taken up with the growing hostility of the Jewish leaders there and with his teaching about judgment. Here Jesus performs three striking actions to portray symbolically the nature of the coming kingdom, much as the Old Testament prophets dramatized God's message in some remarkable symbolic action. Jeremiah (19:1–15) smashed a pot to show that God would smash Israel. Isaiah (20:1–4) wandered naked through Jerusalem to illustrate the coming humiliation of Israel by Assyria. Likewise, Jesus' last actions are prophetic, picturing what is to come. But his actions mean more, because he is more than a prophet: he also acts as Messiah.

#### JESUS ENTERS JERUSALEM ON A DONKEY

To celebrate the entry of a king into a city with great fanfare is a well-known phenomenon of the day.[43] Jesus' entering Jerusalem on a donkey says louder than any words, "God is returning to Jerusalem to become king over Israel and the nations. Jesus is laying claim to David's throne." This event is found in all the Gospels (Matthew 21:1–11; Mark 11:1–11; Luke 19:28–40; John 12:12–19) and is always interpreted in light of Zechariah 9:1–13, which helps us to understand its meaning. In Zechariah, Israel's king is pictured returning to Jerusalem after a military victory. As we have seen, Judah Maccabee rode into Jerusalem (about a century and a half before Jesus' time, following his victories against the Seleucid armies) to joyful shouts of praise. Once there, his first act in Jerusalem was to cleanse the temple of the pagan pollution visited on it by the Greek king Antiochus IV Epiphanes. Yet the worldwide kingdom expected by Israel did not materialize with Judah Maccabee. And so the Jews waited for another king to establish the universal kingdom promised to David and the prophets, a king who would follow in the footsteps of Judah Maccabee and truly fulfill the prophecies of Zechariah. And other "kings" *had* come, following Judah in this practice, laying claim to the throne of Israel. But none of these had brought God's kingdom with him.

Against this background, Jesus' claim to Davidic kingship cannot be clearer. He enacts this same ride into Jerusalem, coming as Messiah to claim the throne of Israel, to bring the kingdom that Judah Maccabee could not bring. The crowds in Jerusalem understand this action and greet the arrival of Jesus with shouts, welcome, and praise (from Psalm 118): "Blessed is the king who comes in the name of the Lord." "Blessed is the coming kingdom of our father David!" (Mark 11:9; Luke 19:38). Yet neither the crowd nor the disciples (John 12:16) understand what kind of king Jesus is. Matthew, writing to Jews who expect a military Messiah, stresses in his account that Jesus comes as a gentle and humble king. He quotes Zechariah: "See, your king comes to you, gentle and riding on a donkey" (Matthew 21:5). The animal chosen for his entry is a humble creature of burden rather than a royal steed suited to military conquest, for Jesus comes in peace. The people of Jerusalem "[do] not recognize . . . God's coming" (Luke 19:44) because they misunderstand the nature of his kingship, which is "one of humility and service rather than political conquest."[44] Within days, the same crowd will be demanding that he be nailed to a cross.

### JESUS ENACTS JUDGMENT ON THE TEMPLE

In his second messianic action in Jerusalem, Jesus visits judgment on the temple (Mark 11:12–17).[45] Since there was always a close connection between religion and politics in the ancient Near East, the entry of a victorious king would often be followed by some kind of action in the temple.[46] In the Gospels' story, the Jerusalem temple is the single most important symbol of Judaism, the place where God dwells among his people. There the sacrificial system allows an unfaithful Israel to repair the breach made in the covenant relationship by sin. Beyond this, the temple is loaded with religious, political, economic, and social significance; above all, it stands as the center of Jewish hope for the coming kingdom. Just as Judah Maccabee once cleansed the temple, Israel believes that God will one day return here to establish his throne, and from here he is to rule his worldwide kingdom (Malachi 3:1). When God returns to his temple, he will come in fiery judgment (3:3, 5). According to Jewish expectation, this judgment will be directed against the pagan Gentiles and against those among the Jews who have compromised with pagan practices. God will "destroy the unrighteous rulers" and "purge Jerusalem from gentiles who trample her to destruction. . . . To shatter all their substance with an iron rod; to destroy the unlawful nations with the word of his mouth" (Psalms of Solomon 17:21, 24).[47]

The Jerusalem crowds wait for Jesus to fulfill these expectations. But Jesus weeps because Israel has misunderstood God's coming, which indeed means judgment—not on the Gentiles, but on unfruitful Israel (Luke 19:41–44). Throughout his ministry Jesus has threatened God's judgment against God's faithless nation; now, during his time in Jerusalem, his teaching increasingly focuses on this topic (Matthew 21:28–25:46; Mark 12–13).[48] When he comes in judgment against the temple, Jesus symbolically enacts all that he has been threatening.

The temple action is framed by Jesus' curse on the unfruitful fig tree (Mark 11:12–14, 20–21), a messianic and prophetic action that symbolizes judgment on an unfruitful nation. In the very place that is the symbolic center of the nation, Jesus drives out those who are selling animals for sacrifice and overturns the tables of the money changers. Jesus temporarily shuts down operations in the temple, possibly prefiguring the ultimate demise of the temple.

Jesus' words interpret his act: the temple is to be a house of prayer for all nations (Mark 11:17), the place to which all people will come to acknowledge Israel's God (Isaiah 56:7–8). God has chosen the people of Israel to dwell among the nations so that *all* nations can enter the covenant with God. But the temple Jesus enters now functions in a quite different way, supporting a separatist cause, cutting Israelites off from their neighbors. Furthermore, the spirit encouraged within the temple is one of violence and destruction: it has become "a den of revolutionaries" (Mark 11:17; authors' translation).[49] Israel has turned its election into separatist privilege instead of obeying its call to be a light to the world. Judgment on this temple must take place so that a new "temple," Jesus' resurrection life in the renewed people of God (cf. John 2:21), can become the light for the nations that God intends.[50]

When we see Jesus' cleansing of the temple in this context, it becomes clear why the Jewish leaders begin to look for a way to kill him. Not only is he challenging their treasured hopes and aspirations and announcing the destruction of their most cherished symbol. He also is doing these things in the name of the Lord, their God! He is acting as if he is God's chosen Messiah. Though the Pharisees, Sadducees, and others who vie to lead Israel can agree on nothing else, they do agree that this man Jesus threatens their whole way of life with his claim of the coming kingdom. This man has to go!

### JESUS SYMBOLIZES HIS DEATH

After his entry into Jerusalem and his cleansing of the temple, Jesus spends much of the rest of the week in heated arguments with the Jewish leaders. Since it is Passover week, Jesus gathers his disciples to celebrate the Passover meal together (Matthew 26:17–30; Mark 14:12–26; Luke 22:7–23). This is the final and most important of the three symbolic actions Jesus performs in Jerusalem: in this meal he dramatizes the climactic event of his kingdom mission.[51]

On the night of Passover, Jesus directs his disciples to prepare the Passover meal.[52] This ritual meal began as a celebration of Israel's redemption from Egypt in Moses' time (Exodus 12). However, for first-century Jews it also symbolizes the coming "new exodus" by which the kingdom of God is to arrive. Looking back to the past victory of God over the Egyptians, Jews of the first century enacted the meal in the hope that soon God would do something similar in their own time. He had freed his people *then* from their bondage in Egypt: surely he would free them *now* from their Roman oppressors. The coming kingdom of God, a new covenant, the forgiveness of sins, their return from exile—all these terms express Israel's hope for what God will do at the climactic moment in their nation's history. And this Passover meal reported in the Gospels looks forward to that moment. But Jesus takes this meal and gives it new meaning. In his actions and words he says that the kingdom they long for is bursting in on them now. The climactic moment of Israel's story is to be his own death: "The meal, focussed on Jesus' actions with the bread and cup, told the Passover story, and Jesus' own story, and wove these two into one."[53]

In the Passover tradition the head of the home interprets the events of the Exodus and their meaning for the present. Jesus thus explains in simple (but startling) words the new meaning of the bread and wine. He takes the bread, saying, "This is my body" (Mark 14:22). Jesus is about to die, and that death will mean life for his people. As the bread of the Passover has always been a reminder of Israel's redemption from Egypt, so Jesus' death will become the means of Israel's ultimate redemption. The cup also takes on new meaning: "This is my blood of the covenant" (14:24). In his death Jesus will bring the new covenant, the forgiveness of sins, the kingdom of God for which Israel longs. Moses sprinkled blood on the people of Israel and confirmed the Sinai covenant with these words: "This is the blood of the covenant" (Exodus 24:8). And a thousand years after Moses, Zechariah prophesied that through a messianic victory God would liberate Israel from exile and renew his covenant with the nation: "As for you, because of the blood of my covenant with you, I will free your prisoners from the waterless pit" (Zechariah 9:11). By "the blood of the covenant" the exile would end and God's kingdom would come. Jesus identifies this "blood of the covenant" with his *own* blood, soon to be shed on the cross. It is through his death that God's kingdom will come.

### Jesus Is Arrested and Tried

Ever since his early ministry in Galilee attracted their attention, Jesus' enemies were plotting his destruction (Mark 3:6). Their hostility reaches its climax with Jesus' outrageous behavior in the temple, and they meet to work out a plan to arrest and kill him (14:2). One of Jesus' disciples, Judas Iscariot, appears unexpectedly and (to their great delight) offers his help: he will locate Jesus at a time when they can arrest him quietly, without fear of the crowd. The Sanhedrin (the ruling council of the Jews in Jerusalem) dispatches a large group of people to carry out the arrest (14:10–11, 43).[54]

Meanwhile, following the Passover supper, Jesus and his disciples go to a place called Gethsemane. Knowing that the final battle for the kingdom is not far off and knowing what this will mean for him personally, Jesus prays to the Father: "Take this cup from me. Yet not what I will, but what you will" (14:36). After his prayer he rouses his sleepy disciples to face an angry crowd of Jewish leaders (led by Judas), with temple guards and Roman soldiers (see John 18:3). Judas greets Jesus with a kiss, thus identifying him in the darkness. One of Jesus' followers quickly draws a sword—they still don't understand that Jesus' kingdom will come in peace and not violence (Mark 14:47). As Jesus is arrested, all but one of his disciples desert him and run for their lives (14:50–52). But at a distance Peter follows the soldiers with their prisoner, to see what will happen.

It is very late at night. There is a brief interrogation of the prisoner before the Jewish leaders, beginning with Annas (the former high priest), who questions Jesus to try to get him to say something incriminating. When Annas fails, he sends Jesus to Caiaphas (the reigning high priest), who allows a crowd of Jewish leaders to interrogate the prisoner. A parade of false witnesses comes before Caiaphas, accusing Jesus of this and that, but their statements contradict one another (cf. Deuteronomy 17:6; 19:15). In exasperation, the high priest himself finally demands, "Are you the Christ, the Son of the Blessed One?" Jesus answers, "I am" (Mark 14:61–62). The court swiftly agrees that this is blasphemy, deserving the death penalty (14:63–64). These middle-of-the-night interrogations are punctuated by mocking comments from onlookers. From time to time, the guards are encouraged to beat their prisoner (14:65; Luke 22:63–65). As dawn comes and the Sanhedrin meets in formal session, the charge of blasphemy is confirmed (Luke 22:66–71). During the trial, Peter is questioned about his relationship with Jesus, but three times he denies knowing him.

Since the Jews do not have the power to put anyone to death (John 18:31), Jesus is led to Pilate (the Roman-appointed procurator) for sentencing. The men of the Jewish Sanhedrin know full well that blasphemy is not a capital crime under Roman law. Instead, they charge Jesus with treason and sedition, claiming that he has been subverting Israel by opposing the payment of taxes to Caesar and by claiming to be a king (Luke 23:2). Pilate is intrigued by this last accusation and asks Jesus: "Are you the king of the Jews?" (Luke 23:3). Throughout the time he spends with Jesus, Pilate vacillates: the Jewish leaders' "charges" against Jesus are unconvincing, yet Pilate's own position as ruler in Palestine is already tenuous. For political reasons he cannot afford to upset the Jews. Though he can find no legal basis for passing a sentence of death against this man, he sees that the Jews will not tolerate Jesus' release. Pilate tries to duck the issue, first by sending Jesus off to Herod, then by offering the Jews an amnesty for one Jewish prisoner. He says he will release either this man Jesus or another Jew who sits in jail waiting for death, a revolutionary named Barabbas. But the crowd cries, "Crucify him!" and frustrates Pilate's attempt to reason with them. Pilate then orders that Jesus be scourged as his sentence of punishment, hoping that this will be enough for the Jews and that he can then release the prisoner. The Roman soldiers mock and brutally scourge Jesus, beating him with fists and whips. After this he is returned to Pilate, who again tries to release him, but it does not work. The Jews chant, "Crucify him! Crucify him!" Finally, reluctantly, Pilate agrees. Jesus is sentenced to death and led away to be nailed to a Roman cross, to hang there until he dies.

## In His Death Jesus Secures the Victory of God's Kingdom

In this brutal event we see the mightiest act of God. The Bible tells of God's great deeds in human history to restore his creation. Again and again the psalmists call God's people to praise God for these things: "Shout with joy to God, all the earth! Sing to the glory of his name; offer him glory and praise! Say to God, 'How awesome are your deeds!'" (Psalm 66:1–2). But when we follow the story of God's works in history and arrive at the death and resurrection of Jesus Christ, we see the *most* awesome of all God's works of redemption. It is at the cross that God delivers the deathblow to human sin and rebellion and accomplishes the salvation of his world. Yet the crucifixion hardly seems like a *victory* for God, especially not when we see this event in the context of first-century Roman culture.

### Jesus Dies on a Cross

The Romans would force a condemned criminal to carry the heavy horizontal beam of his own cross to the place where he is to be crucified. But Jesus' sleepless night, the cruel mockings, and especially the brutal beatings have taken their toll. Jesus stumbles under the weight of the beam, and Simon of Cyrene is dragged from the crowd and forced to carry it. The grisly parade carries on to Golgotha, "the Place of the Skull," where Jesus is offered a sedative (wine mixed with myrrh), which he refuses. At nine o'clock in the morning, Jesus is stripped naked and nailed by his wrists and feet to a cross set between two other men (revolutionaries, also brought here to die). As the soldiers drive the nails through his flesh, Jesus says, "Father, forgive them, for they do not know what they are doing" (Luke 23:34).

His clothes are divided among the soldiers, and they write a mocking accusation on a piece of wood and fix it to the cross above his head: "This is Jesus, the King of the Jews." To the Roman, calling yourself "king" is treason, a challenge to Caesar's sovereignty; to the Jew, it is blasphemy; and to any one who looks back on this crucifixion through the lens of the resurrection, this "accusation" is, ironically, merely the plain truth!

The Jewish leaders who have hounded Jesus and conspired to have him killed now heap scorn and insults on him: "He saved others, but he can't save himself! He's the King of Israel! Let him come down from the cross, and we will believe him" (Mark 15:31–32 paraphrased). One of the criminals joins in this jeering from his own cross beside Jesus, but is rebuked by the condemned man on the other side: "We are getting what our deeds deserve. But this man has done nothing wrong." He then turns to Jesus and says: "Remember me when you come into your kingdom" (Luke 23:40–42). Jesus acknowledges his faith; indeed, this man will inherit the kingdom of God.

At noon and for the following three hours, darkness covers the whole land. Jesus cries out in agony, "My God, my God, why have you forsaken me?" (Mark 15:34). The One whom Jesus has always called "Father" has turned his back on his own Son, because at this moment Jesus bears the sin of the world. Jesus thus does not address him as "Father" but only as "my God." And then Jesus' life ends with a loud cry: "It is finished! Father, into your hands I commit my spirit" (Luke 23:46). Having at last accomplished God's will, Jesus' work is complete; he can again place himself in the hands of his loving Father.

A Roman centurion stands nearby to ensure that these crucifixions are accomplished without interference from the Jewish crowd. When he sees the manner of Jesus' dying and hears his words, this tough professional soldier, an officer in charge of a hundred troops in the army of occupied Palestine, blurts out, "Surely this man was God's son!" (Mark 15:39 NRSV). At the same moment, something strange happens back in the city, a long way from Golgotha, deep within the Jerusalem temple itself. There the heavy curtain that separates the holy of holies from the outer chambers, veiling the place of God's presence from the people, is torn from top to bottom, but not by human hands (Mark 14:38). The death of Jesus has opened a way into the very presence of God (cf. Hebrews 4:16).

### Crucifixion in the Roman Empire

"They brought Jesus to . . . Golgotha, . . . and they crucified him" (Mark 15:22–24). It is difficult for us, living some two thousand years later, to comprehend just how horrifying and loathsome the idea of crucifixion was for the first-century onlooker: "an utterly offensive affair, 'obscene' in the original sense of the word."[55] Those who enjoyed the privilege of Roman citizenship could not by law be crucified. This means of torture and death was reserved only for slaves and foreigners, for the worst criminals, in the judgment of the Romans. The physical suffering was terrible and drawn out as long as possible—for many hours, or even days.[56] In the process the victim was utterly degraded,[57] hanging naked to public view and suffering the jeers and taunts of bypassers. For the Roman citizen particularly, but also for subject peoples within the Roman Empire, the cross was a potent symbol of humiliation and agony.

And yet the early church had the temerity to point to this event—the crucifixion of their leader—as the mighty act of God. What utter foolishness![58] Little wonder that the church was mocked by its opponents. A drawing scratched on a wall (graffito) from the early Roman Empire shows the body of a man with the head of an ass nailed to a cross, and a man worshipping it. Scrawled below is the mocking caption, "Alexa-

**Figure 21** *Ass on a Cross*

menos worships god." Apparently some slave or child was poking fun at someone with this early cartoon. How stupid, how absurd, to worship a crucified god! The claim that Jesus' death was a mighty act of God must have seemed utter foolishness anywhere within the first-century Roman world.

The Romans were not alone in this opinion. The sheer horror and degradation of death by crucifixion made it impossible also for Jews to accept this as an event that might reveal the hand of their God. Hadn't the Old Testament prophecies spoken of the Messiah coming in glory and victory? Surely he was to be a great and mighty ruler, dispensing justice to a new world empire. His kingdom was to stretch from one end of the earth to the other. As the *Jewish Encyclopedia* puts it, "No Messiah that Jews could recognize could suffer such a death; for 'he that is hanged is accursed by God'" (Deuteronomy 21:23; cited in Galatians 3:13). Moreover, the cross was the place where all those who rebelled against the Roman Empire—including many false messiahs—ended their lives. For the Jews, "crucified Messiah" was an oxymoron. The cross as God's mighty act was (and is) a stumbling block to them (1 Corinthians 1:23).

### Crucifixion in the New Testament

The New Testament is unique in ancient literature in interpreting the crucifixion in a positive way, as the greatest of God's actions in history. Paul proclaims that "the message of the cross is foolishness to those who are perishing, but to us who are being saved it is the power of God" (1 Corinthians 1:18). But he and the other New Testament writers are entirely aware that their view of this event attracts scorn. To the Romans, the cross is utter *foolishness*: crucifixion is merely the worst of the punishments routinely meted out to Rome's enemies. They are humiliated, defeated, tortured beyond human endurance, exposed in their weakness—and then they die. Beyond that, the cross is a random act of cruelty.

Yet the early church makes the bold and fantastic claim that the cross is the central act of God in all of human history! This boldness is the product of a radically different perspective because the church looks at the cross *through the lens of the resurrection*.

It is Jesus' return from the dead that validates his claim to be God's anointed Messiah. When one begins to look at the cross through the lens of the resurrection, what at first appears to be foolishness is really the *wisdom* of God. What seemed to be weakness is really the *power* of God, conquering human rebellion and Satanic evil. What appears to be humiliation is a revelation of the *glory* of God. God's self-giving love, mercy, faithfulness, grace, justice, and righteousness are revealed in the event by which God accomplishes the salvation of his creation. What seems to the world to be Jesus' defeat, the early church proclaims to be his surpassing *victory* over all the enemies who stand opposed to God's good creation. This apparently meaningless act of violence and cruelty in fact reveals the fullest *purpose* of God: his judgment against sin, and his power and will to renew the creation. Seen in one way, the cross is a token of foolishness, weakness, humiliation, defeat, absurdity. Seen in another way, by those who know that Jesus is alive again from the dead, the cross is full of God's wisdom, power, glory, victory, and purpose.

In the cross, Jesus acts to accomplish his purposes for all of history—to save the creation. Too often we reduce the significance of the cross to the fact that "Jesus died for *me*." Believers *do* share in the accomplishments of his death, and so we can say this with joy and confidence. Yet God's purposes move beyond the salvation of individuals. In the death of Jesus, God acts to accomplish the salvation of the entire creation: Jesus dies for the world.

The idea that the cross is the means by which God accomplishes salvation is clear both in the way the Gospel writers choose to tell their story and in the images the Epistles use to interpret it.[59] All four Gospel writers devote enormous space to it, as the culmination of Jesus' ministry (Matthew 20:28; Mark 10:45; Luke 24:25–27; John 12:23–28). Yet each tells the story in his own way, with an emphasis suited to his own audience.[60] Mark presents the crucifixion as the means by which Jesus offers salvation to a new community who will follow him in sacrificial discipleship. Matthew (writing to the Jews) narrates the story of Jesus' death as the rejection of God's Messiah by his own people—yet the crucifixion proves his claim to royal status and inaugurates a new order for *all* nations. Luke tells the story of the cross with two themes in mind: (1) As a prophet, Jesus' pursuit of justice brings Satanic opposition and rejection by the people. (2) The crucifixion *must* take place because it is the central event of world history. John "overcomes the scandal of the cross by interpreting it in terms of Jesus' exaltation." Jesus is lifted up on the cross to die, but in that very act he is exalted and glorified in his love.[61]

The Letters to young churches in the New Testament use many images to interpret the universal significance of Jesus' death. Here we briefly note three. The first is the image of *victory*, which John Driver calls the "conflict-victory-liberation motif."[62] The crucifixion is a token of the great spiritual battle between God and Satan. Jesus wins the battle and grants liberation from slavery to Satan to those for whom he fought. The second image is of *sacrifice* and derives from the Old Testament practice in which an unblemished animal was slain in place of the guilty sinner.[63] *Then*, the sinner was restored to covenant fellowship with God because that animal took away their sin. *Now*, Jesus is the Lamb of God who takes away the sin of the world (John 1:29). The final image depicts Jesus as *representative man*, one who acts on behalf of an entire nation. Jesus grapples with Satan, sin, and death and conquers them as he dies on behalf of all people. He dies for the sake of the entire cosmos, bearing God's judgment on a creation that has become corrupted and polluted by sin. We share in that victory over sin, even as we share in Jesus' triumph over it (Romans 6:1–11).

The cross represents the climactic victory of the kingdom of God. God's rule was disrupted by human rebellion and all that came with it: demonic power, sickness, suffering, pain, and death—every kind of evil. The root of all opposition to God's rule was human rebellion, and that could be destroyed *only* at the cross.

## In His Resurrection Jesus Inaugurates the Kingdom of God

An atheist, a committed disciple of the "truth" of Communism, once gave a speech to an enormous crowd in the former Soviet Union. He mocked the Christian faith, saying it was all mere fantasy. It was not Jesus but the program of Marx and Lenin that was destined to bring history to its appointed purpose. The atheist was eloquent and withering in his scorn for Christianity. When he finished, an Orthodox priest asked if he could say just two words in reply (his two Russian words are translated by three words in English). The priest shouted, *"Christ is risen!"* and the crowd roared back the response carried with them from their childhood: *"He is risen indeed!"* For a world so twisted by evil and enslaved by sin, what other message could there be? *Christ is risen*. In the resurrection of Jesus Christ, a new world is dawning. The night of evil has ended. The light of God will fill the whole earth again. The resurrection stands at the center of the Christian faith.

### Jesus Rises from the Dead

After Jesus' death, Pilate gives permission to Joseph of Arimathea and Nicodemus to take the body from the cross, prepare it for burial, and lay it in a tomb. Some women who have been followers of Jesus watch to see where he is buried (Mark 15:42–47; John 19:38–42). Jesus' crucifixion naturally has left his disciples perplexed and despondent. Everything they have hoped for seems lost. One of them, walking from Jerusalem to Emmaus, puts it this way: "We *had hoped* that he was the one who was going to redeem Israel" (Luke 24:21, italics added). *"Had hoped"*—past tense, future indefinite. With a dead leader and a lost cause, the disciples must decide what to do next, and they are exceedingly afraid. But all this soon begins to change. With the discovery of the empty tomb, the angelic announcement of his resurrection, the appearances of the risen Lord, and the testimony of those who actually see Jesus alive again—the conviction grows among his followers that Jesus *is* truly risen from the dead.

The women who have observed Jesus' burial are the first to come to the tomb, to anoint his body, but they do not know how they will manage to roll the heavy stone away from the entrance. When they arrive they find the stone already rolled out of the way, and angels are there! The women are naturally terrified, but one of the angels calms them, then reveals that Jesus' body is no longer in the tomb: he is alive, risen from the dead. The angel reminds them of Jesus' own words: "The Son of Man must be delivered into the hands of sinful men, be crucified and on the third day be raised from the dead" (Luke 24:7–8). Then the angel instructs the women to tell the other disciples that Jesus will meet them in Galilee, as he has promised (Mark 16:1–8; Luke 24:1–8).

Still trembling and bewildered—yet joyful—the women return to the city. At first they tell no one. When they do tell the other disciples, their story seems like nonsense. Nevertheless, Peter and John go to the tomb and verify what the women have reported: the tomb is indeed empty (Luke 24:9–12; John 20:1–8). The two disciples leave, wondering what is going on. (They may even think that this just means more trouble for Jesus' followers.) The Gospel of John tells us that, at this point in the story, the disciples still do not understand from Scripture that Jesus had to rise from the dead (John 20:9). For any Jew, the idea of one person being resurrected in the middle of history is inconceivable. Thus, when Jesus told them that he would rise from the dead, they discussed among themselves what "rising from the dead" could possibly mean (Mark 9:10).

The appearances of Jesus move them toward full acceptance of the truth. What we find in the Gospel records are not naive and credulous disciples who badly want to believe that Jesus is alive. Rather, we find highly skeptical disciples who are only gradually convinced of the truth—by Jesus' appearances to them. Jesus appears to Mary and the other women (John 20:11–18), to two disciples walking along the road to Emmaus (Luke 24:13–35), to the small band of disciples (several times: Luke 24:36–48; John 20:19–25, 26–29; 1 Corinthians 15:5), and to a larger gathering of his followers (1 Corinthians 15:6). By this means the disciples come to accept the fact that Jesus is indeed alive, raised from the dead. *But what does it all mean for them?*

### Resurrection in Jewish Thought

What did Jesus' followers understand about resurrection?[64] The term that we translate as "resurrection" is first used in Jewish literature metaphorically, to describe the renewal of Israel after its return from exile

(Ezekiel 37:1–14; Isaiah 26:19). At the end of the Old Testament (Daniel 12:2) and throughout the intertestamental period, the language of "resurrection" is used literally to describe the event of physical life actually returning to a body that has been dead. The Jews believed this would take place in the last day, not as an event occurring to an individual, but as the whole company of God's people would be fully restored to life in a renewed creation. From that time "the resurrection" became a vivid image in Jewish thought, implying the coming of the end of the age and the renewal of the cosmos, in which God's people would participate by their own return to physical life. The resurrection of human bodies was but one element in that cosmic renewal, but the language of "resurrection" was also used to refer to the whole of it:

> "Resurrection," while focusing attention on the new embodiment of the individuals involved, retained its original sense of the restoration of Israel by her covenant god. As such, "resurrection" was not simply a pious hope about new life for dead people. It carried with it all that was associated with the return from exile itself: forgiveness of sins, the re-establishment of Israel as the true humanity of the covenant god, and the renewal of all creation. . . . Thus the Jews who believed in resurrection did so as one part of a larger belief in the renewal of the whole created order.[65]

The idea of the resurrection of the body was therefore intricately woven together with the Jewish concept of the renewal of creation as a whole and the coming of the kingdom of God.

### Jesus' Resurrection: The Beginning of the Age to Come

All the Gospels give eyewitness accounts of those who experience the living Jesus after he is bodily raised from the dead. But if this kind of thing—the dead returning from their graves—is not supposed to happen until the end of history, what is going on (cf. Mark 9:10, 32)? The early followers of Jesus struggle with the meaning of this new reality, seeking to interpret it too (like the crucifixion) "according to the Scriptures" (1 Corinthians 15:4). We find their conclusions about it in their preaching in Acts, in the narratives of the four Gospels, and in the New Testament Letters.[66] The early church joyfully proclaims the resurrection of Jesus to be *good news*, an event with cosmic consequences, the beginning of God's renewal of creation.

The words of Jesus in John 11 help us make a start in understanding the resurrection. When Jesus says to Martha that Lazarus will rise again, Martha responds: "I know he will rise again in the resurrection at the last day." Jesus responds, "I am the resurrection and the life. He who believes in me will live, even though he dies; and whoever lives and believes in me will never die" (John 11:23–25). The resurrection of Jesus has implications beyond his own return to life. In Jesus' death and resurrection, he acts on behalf of all of us and of the whole creation. He *is* the resurrection: in dying he takes upon himself the judgment of the world. In rising from the dead, he inaugurates the renewal of the whole creation, including the physical bodies of men and women. Therefore, whoever believes in Jesus will live and share in his resurrection.

Jesus' return from the grave is the dawn of the new day: God's people and all creation will share in his resurrection life. Three images in the New Testament picture the close connection between Jesus' *representative* resurrection and our own. First, Christ is the *firstborn* from the dead (Colossians 1:18; Revelation 1:5). His siblings (believers like you and me) will follow their elder brother in his new life. Second, Christ is described as the *firstfruits* (1 Corinthians 15:20, 23), the first part of the agricultural harvest to be brought in as a guarantee that the whole harvest is to follow. Third, Jesus is pictured as the *"pioneer* of [our] salvation" (Hebrews 2:10 NRSV), the one who goes ahead into new territory to lead the way and mark the trail. Jesus has led the way for us into the age to come, marked our path into the kingdom of God. We can enter that kingdom as we follow him—enter first in foretaste on this side of the completed kingdom and at last enter it fully on the new earth.

### Jesus Commissions His Disciples

After the resurrection, Jesus gathers his disciples and charges (or "commissions") them to carry on the task that he has begun.[67] Again, each of the Gospels looks at this last commission in a different way, according to its intended audience.[68] Matthew, whose Gospel highlights the conflict between Jewish authorities and Jesus, reports these words from the risen Christ: "All authority in heaven and on earth is given to me" (28:18). Jesus is vindicated! Matthew underscores the cosmic scope of Jesus' authority with a fourfold repetition of the word *"all."* Jesus is given *all* authority. His followers are to make disciples of *all* nations. They are to teach the disciples to obey *all* Jesus has commanded. And Jesus will be working among them *all* the days that remain for the earth (Matthew 28:18–20). Behind this statement of Jesus' authority is Daniel 7:14, which says that one like a son of man is given all authority to rule the nations. What will Jesus do with this supreme authority and sovereign power? Will he use coercive and violent power to crush the enemies who have rejected him? Apparently not: "Therefore," Jesus continues (in effect), *"because I have been given this cosmic authority*, make disciples." Through the unpretentious and humble mission of the church in making disciples, the exalted Christ, the Lord with all authority, will "subdue" his enemies—in love. The former "enemy" is to be baptized into the community of disciples and there taught the way of Jesus.

In the Gospel of John, Jesus is portrayed as the One sent by the Father into the world to bring life. On the evening of resurrection Sunday, Jesus appears among his disciples and tells them to continue what he has been doing: "As the Father has sent me, I am sending you" (John 20:21). It is easy here to miss the "*as.*" *In the same way* that Jesus himself carried out his mission, the newly gathered community is to carry out its mission. Specifically, it is to deliver the good news, which includes the forgiveness of sins (20:23). This mandate is bracketed by two actions that help to deepen our understanding of its meaning. *Before* Jesus speaks these words, he shows the disciples his wounded hands and side, the marks of his conflict with evil, as if to say, "You too will encounter evil in your mission; you too will suffer. Your mission is to be carried out in the shadow of my cross, and in that shadow there will be conflict and suffering." *After* commissioning the disciples, Jesus breathes on them to symbolize the giving of life (cf. Genesis 2:7; Ezekiel 37:5–10) and says, "Receive the Holy Spirit." To accomplish Jesus' mission, the disciples must receive Jesus' resurrection life—the Holy Spirit—by whose power alone their task can be carried out (John 20:19–23).

In the Gospel of Luke, Jesus commissions the disciples to be "witnesses," a word from the justice system identifying someone called to testify to what he or she has experienced. This new community is expected to testify, first to the death and resurrection of Jesus Christ, and then to his offer of repentance and forgiveness for all peoples. Again, Luke emphasizes that this witness cannot begin until the Father has sent the promised Spirit and clothed Jesus' followers with the power they will need to carry out the task (Luke 24:46–49; cf. Acts 1:8).

### More to Come—but What?

Jesus' entry into human history—his earthly life, his death, and his resurrection from the dead—marks the climax of the biblical story. Jesus reveals the coming kingdom by his way of life, his words, and his actions. At the cross he challenges and conquers evil itself. The new day of resurrection for all creation dawns when Jesus rises from the dead. Does this mean the kingdom of God is about to come immediately in its fullness? In his last commission, is Jesus instructing his disciples to complete the task of "gathering in the nations" and so to prepare themselves for the end? They thought so, at least initially (Acts 1:6). But if the coming of the kingdom is *not* to be immediate—what then?

How should the followers of Jesus live in the meantime? What should they—and we—do?

While Matthew, Mark, and John end their stories of Jesus with the resurrection, Luke continues his narrative in the book of Acts. To this book we now turn for the answers to the disciples' early questions about the timing of his kingdom's coming and their own place in his continuing mission.

# Act 5

# Spreading the News of the King
## The Mission of the Church

The goal of God's redemptive work is to restore his creation from the effects of sin upon it. In his death Jesus has conquered sin, and in his resurrection he has inaugurated a new era of salvation and recovery. The kingdom banquet is ready to be enjoyed, but it does not begin just yet. More peoples must first be gathered to the banquet table so that they too may taste of the renewing power of the coming age. This in-between time, after Jesus' first coming and before he comes again, is a time of mission for the exalted Christ, the Spirit, and the church.

### Scene 1: From Jerusalem to Rome

Luke is the only one of the four Gospel writers to carry the story past Jesus' death and resurrection. The book of Acts is really the second volume of Luke's Gospel, telling the story of the coming of God's kingdom during the three decades following Jesus' resurrection.[1]

The work of the exalted and reigning Christ is to pour out salvation on the world. Luke's opening words in the book of Acts suggest this: "In my former book, Theophilus, I wrote about all that Jesus *began* to do and teach until the day he was taken up to heaven" (Acts 1:1–2, italics added). The clear implication is that this second volume of Luke's story is about all that Jesus *continues* to do and teach, even after he has returned to the Father. Jesus' work now is primarily through his Spirit, who distributes all the gifts of his kingdom, "filling" the church and giving power to a community of Jesus' followers, through whom he brings his message of salvation to the world. While he was alive on the earth, Jesus mostly confined his work to Israel; the exalted Christ now extends his ministry "to the ends of the earth" (1:8). This second part of the gospel story is about *the continuing mission of the exalted Christ by the agency of his Spirit to give salvation to the church and through the church to the whole world*. We who stand in historical continuity with that early church have also been taken up into its mission. Their story is also *ours*.

### Christ Is Exalted to the Right Hand of God

As the book of Acts begins, the risen Christ appears to his disciples over a period of forty days, during which time there is much talk of the kingdom of God and the coming of the Spirit (1:3–5). The disciples ask Jesus the obvious question: "Lord, are you at this time going to restore the kingdom to Israel?" (1:6). His answer is significant: "It is not for you to know the times or dates the Father has set by his own authority. But you will receive power when the Holy Spirit comes on you; and you will be my witnesses in Jerusalem, and in all Judea and Samaria, and to the ends of the earth" (1:7–8). It is not for the disciples to know when the end will come (cf. Mark 13:32), but until then—until Jesus returns—the Spirit is to bring the life of the kingdom through the witness of Jesus' followers to all nations.

Then Jesus is taken up into heaven (Acts 1:9), or "exalted to the right hand of God," as Peter says later (2:33; 5:31). This is coronation day! The Messiah now shares the throne of God over all creation and all peoples.

It is important to understand the significance of that *place* described as "the right hand of God." Though many Jews believe that the Messiah will share the throne of God, they expect God's throne to be in Jerusalem, from which the Messiah will rule a worldwide Jewish empire. However, the throne of the Messiah as Peter describes is not in Jerusalem at all: it stands entirely above the world, in heaven at the right hand of God. This is the place of *highest* authority and honor. God's kingdom has no boundaries of any kind. Jesus does not merely sit on the throne of our hearts and reign there: that is much too narrow a concept of his authority. Jesus reigns over *all* of human life, all history, and all nations.

The *name* given to Jesus as he ascends to rule from God's right hand is equally significant. An early Christian confession states:

> God exalted [Jesus] to the highest place
> and gave him the name that is above every name,
> that at the name of Jesus every knee should bow,
> in heaven and on earth and under the earth,
> and every tongue confess that Jesus Christ is Lord,
> to the glory of God the Father. (Philippians 2:9–11)

This "name" becomes the central confession of the early church: Jesus is *Lord*, a title that speaks of supreme authority (*kyrios* in Greek; Acts 2:36; Romans 10:9; 1 Corinthians 12:3). There were many lords in the Roman Empire, each having authority within a limited sphere: the paterfamilias was lord over his household, the centurion was lord over a hundred troops, and so on. However, in the Roman Empire, Caesar himself was supreme. Roman military commanders and others were required to confess, "Caesar is Lord." But the early Christian church could *not* say this since they believed that Caesar's authority extended only as far as the political affairs of Rome and even in that was subordinate to God's authority through Christ. It was not Caesar but Jesus who was *Lord* over all the earth. The early church's refusal to say otherwise set them on a collision course with Roman authority and led to much conflict and suffering.

When Peter (in Acts 2:32–36) says that Jesus has been raised to the right hand of God, he quotes Psalm 110:1: "The Lord said to my Lord: 'Sit at my right hand until I make your enemies a footstool for your feet.'" This verse defines the mission of the exalted Christ: to subdue all his enemies. The psalm goes on to speak of the Lord extending his mighty scepter throughout the whole earth, ruling in the midst of his enemies, crushing lesser kings in his wrath, judging the nations, and heaping up the dead. It seems that God's kingdom is to come by violent military power over Israel's political enemies. Yet this is not what happens, either before or after Pentecost. Jesus uses his authority in a very different way.

In his earlier teaching, Jesus has already redefined both the "enemies" and their "subjugation." The real "enemy" of God's kingdom is not Rome, but the powers of evil that stand behind all opposition to God's rule.[2] Subjugation will not come about by military force but by the loving power of the gospel. To "subdue his enemies" means to give them the salvation he has accomplished: "as enthroned one (Messiah), as the Benefactor of the people (Lord), the exalted Jesus now reigns as Saviour, pouring out the blessings of salvation including the Spirit . . . to all."[3]

Act 5 of our book looks at the continuing story of the gospel especially as Luke narrates it in Acts.[4] Our purpose is to discern how the exalted Christ carries out his mission—and how *we* are involved.

## *The Exalted Christ Pours Out His Spirit*

After Jesus ascends to the Father, Jesus' work begins with the outpouring of his Spirit. The Old Testament promised that in the last days the Spirit would be poured out—on the Servant Messiah (Isaiah 42:1), on Israel (Ezekiel 37:14), and on all people (Joel 2:28–32). The Spirit has been poured out on Jesus at the beginning of his ministry but is not to be given in fullness until his exaltation (Luke 3:21–22; John 7:39). After the resurrection, Jesus promises that the Holy Spirit will be poured out on his followers and tells them to wait in Jerusalem (Luke 24:49; Acts 1:4–5).

This mighty act of God occurs about ten days after Jesus' ascension, on the Jewish Feast of Pentecost. The timing is significant in two distinct ways. Originally this feast was a time for Israel to bring the firstfruits of its harvest to God in anticipation of the whole crop that would be gathered in (Exodus 23:16; Deuteronomy 16:9–12). God chooses this day to give the Spirit, which is the *firstfruits* of the coming kingdom of God (cf. Romans 8:23). By the second century before Christ, the Feast of Pentecost had lost its original focus as a harvest festival.[5] Instead, it celebrated the promise God had given to Abraham, that his descendants "might become an elect people . . . and an inheritance from all of the nations of the earth from henceforth and for all the days of the generations of the earth forever."[6] Thus, in Jesus' day the Feast of Pentecost celebrated the *covenant renewal* of Israel and the *inclusion of the nations* within the covenant made between God and Abraham. Now, at this Feast of Pentecost, the Spirit comes in fulfillment of that expectation and hope.

As Jesus' disciples are gathered on the day of Pentecost, a violent wind suddenly fills the house (Acts 2:1–4). Tongues of fire rest on their heads, and all are filled with the Holy Spirit. These two signs of the Spirit's presence—wind and fire—are significant. In Ezekiel's parable of the "dry bones," the Sovereign LORD says, "Come from the four winds, O breath, and breathe into these slain, that they may live." He promises to put his Spirit in them so that they may live. Wind represents the power of God to bring new life (Ezekiel 37:9, 14). In fact, the Hebrew word for Spirit in the Old Testament (*ruach*) and the Greek word for Spirit in the New Testament (*pneuma*) can mean "wind" or "breath." Similarly, fire often represents the presence of God, as when the pillar of fire showed his presence during the exodus from Egypt (Exodus 3:2; 13:21–22; 19:18). Here at Pentecost the Spirit of God comes with the sign of fire as a token of the *powerful presence of God* bringing the life of the kingdom.

During this feast time, Jerusalem is full of people from many parts of the Roman Empire, and a third sign of the Spirit's presence comes when the disciples begin to speak in different languages, making the good news available to people from various nationalities in their own languages. The gospel is no longer confined to the Jewish nation and the Hebrew language: God's rule begins to work outward from Israel to the nations, as Jesus has promised it would.

This remarkable event—people speaking in languages they have never learned—is amazing, bewildering to those who witness it. *What can be happening?* Peter stands up and delivers a sermon that explains the significance of what has happened to Jesus' followers (Acts 2:14–36). This event is in fulfillment of Joel's prophecy that the Spirit will be poured out in the last days (2:16–21). These "last days" have arrived, ushered in by Jesus of Nazareth. His own life has revealed the kingdom of the "last days," and yet he has been nailed to the cross according to God's plan (2:22–23). But God has since raised Jesus from the dead: the disciples are eyewitnesses of this fact (2:24–32). This same Jesus, once crucified, has now been exalted to the right hand of God and reigns there, putting all enemies beneath his feet. He is Lord and Messiah. Having received the promised Holy Spirit from his Father, Christ has now poured out the same Spirit on his disciples (2:33–36).

The exalted Christ will now work by his Spirit, who thus becomes the primary actor in the book of Acts.[7] The Spirit sends the good news to the ends of the earth, brings new converts into the community, guides and empowers the apostles and the church to carry out their mission, and acts in judgment both inside and outside the church.[8]

### The Spirit Forms a Community

The Spirit's first work is to form a community to share in the salvation of the kingdom and to be a channel of that salvation to others. This is the next part of the story that Luke tells (Acts 2:37–47).

When Peter concludes his sermon explaining the meaning of the event of Pentecost, the people's immediate response is to ask, "What shall we do?" They understand that they have killed the Messiah! Peter responds, "Repent and be baptized, every one of you, in the name of Jesus Christ for the forgiveness of your sins. And you will receive the gift of the Holy Spirit" (2:38). God requires those who respond to *repent*—turn from idolatry and orient their lives to Christ and his coming kingdom—and be *baptized* into this community that now has received *the* gift of the kingdom—the Holy Spirit. Within this community, the Holy Spirit brings the blessing of forgiveness. Responding to Peter's sermon, about three thousand people are immediately added to the young church. In the next section of his book, Luke describes the life of this early church community. This is not merely a history lesson but also a blueprint for what the church ought to be in every age.

As Luke describes the young church, it has three defining qualities. The first is *devotion*: this new community devotes itself to the apostles' teaching, fellowship, the breaking of bread, and prayer so that they might more and more experience the life of the kingdom (2:42). The church's second defining quality is that *the life of Christ is manifested* both in the lives of individual members and in the life of the community considered as a whole. The church is thus known by convincing signs of God's saving power within it (2:43), by justice and mercy in its communal relations (2:44–45), by joyful conviviality (2:46), and by worship (2:47). Third, as the liberating life of the kingdom becomes more and more evident in the church, we hear that the exalted Lord "[adds] to their number daily those who are being saved" (2:47). This too fulfills Old Testament prophecies about God's kingdom. The prophets picture the drawing power of a renewed Israel (Isaiah 60:2–3; Zechariah 8:20–23): "A decisive element of the prophetic conception of the pilgrimage of the nations to Zion is that the Gentiles, fascinated by the salvation visible in Israel, are driven of their own accord to the people of God. They do not become believers as a result of missionary activity; rather, the fascination emitted by the people of God draws them close."[9] This newly formed community of the early church is *attractive* to outsiders. The life of the believing community radiates the light of the kingdom and thus draws people from darkness (cf. Ephesians 5:8; 1 Peter 2:9).

Though the Spirit-filled community of Acts 2 is in one sense new to history, it also stands in historical continuity with the Old Testament nation that had its origins in Abraham. God formed Israel to be a light to the nations, but the Israelites failed to live up to their calling, so God sent them into exile. Nevertheless, he promised to gather his people again one day, pouring out his Spirit on them so they might at last fulfill their calling. The prophets looked forward to the day when Israel would be regathered. Now, in Jesus, the regathering has begun. He has appointed twelve apostles, representing the twelve tribes of Israel, to be the foundation of his kingdom, the new nation of God's people. At Pentecost, in response to Peter's preaching and the power of the Holy Spirit, three thousand people are added to that foundation. The remainder of the book of Acts tells the story of how this new community of believers continues Jesus' mission of gathering the lost from within Israel, then moves beyond old ethnic and cultural barriers to gather Samaritans and Gentiles into the kingdom.[10]

### The Church Witnesses in Jerusalem

After its start (Acts 2), the story of the church's witness continues in Jerusalem (3:1–6:7), reaches outward to Judea and Samaria (6:8–11:18), and eventually moves from the fringes and provinces of the Roman Empire to Rome itself (11:19–28:31), as Jesus himself has promised (1:8). Acts 3:1–6:7 tells more about the first stage of this witness of the Spirit through the apostolic community—the beginnings, in Jerusalem.

We have noted three agents of this witness: it is the work of the *exalted Christ* by the *Spirit* through the *church*. But the book of Acts describes how this witness comes also through *the word of God*. In each major section of Acts, we read the clause, "So the word of God spread," or something similar (6:7; 12:24; 19:20).[11] The gospel message spreads from Jerusalem to Rome, gathering an increasing number of adherents as it is embodied in their community, enacted in their lives, and explained in their words.

After the Spirit is poured out (2:1–13), the first believing community is formed in Jerusalem in response to Peter's proclamation of the good news (2:14–47). This band of believers follows Jesus in witnessing to the kingdom as he has done. In Luke's account this witness by the *actions* as well as the *words* of the believers begins with Peter and John visiting the temple. On the way they heal a man crippled from birth (3:1–10). This immediately draws a crowd, and Peter takes the opportunity to proclaim the good news once more: In the death and resurrection of Jesus Christ, the Old Testament story has reached its climax (3:11–26).

The words and actions of these two disciples immediately bring a hostile reaction and *suffering* just as Jesus' own words and actions have done. The Jewish leaders arrest Peter and John, put them in jail, then bring them before the Sanhedrin to account for their "disruptive" preaching. This gives Peter another opportunity to proclaim the good news of Jesus. The men of the Sanhedrin find themselves in a bind. They want to punish Peter and John, but a miracle (the healing of the crippled man) has taken place that they dare not deny. So they merely warn Peter and John to stop spreading the gospel, but the two reply, "Judge for yourselves whether it is right in God's sight to obey you rather than God. For we cannot help speaking about what we have seen and heard" (4:19–20).

After their release, Peter and John return to the church community to report what has taken place, and the church immediately turns to *prayer*. They ask the Sovereign Lord to grant them continued boldness and power in their witness in the face of hostility (4:23–31). The response is dramatic: "After they prayed, the place where they were meeting was shaken. And they were all filled with the Holy Spirit and spoke the word of God boldly" (4:31). Through prayer the Holy Spirit works a powerful witness. Jesus is the example for praying frequently, and now his church follows him in prayer.

As more and more people believe and are added to the number of Christ's followers (5:14), the success of this movement fills the Jewish leaders with jealousy and fury. They arrest the apostles and want to kill them, but the Pharisee Gamaliel counsels caution. He suggests that if this is a movement with a merely human origin, it will fizzle; but if it is of God, then the Jewish leaders do not want to be found fighting against it (5:33–39). The Sanhedrin listens, warns the apostles again not to speak of Jesus, and then has them beaten before releasing them. But the apostles receive such brutal treatment with joy because they have been counted worthy to suffer for the name of Jesus (5:41). Their witness continues: "Day after day, in the temple courts and from house to house, they never stopped teaching and proclaiming the good news that Jesus is the Christ" (5:42). Mere human opposition cannot stop the spread of the gospel because the growth of the church and the coming of the kingdom are the *work of God*. The Sovereign Lord is active by his Spirit and in his word to draw people to faith. In the story of Acts we see "the mighty acts of God contending with forces hostile to the Christian gospel."[12] But neither the Sanhedrin nor Herod (Agrippa I) nor any other political authority is able to silence the powerful witness of the gospel (chapters 3, 5, 12).

Much of Acts is taken up with the witness of the apostles. Yet it is the *life of the community* as it embodies the powerful working of the Spirit that authenticates the truth of the good news.[13] That vibrant and sharing life attracts more and more people from outside the community to join with those who already possess this new life.[14] The apostles can proclaim the gospel to any who will listen, but it is through observing the life of the Christian community that many people are convinced of its truth (4:32–37). The apostolic witness depends on a community that verifies the truth of the gospel with its winsome lifestyle. Thus, when the testimony of the church's communal life is threatened, the apostles act quickly and decisively (6:1–6). In the daily distribution of food, Greek-speaking Jewish disciples complain that their widows are being overlooked. The apostles quickly recognize that this is unjust. They propose that the church appoint seven godly men to oversee the distribution of food and other care for the needy, while the apostles themselves continue to devote their attention to the word and prayer. These seven are the first deacons of the church. Thus begins a tradition of caring for bodily needs within the church, a practice that will continue to be a powerful witness to the compassion, mercy, and justice of the gospel—attracting even priests. "So the word of God spread. The number of disciples in Jerusalem increased rapidly, and a large number of priests became obedient to the faith" (6:7).

The disciples' witness to the good news in Jerusalem and the gathering of a believing community fulfills Old Testament prophecies about gathering scattered Israel. But the same prophecies have also promised that God's salvation will extend to *all* nations. At this point in the story of the early church, it remains largely a Jewish community (though some Gentiles are beginning to join). The next important development in the story is that the gospel moves increasingly to those outside the Jewish context[15] beginning with God-fearing Gentiles who already worship in the synagogue.

### The Church Witnesses in Samaria and Judea

The good news of the kingdom cannot remain locked up in Jerusalem. It must reach "to the ends of the earth."

> Acts narrates the progress of the gospel from a small gathering of Jewish disciples of the earthly Jesus in Jerusalem, across formidable cultic, ethnic, relational, and geographical boundaries, to Paul's bold and unhindered preaching of the risen and ascended Jesus to Gentiles in Rome. Acts is unmistakably a story of missionary expansion, which is announced in 1:8 and confirmed along the way with the so-called progress reports.[16]

As the gospel spreads from Jerusalem and into the provinces of Judea and Samaria (6:8–12:24), the responsibility for witness moves beyond the apostles to include others in the community. Special examples are Stephen and Philip, who are among the seven appointed in the Jerusalem church (6:1–6). Soon it is not only church leaders who spread the good news: "ordinary" Christians also are involved in witness.

Stephen, one of the seven men appointed to care for the widows, carries out a powerful witness in his words and actions among the Jewish synagogues in and around Jerusalem and perhaps even further afield. Now the Jews who have rejected Jesus begin to oppose Stephen. Unable to stand against Stephen's wisdom and the Spirit at work in him, his enemies plot against him and make false accusations before the Sanhedrin (6:8–15). Stephen's appearance there allows him to proclaim the good news about Jesus Christ (7:1–53).[17] He tells the Jewish leaders the story of their own nation—with the events of Jesus' life as the climax and fulfillment of that story. The leaders themselves, Stephen claims, are like the rebellious Israel of the Old Testament, who constantly opposed God's work: "You stiff-necked people, with uncircumcised hearts and ears! You are just like your fathers: You always resist the Holy Spirit!

Was there ever a prophet your fathers did not persecute? They even killed those who predicted the coming of the Righteous One. And now you have betrayed and murdered him" (7:51–52). The Jews, enraged by Stephen's accusations, gnash their teeth, cover their ears, and rush at Stephen, shouting him down. They drag him out of the city and stone him to death. But Stephen (like Jesus) dies with words of forgiveness for those who take his life (7:54–60; cf. Luke 23:34).

Great persecution then breaks out against the church in Jerusalem. Disciples leave for the surrounding areas of Judea and Samaria, but "those who had been scattered preached the word wherever they went" (8:4). Though the church certainly has not planned this "missionary expansion," the scattering *is* being used by the Spirit. All those who are driven out of Jerusalem by this persecution begin to spread the good news. No longer is it only the official spokesmen of the church who make the gospel known (8:4; 11:19–21; cf. 1 Thessalonians 1:8). As the book of Acts tells the story, the spread of the gospel might seem to be mostly the work of the apostles as they are directed and guided by the Spirit. Yet here and there are reports showing that the lion's share of evangelism was the work of ordinary believers, the "informal missionaries" of the early church: "The great mission in Christianity was in reality accomplished by means of informal missionaries."[18] This "spontaneous expansion of the church . . . follows the unexhorted and unorganized activity of individual members of the Church explaining to others the Gospel which they have found for themselves."[19]

One of those who finds himself driven out of Jerusalem by the great persecution is Philip. He journeys to Samaria (Acts 8:5–25) and later encounters an Ethiopian eunuch, with whom he shares the good news (8:26–40). About the same time, a church for Jews *and* Gentiles is planted in Antioch by unnamed Christians who also have been scattered by the persecution (11:19–21; cf. Galatians 2:11–14). The Spirit is using the enemies of the church to scatter its members throughout the Roman Empire. Thus, instead of thwarting the spread of the gospel, these enemies actually have a hand in spreading it!

Undoubtedly the most important event to arise out of this period of persecution is the conversion and call of a man from Tarsus named Saul (Acts 9:1–30). Saul was present when Stephen was stoned to death—he may even have been in charge (8:1)—and now he leads the Sanhedrin's campaign of persecution against the young church. He is conveying its instructions to synagogues across Palestine and beyond, authorizing him to capture disciples of Jesus and return them to Jerusalem for trial. However, on the road to Damascus, a blinding light strikes Saul. He hears a voice saying, "Saul, why do you persecute me?" After Saul asks, "Who are you, Lord?" he hears: "I am Jesus, whom you are persecuting" (9:4–5). As his followers suffer, Jesus suffers. From this event, Saul becomes a follower of Jesus Christ. He will play an important role in the spread of the gospel to Gentiles as the Lord's "chosen instrument to carry [Jesus'] name before the Gentiles and their kings and before the people of Israel" (9:15).

As the believers scatter and share the good news throughout Judea, Galilee, and Samaria, churches spring up. Following the conversion of Saul (whose Roman name is Paul; 13:9), we read this summary: "Then the church throughout Judea, Galilee and Samaria enjoyed a time of peace. It was strengthened; and encouraged by the Holy Spirit, it grew in numbers, living in the fear of the Lord" (9:31).

As the gospel spreads beyond Jerusalem, it reaches mostly to Jewish synagogues throughout Palestine and beyond. There are Jews living throughout the Roman Empire, and in those very places there are synagogues. Thus the very early church maintains its close association with Jewish culture. But that is about to change.

While Peter is traveling about Judea and reaches Joppa by the sea, he sees a vision in which a sheet with all kinds of unclean animals descends from heaven (10:9–16). Peter hears a voice commanding him to kill and eat, but he responds: "Surely not Lord! . . . I have never eaten anything impure or unclean." The Lord insists, "Do not call anything impure that God has made clean" (10:14–15). Three times Peter receives this vision. He obviously is thinking of the dietary laws that God commanded in the Old Testament. By now they function among the significant boundary markers between Jews and Gentiles. While Peter is wondering about the meaning of his vision, some men sent by Cornelius, a God-fearing Gentile centurion, arrive to invite Peter to Cornelius's home in Caesarea. Cornelius also has a story to tell: he has seen an angel who instructed him to send for Peter. He concludes, "Now we are all here in the presence of God to listen to everything the Lord has commanded you to tell us" (10:30–33). So Peter begins to tell the good news of Jesus to a Gentile household. While he is speaking, the Spirit falls upon *all those* listening, and Peter and the other Jewish Christians are astonished to see for themselves that God pours out the Spirit even on Gentiles. Cornelius and his household then are baptized in the name of Jesus (10:44–48). When Peter returns to Jerusalem, the church community there criticizes him for eating with Gentiles. Peter explains the visions he and Cornelius have received, and the fact that the Spirit himself has ratified the faith of these Gentiles. After that, the Jewish believers in the Jerusalem church have no further objections (11:1–17). They praise God that he "has granted even the Gentiles repentance unto life" (11:18).

This section of Acts, describing the unplanned spread of the gospel beyond Jerusalem, ends with another story of opposition and persecution.

Herod (Agrippa I) has already had James (the brother of John) put to death, and now he arrests Peter with the same intention for him. But in response to the church's prayers, God sends an angel to free Peter from Herod's prison—much to the surprise of the praying church (12:1–19). In a follow-up story, Herod is struck down by God and dies a painful death because he has blasphemously accepted worship as a god (12:19–23; cf. Daniel 4:28–37). The message is clear: no human being, no opponent of any kind, can stand in the way of God's redemptive work. Herod dies, "but the word of God [continues] to increase and spread" (12:24).

### The Church Witnesses to the Ends of the Earth (Rome)

Though the gospel has begun to move outside of Jerusalem, it has mostly spread among the Jews scattered throughout the Roman Empire. But something new begins to take place in Antioch, where believers— made up of Jews and Gentiles—have come together to form a church community (Acts 11:19–21). When the mother church in Jerusalem hears about this, they send Barnabas to see what is happening in Antioch. Barnabas sees clear evidence of the grace of God working among the Antiochian believers and encourages them to continue in their faith. In fact, this church is destined to become the base for a large-scale missionary project that will send Paul with the gospel of Christ to large parts of the Roman Empire. While the church at Antioch is worshipping, the Holy Spirit says, "Set apart for me Barnabas and Saul for the work to which I have called them" (13:2). After fasting and praying, the leaders of the church place their hands on Saul and Barnabas and send them off to preach the gospel in other cities of the Roman Empire.[20]

Here for the first time we see a planned effort to take the gospel to places where it has not yet been heard. This church still carries out its own mission in the place where it has been set—here, in Antioch. But now it also lifts its gaze to "the ends of the earth" in obedience to God's calling. The first major move outward from Jerusalem has been an *unplanned expansion* of the gospel into Judea, Samaria, and certain Gentile areas (6:8–12:25). Now we see *organized expansion* from the church at Antioch into Asia Minor and Europe under Paul's leadership (12:25–19:20).[21]

Paul, the great Christian missionary figure, has been introduced to us as Saul the Pharisee, the ruthless persecutor of the church in its early days. After Saul's vision of the risen Christ, he experiences a dramatic conversion and answers God's call "to carry [his] name before the Gentiles and their kings and before the people of Israel" (9:15). Later Paul himself will explain that the Lord said to him, "I have made you a light for the Gentiles, that you may bring salvation to the ends of the earth"

(Acts 13:47; cf. Isaiah 49:6). Paul is the central human witness of the gospel story in Acts from chapter 13 to the end, and thirteen Letters in the New Testament also have Paul's name on them. It thus might *seem* that Paul is the main character in the latter half of the book of Acts. But that is not quite accurate: the *Spirit* dominates this story, with Paul as his instrument. The Spirit sends Barnabas and Saul/Paul on their way (13:4), forbids Paul to preach in the province of Asia (16:6), keeps him out of Bithynia (16:7), compels him to go to Jerusalem (20:22), empowers him (13:9), and warns him of dangers (20:23). Mission is first of all a work of the Spirit.

Paul's missionary work includes planting new churches and building them up to radiate the light of the gospel. Paul's goal is to establish witnessing kingdom communities in every part of the Roman Empire (Romans 15:17–22). He also takes time to establish these communities on a firm foundation. Paul passes along the gospel and the Scriptures, establishes leadership to oversee the community's growth, and institutes the Lord's Supper.[22] Often in his travels he will return to churches he has founded or built up, to further encourage them to faithfulness (as in Acts 15:41). He also writes New Testament Letters (or *Epistles*) to these young churches for the same purpose.

Paul makes three journeys into Asia Minor, Greece, and Macedonia to plant and build up churches. His regular practice is to begin at the local synagogue, since he well knows the Old Testament prophecies that God's renewal is to start with Israel and that the Gentiles will then be drawn in (Romans 1:16). In his first journey, Paul travels with Barnabas (and also, for a short time, with Mark) from Antioch to Cyprus. Here a proconsul is converted, but Luke adds few other details of what happens on this island (13:4–12). From Cyprus, Paul and Barnabas travel to Pisidian Antioch in the province of Galatia, where Paul proclaims the gospel in the synagogue. Some of his Jewish hearers (and some Gentile converts to Judaism) accept the good news, but others do not. Many people, both Jews and Gentiles, invite Paul to remain with them to explain his message further, but the leaders of the Jewish community violently oppose them. Paul then turns his attention to the Gentiles, many of whom believe and are filled with the Spirit (13:13–52). The Jewish establishment once again stirs up trouble against Paul and Barnabas and expels them from their city.

In Iconium a similar pattern emerges: a great number of Jews and Gentiles believe the gospel, but again official Jewish opposition drives Paul and his companions out (14:1–7). In Lystra, Paul and Barnabas heal a lame man—and the pagan citizens of that town believe that Zeus and Hermes have come to them! Paul preaches the good news, but Jewish opponents who have followed them from Iconium harass Paul

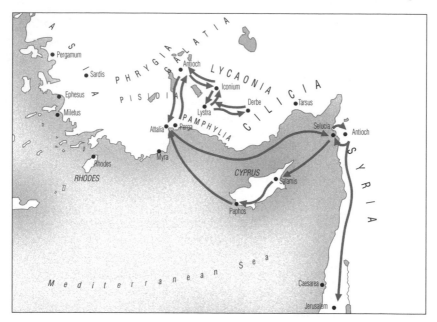

**Figure 22**  *Paul's First Missionary Journey*

and have him pelted by stones in an attempt to kill him. When at last he recovers from this ordeal, Paul leaves with Barnabas for the city of Derbe (14:8–20). After preaching the gospel there and winning a large number of disciples, they retrace their steps through Lystra and Iconium, return to Antioch of Pisidia (14:21–23), and then to Antioch of Syria, where they report to the sending church (14:24–28).[23]

As we have seen, Paul's habitual practice is to begin a new work by preaching first in the synagogue and then moving outward as resistance arises. The Jews he encounters in his travels generally oppose his preaching, while the Gentiles are more receptive. Hence, the churches Paul plants and nurtures in his first journey are mostly made up of Gentile believers. It may well be difficult for us today to understand how hard it was for the Jews of the first century to give up traditions that had for so long safeguarded their religious identity as *distinct from* the pagan Gentiles. Paul now calls them to *accept* Gentile believers as equal partners in this renewed "Israel" of God's kingdom. It is not surprising, then, that struggles between Gentiles and Jews mark this early period of the church's story. In particular, the Jewish Christians who have formed the first communities of believers (in Jerusalem and just beyond it) are at first convinced that Gentile converts to faith in Christ should at least be required to obey the law of Moses. The Jewish believers expect Gentile

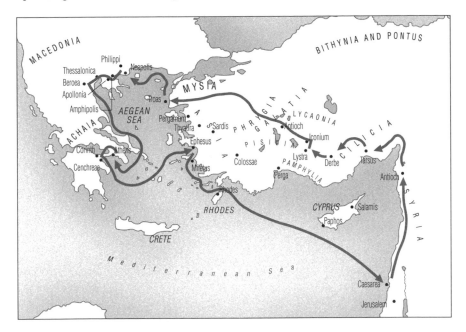

**Figure 23** *Paul's Second Missionary Journey*

believers to submit to the rite of circumcision as if they have been born into the Jewish covenant with God. A group of these "Judaizers" even travels from place to place in Galatia, visiting churches planted there by Paul and attempting to convince Gentile Christians that they should live as Jews. But Paul fires off an angry and impassioned letter to the Galatian churches, urging them rather to remain constant in their faith: salvation is in Christ alone, not in the works of the law. This doctrinal struggle builds until a council is held in Jerusalem, which concludes that Gentiles should be admitted to the church as equal members, without having to observe the rules of the Judaizers (Acts 15). Though this decision brings peace for a time within the churches, it is by no means the end of this particular controversy.

Paul's second journey is notable for a couple of reasons (15:36–18:22). First, his strategy changes somewhat. He chooses to spend more time in each region's important cities, soundly establishing churches there.[24] Moreover, on this journey he visits churches in most of the places that will eventually receive one of his pastoral letters: Philippi, Thessalonica, Corinth, and Ephesus.

After a dispute between himself and Barnabas, Paul sets out on his second journey accompanied by Silas and later also by Timothy. They travel westward from Antioch (in Syria) and through the Roman prov-

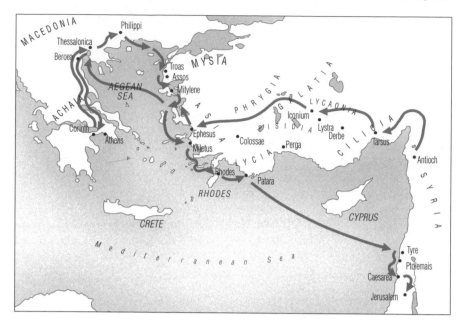

**Figure 24** *Paul's Third Missionary Journey*

inces of Cilicia, Galatia, and Asia (between the Mediterranean and the Black Seas). After Paul sees a vision of a man from Macedonia begging for help, they cross the Aegean Sea to the Greek peninsula in obedience to the Spirit's prompting. They plant churches in Philippi, Thessalonica, Athens, and Corinth. After a year and a half of ministry in Corinth, Paul and his coworkers return to Antioch (15:36–18:22).

In Paul's third journey he begins by retracing his steps through Cilicia, Galatia, and Phrygia, strengthening the churches in those regions (18:23). His primary goal now is to establish a church in the important city of Ephesus, which he visited briefly at the end of his second journey. Through instruction and mighty deeds (including miracles of healing), Paul is successful in planting a church there, which challenges the flourishing occult practices and pagan worship in that city. He stays on at Ephesus for over two years (19:1–41), during which time "the word of the Lord [spreads] widely and [grows] in power" (19:20). While in Ephesus, Paul writes at least four letters to the church at Corinth (two of which have been preserved in our Bible), addressing a number of questions about what it means to embody the gospel in the pagan setting of Corinth. He also works through some personal problems between himself and that church.

Upon leaving Ephesus, Paul travels through Macedonia and Greece, encouraging the churches established in Athens, Corinth, Berea, Thessalonica, and Philippi (20:1–6). He stays at least three months in Greece, and from here he also writes to the Christians at Rome. This is Paul's most famous letter and the one that has had more influence in church history than any other: the Letter (or Epistle) to the Romans. Paul has never visited Rome, and so his tone in this letter is more formal as he deepens the Roman Christians' understanding of the gospel and of the relationship between Jews and Gentiles. From Greece, Paul sails to Troas and then once again to Ephesus, where he strengthens the leaders there before bidding them a tearful farewell (20:7–38).

Paul completes his last journey by returning to Jerusalem, where he reports the news of his missionary journeys to the church (21:17–26) and where he is arrested by the Romans at the instigation of the Jewish authorities (21:27–36). The remainder of the book of Acts shows Paul in his various judicial hearings and trials, as he moves from Jerusalem to Caesarea and then on to Rome. Even these trials afford Paul opportunities to proclaim the good news to many, including various rulers (cf. 9:15). During his time in Rome, he writes letters to the churches in Philippi, Ephesus, and Colossae, as well as his letter to Philemon (the owner of a runaway slave whom Paul had led to Christ). In Acts, Luke is reporting the acts of the exalted Christ by the Spirit through the early church. He ends this story by telling us that Paul spends two years in Rome under house arrest, boldly preaching about the kingdom of God and the Lord Jesus Christ.

## *Paul Unfolds the Gospel in His Letters*

### PAUL IN THE BIBLICAL STORY

Paul plays a hugely significant role in the biblical story. He is the central human figure in the latter part of Acts, bringing the gospel from its original Jewish setting out into the Gentile world. Paul is above all a "missionary," bringing the good news to places where it has not yet been heard. Paul also has a missionary pastor's heart. He longs to see each of the churches he has planted go on to flourish and become a vibrant, witnessing community that will faithfully point to the coming kingdom of God in life, word, and deed. After planting a church, he often stays for some time to instruct the newborn Christians there in what it means to embody the good news. In subsequent travels he often returns to further instruct them in the way of kingdom living. His letters to the young churches unfold the significance of the gospel for their new life in Christ. If we are to understand Paul's teaching in his letters, we must see him first as a missionary whose primary motive is to nourish the churches he has planted so that they become faithful witnesses to the kingdom.[25]

Paul writes his letters to unfold the significance of the good news of Jesus Christ for particular churches in particular historical situations.[26] The letters build on, flow from, and explain the good news of what God has done for the world in the historical events of the life, death, and resurrection of Jesus Christ. Paul unfolds the meaning of the good news in detail and its implications for the church's new life in Christ. He also connects the gospel with the Old Testament story setting, establishing its truth against the errors of false teaching, and setting his own authority as an apostle against the errors of the false teachers. Each of Paul's letters addresses a different church with its own problems and questions. In this present chapter we cannot discuss all the details but will briefly describe the *structure* of Paul's teaching.[27]

### PAUL'S TEACHING: THE KINGDOM OF GOD HAS DAWNED IN CHRIST

Trained as a Pharisee, Saul of Tarsus has been taught to think of human history as divided between "the present age" and "the age to come."[28] In Jewish thinking, "the present age" is dominated by sin, evil, and death, but in "the age to come," God will return to Israel and usher in his kingdom. When a group of people in Jerusalem begins to make the claim that, in the crucified Jesus, this kingdom has already come, Saul is incensed. He attacks this heretical sect with zealous ferocity. But everything changes for Saul when the risen Jesus personally confronts him. If Jesus *is* the Jewish Messiah alive from the dead (and Paul never wavers from this belief, once he has met the risen Jesus for himself), that means the age to come *has* dawned, the kingdom of God *is* here. The newborn Christian and former Pharisee must rethink all he *thought* he knew.

And this is Paul's starting point: *the kingdom of God, "the age to come," has arrived.*[29]

> The whole content of Paul's preaching can be summarized as the proclamation and explication of the eschatological day of salvation inaugurated with Christ's advent, death, and resurrection. It is from this principal point of view and under this denominator that all the separate themes of Paul's preaching can be understood and penetrated in their unity and relation to each other.[30]

The salvation promised by the Old Testament prophets has begun; the old age is passing away, and the new has come (2 Corinthians 5:17).

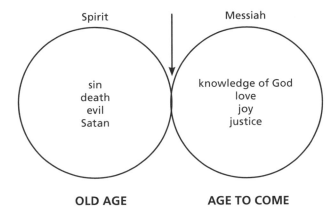

**Figure 25** *Jewish Expectation*

The fullness of times has arrived (Galatians 4:4), and *now* is the day of God's salvation (2 Corinthians 6:2).

Furthermore, the kingdom of God has arrived *in the death and resurrection of Jesus Christ*. Two great figures stand at the entrances to two worlds: Adam stands at the gate of the old world, Jesus at the gate of the new. Adam's first sin inaugurated the old age and brought sin, death, and condemnation. Now in Jesus a new day of righteousness, life, and justification has come (Romans 5:12–21). If we are "in Adam," we are part of the old age and under its sway. But if we are "in Christ," we are part of the age to come and can already experience God's life-giving power.

What prompts the great change in Paul's thinking about the kingdom is a new understanding of the resurrection. On the road to Damascus, the risen Jesus personally encounters Paul.[31] To Paul (thinking as a carefully trained Jew of the first century), resurrection *means* rising bodily into the life of the "age to come." Since Jesus is alive again and the kingdom has come, "the age to come" has arrived. "Because Jesus was the Christ, his resurrection is not, as previous raisings of the dead, an isolated occurrence, but in it the time of salvation promised in him, the new creation, dawns in an overwhelming manner, as a decisive transition from the old to the new world (2 Cor[inthians] 5:17; cf. v. 15)."[32] Paul speaks of Jesus as the firstborn among many brothers (Romans 8:29), the firstfruits of those who have died (1 Corinthians 15:20). Jesus is the beginning—the pioneer—of the resurrection life, who has opened up the way for others to follow (Colossians 1:18).

For Paul, this new view of the resurrection demands a similarly new view of the crucifixion. From the Old Testament he knows that "cursed is everyone who is hung on a tree" (Galatians 3:13; cf. Deuteronomy 21:23). But since this Jesus *is* the Messiah, and he *is* raised from the dead, the cross itself must be reexamined through the lens of the resurrection. Since the resurrection means the beginning of the new, Christ's crucifixion must mean the end of the old (Romans 6:1–11). For the sake of the world, Christ has taken upon himself God's curse, the guilt and power of sin that has ruled the old age (Galatians 3:13–14). Paul now proclaims that God used the cross to bring the old age to a close. The cross marks God's victory over the powers of sin and evil that rule the world in the present age (Colossians 2:15). Though such an idea might be a stumbling block to the Jews and seem utter foolishness to Gentiles, it is in fact (Paul maintains) the wisdom and power of God (1 Corinthians 1:18–2:5).[33] Paul employs a plethora of images to unfold the significance of that central event, at least several dozen.

But if the old has passed away and the new has come, why do evil and death remain in the world? Paul's letters are charged with the same tension between the "already" and "not yet" aspects of the kingdom of God that we have seen in Jesus' own teachings, but with some differences in emphasis. For Paul, the kingdom is *here already* in that Jesus' death brings an end to the old and his resurrection inaugurates the new. The Spirit is described as a *deposit* (or down payment) on the coming kingdom (2 Corinthians 1:22; 5:5; Ephesians 1:14). A deposit is not merely an IOU or promise for the future; instead, it is a real payment given now as a guarantee that in the future the rest will be paid. The Spirit is also pictured as *firstfruits*, the first part of the harvest, ready to be enjoyed now, and tangible evidence that the remainder of the harvest will also come (Romans 8:23).

The kingdom has *not yet* arrived for us in its fullness. We remain in a world that has not yet been fully delivered from the influence of evil, demonic power (2 Corinthians 4:4). We are still surrounded by the darkness of sin and rebellion against God (Ephesians 2:2–3), even while we anticipate the full revelation of God's kingdom in which those things shall be no more. Thus, in Paul's thought there is no clearly marked threshold between "the present age" and "the age to come." We live in the "in-between" time, in which the two ages overlap. Paul goes on to explain that these two ages are allowed to coexist within God's plan so that the church's work of mission—the gathering of the nations to the God of Israel—can be accomplished before the final revelation of the kingdom.[34] In fact, God gives this in-between time to the church as its own, to fulfill its calling as his witness to the coming of the kingdom.[35]

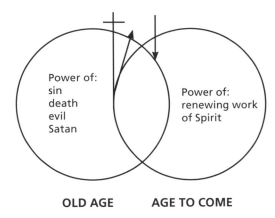

**OLD AGE          AGE TO COME**

**Figure 26** *Fulfillment in the Gospels*

### Nurturing the Growth of Our New Life in Christ

As we have seen, Paul's first concern as a missionary is to bring the gospel where it has not yet been heard. For Paul, the gospel is not simply a record of historical events nor some new religious teaching or doctrine. It is the very power of God to bring salvation, to bring men and women into the kingdom of the age to come. Paul thus feels an obligation and is always eager to tell the gospel story (Romans 1:14–15). He is compelled to preach the gospel: "Woe to me if I do not preach the gospel!" (1 Corinthians 9:16). As his hearers respond in faith and are baptized to signify their "death" to the old way of life and their "resurrection" to new life in Christ among his people, newborn churches are established wherever Paul travels through the Roman Empire.

But these infant churches cannot simply be left to fend for themselves. They are witnessing to the reality of God's kingdom while living out their lives in the present age, facing the evil still at work in the world before the kingdom comes in its fullness. Hence, Paul's second concern as a missionary is to bring these communities of believers to maturity in their faith and witness. Paul's writings use two images to capture this process of coming to maturity. First, the church is pictured as the new temple of God, where he now lives by the Holy Spirit (1 Corinthians 3:16; Ephesians 2:21–22). Its foundation is the gospel itself, and its coming to maturity is the process of building on that foundation (Ephesians 4:12). Second, the church's coming to maturity is likened to the organic growth of a human body (from infancy to adulthood, Ephesians 4:15) or of a field crop (1 Corinthians 3:5–9), "rooted" in Jesus Christ (Ephesians 3:17; Colossians 2:7) and being cared for so that the church might come to fruitful maturity.

The church's life *begins* by receiving the life of the Spirit through the gospel: it is established upon Christ and rooted in him. But the church's life also *continues* by faith in the gospel (Galatians 3:2–3; Colossians 2:6–7) as the believers are brought along by the Spirit to completion, adulthood, fruitfulness: the "fullness of Christ" (Ephesians 4:11–16). Paul discusses at length the various gifts and ministries given to the church by the Spirit to bring it to maturity.[36]

### New Life and New Obedience

Moving toward fullness in Christ is an ongoing task. Paul thus repeatedly exhorts the newly established churches to live a life worthy of the gospel. The pattern of this exhortation recurs in Paul's letters to the churches. First he tells them *what God has done* to give them new life, and then he tells them *what they must do* to live according to that new identity. Since God has given them new life in the kingdom of God, they are to live as obedient citizens of that kingdom.

The church's new life is based on what God has done in the death and resurrection of Jesus Christ. In Christ's death, God has defeated the powers that rule "this present age"—sin, evil, and death. In Christ's resurrection the "age to come" has begun, with its promise of life, love, and peace (Romans 6:1–11). The church's new life is also empowered by the Spirit, which lives within the community of believers and constantly brings new life to it (Romans 8; Galatians 5). This, says Paul, is the new life of the Christian, begun by Christ's work on the cross, lived out in the Father's kingdom, and shaped by the Spirit's power.

At the heart of this new life is a new relationship to God, which Paul describes in terms of righteousness, reconciliation, and adoption.[37] First, since God is the righteous Lawgiver and Judge, we who follow rebellious Adam are estranged from him by our sin; we too are guilty. But Paul proclaims the good news that (for those who have faith in Jesus) our "guilty" verdict has been overturned. There is a new verdict: we have *already* been declared righteous—on the basis of the death of Jesus Christ (Romans 3:21–31; Galatians 2:15–16; 3:6–14).[38] As far as the Christian is concerned, God's final judgment has *already taken place!*[39] With our guilt removed, we stand in a right relationship to God.

Second, since we were once estranged from God by our sinful rebellion, we need to be reconciled to him. Reconciliation, long thought to become available only at the end of time with the coming of God's kingdom, is a gift freely offered even now (2 Corinthians 5:18–19; Colossians 1:20).[40] Reconciliation removes the sin that has put God's world at enmity with him and leads to peace. This means the restoration of the *shalom* and harmony of God's original created order for the whole world and especially for humankind (Romans 5:1). Third, we who are born into the sinful race of Adam are restored to God by receiving his gift of adoption (Galatians 4:4–5; Ephesians 1:4).[41] The same Spirit that lived in Jesus is poured into our *own* lives and enables us to call God "Abba, Father," as Jesus did (Romans 8:14–15).

This is the church: a people who live in a new world with a new identity and a new relationship to God. Thus, Paul commands the church to live more and more the new life of God's kingdom, to "take off" the old self (as if it were soiled clothing) and to put on the new (Ephesians 4:22–24; Colossians 3:9–10). In other words, they are to bid farewell to the way of life that was shaped by their experience of "this present age" and to embrace a new way of life as part of "the age to come." And with this new life comes a call to a new kind of obedience to God's law in every part of life, an obedience rooted in love.[42]

This call to obedience has in view the restoration of the *whole* of human life. Ridderbos calls this "totalitarian character of the new obedience . . . the most essential and characteristic feature" of Paul's understanding of our new life in Christ.[43] Christ rules over all creation and redeems all creation (Colossians 1:15–20). Thus, all human life, including even the mundane activities like eating and drinking, should be lived to the glory of God (1 Corinthians 10:31). Since the whole of our bodily life is to be devoted to God (Romans 6:13; 12:1–2), whatever is done in word or deed should be done in the name of the Lord Jesus, giving thanks to God the Father (Colossians 3:17). This comprehensive obedience is also rooted in the goodness of the creation, which is being redeemed (1 Corinthians 10:26; 1 Timothy 4:1–5).[44] Paul is aware that the whole of human life, though created by God and redeemed by Christ, has also been polluted by sin. So he warns that, though believers have liberty to enjoy God's good creation, they must be careful not to be contaminated by the sin that infects it (1 Corinthians 6:12).

The church's new life of obedience in Christ adopts as its standard of behavior the law of God given in the Old Testament.[45] The problem with the law is that its high standards could never be met by any persons acting in their own strength. However, "what the law was powerless to do in that it was weakened by the sinful nature, God did by sending his own Son in the likeness of sinful humanity to be a sin offering. And so he condemned sin in our sinful nature, in order that the righteous requirements of the law might be fully met in us, who do not live according to the sinful nature but according to the Spirit" (Romans 8:3–4).

This new life of obedience in Christ is characterized in Paul's writings as a life of love (Ephesians 4:15–16; Colossians 2:2).[46] Here Paul builds on Jesus' teaching, especially as it is recorded in the Gospel of John (John 15:1–17). Jesus describes the continuing relationship that the disciples will have with him after his departure in terms of a vine and its branches. As the sap of the vine flows to the branches, they bear fruit. As the life of Christ flows from himself to his disciples, they too will bear "fruit," the most important of which is love. To live and remain in Christ means to love and obey him. Twice he says, "This is my command: Love each other as I have loved you" (John 15:12 and 17 conflated). This love coming as the "fruit" of the new life of the Spirit takes many forms and in Paul's letters is often bound together with joy and peace to form a triad (Romans 5:1–8).[47] Love also comes through in other characteristic qualities of the kingdom: humility, patience, kindness, goodness, faithfulness, gentleness, self-control, righteousness, and gratitude.[48]

### FOR THE SAKE OF THE WORLD

The church's new life and new obedience are for the sake of the world. When the church's new life of the Spirit becomes evident to unbelievers, they too are convinced of the truth of this "good news" and so are drawn to Christ.[49] As Paul struggles to nurture a community that faithfully embodies the new life of the kingdom, he always has his eye on those outside the church. In describing the church's life of love, joy, generosity, and forgiveness, Paul says, "Be careful to do what is right in the eyes of everybody" (Romans 12:17). The church's gentleness and grace are to be evident to all people (Philippians 4:5; Colossians 4:5–6). Believers are urged to work hard "so that [their] daily life may win the respect of outsiders" (1 Thessalonians 4:12) and to devote themselves to doing what is good for all people (Titus 2:7–8). Their conduct is to be "worthy of the gospel of Christ" (Philippians 1:27) so that, in the midst of the dark depravity of the Roman Empire, their witness to the gospel of God's kingdom will "shine like stars" (Philippians 2:15). Bosch speaks of Paul's concern for the witness of the church: "The Christians' lifestyle should not only be exemplary, but also winsome. It should attract outsiders and invite them to join the community. . . . Their 'exemplary existence' is a powerful magnet that draws outsiders toward the church."[50]

The witness of the church is to spill over into the public life of culture, demonstrating that the salvation of the "age to come" is comprehensive in scope. Bruce Winter shows that the New Testament church is to be involved in the public life of their nation and seek its welfare.[51] In Philippians (1:27–2:18), Paul discusses "the obligation of Christians to 'live as citizens' in the world of *politeia* [the public life of the state] in a way that is worthy of the gospel."[52] By being visible and involved in the life of the surrounding culture while avoiding the pollution of that culture's pervasive idolatry, Christians will "shine like stars" "in the midst of a crooked and perverse generation" (2:15).

### THE COMING OF THE LORD

Paul's letters are, as we have seen, charged with the tension between the *already* and *not yet*. Though the kingdom of God has entered human history, the fulfillment of God's redemptive work awaits Christ's return. The kingdom is *real* in the present life of the church, but anticipation of its future completion is also the church's great hope. "The certainty that in Christ the day of salvation, the acceptable time, has dawned, does not mean the end of redemptive expectation, but only makes it increase in intensity."[53] Paul says: "We know that the whole creation has been groaning as in the pains of childbirth right up to the present time. Not only so, but we ourselves, who have the firstfruits of the Spirit, groan inwardly as we wait eagerly for our adoption as sons, the redemption of our bodies. For in this hope we were saved" (Romans 8:23–24). The believer lives in hope, and this hope is a spur to growing obedience and comfort while living in the present evil age.[54]

## *Continuing the Early Church's Story*

The last we hear of Paul is that he is in Rome, living in his own rented house while he waits to be put on trial. Though under house arrest, he is free to welcome all visitors: "Boldly and without hindrance he [preaches] the kingdom of God and [teaches] about the Lord Jesus Christ" (Acts 28:31). This open proclamation in Rome indicates that the gospel is poised to move from the center of the Roman Empire to all its parts. Here Luke draws to a close his story of the church's mission in the first decades.[55]

It is fitting that Luke's second book should end here, with Paul still vitally engaged in the missionary task given him by God on the road to Damascus, because the story of Acts has not ended. It must continue until Jesus himself returns to bring it to completion. "The ending of Acts is truly an opening to the continuing life of the messianic people, as it continues to preach the kingdom and teach the things concerning Jesus both boldly and without hindrance."[56] The work was begun by Jesus and his disciples, carried on by the early church after his ascension, and spread throughout the Roman Empire by Paul and others. It is moving toward completion even now:

> Still to be accomplished in the contemporary life of the church is the divine intention revealed to Paul and Barnabas at Pisidian Antioch midway through the narrative of Acts (13:47): "I have set you to be a light for the Gentiles, that you may bring salvation, to the uttermost parts of the earth."[57]

In his Gospel, Luke tells the story of "all that Jesus *began* to do and teach" (Acts 1:1). In the book of Acts he tells how Jesus' followers carry on that work in the early days of the church. In *this* story we too have a part, for we are invited—urged—to become a part of the story of the church, to follow Jesus and continue the kingdom mission in the steps of his earliest followers.

## Scene 2: And into All the World

The church of the first century is almost two thousand years removed in time and (for most of us) half a world away in distance. Jesus lived in Palestine, died, and rose again there a little before most of the events recorded in the book of Acts. The ancient nation of Israel sought to walk with God while conquering and settling a homeland in Canaan more than a thousand years before that. The biblical accounts of how all these different people struggled to live faithfully in their distant times and places may seem to have little to do with you and me.

Yet it is not so. The world of the Bible is *our* world, and its story of redemption is also *our* story. This story is waiting for an ending—in part because we ourselves have a role to play before all is concluded. We must therefore pay attention to the continuing biblical story of redemption. We must resist the temptation to read the Scriptures as if they were a religious flea market, with a basket of history and old doctrines here, a shelf full of pious stories there, promises and commands scattered from one end to the other. Some readers of the Bible turn it into little more than an anthology of proof texts assembled to support a system of theology. Others seek only ethical guidance, ransacking the Old Testament for stories of moral instruction. Still others look just for inspirational or devotional messages, for comforting promises and lessons for daily living. The result may be that we lose sight of the Bible's essential unity and instead find only those theological, moral, devotional, or historical fragments we are looking for.

But all human communities, including our own, *live out of some comprehensive story* that suggests the meaning and goal of history and that gives shape and direction to human life. We may neglect the biblical story, God's comprehensive account of the shape and direction of cosmic history and the meaning of all that he has done in our world. If we do so, the fragments of the Bible that we *do* preserve are in danger of being absorbed piecemeal into the dominant cultural story of our modern European and North American democracies. And the dominant story of modern culture is rooted in idolatry: an ultimate confidence in humanity to achieve its own salvation. Thus, instead of allowing the Bible to shape *us*, we may in fact be allowing our culture to shape *the Bible for us*. Our view of the world and even our faith will be molded by one or the other: either the biblical story is our foundation, or the Bible itself becomes subsumed within the modern story of the secular Western world. If our lives are to be shaped and formed by Scripture, we need to know the biblical story well, to feel it in our bones. To do this, we must also know our own place within it—where *we* are in the story.

### What Time Is It?

Brian Walsh and Richard Middleton have suggested that our lives are shaped by the answers—explicit or implicit—we give to four great questions: (1) *Where are we?* What kind of world do we live in? (2) *Who are we?* What does it mean to be human? (3) *What is wrong?* What is the fundamental problem with the world? (4) *What is the remedy?* What will fix the problem?[58] N. T. Wright adds: (5) *What time is it?* At what point in the story do *we* enter it?[59] These questions are answered by whichever story about the world we adopt. If the biblical story is to be the basis for the whole of our lives, it is here that we must find the answers to these five fundamental questions.

Wright has provided a helpful illustration of how the Bible *as story* can truly have ultimate authority in our lives.[60] He imagines that the script of a "lost" Shakespeare play is somehow discovered. Although the play originally had six acts,[61] only a little more than five have been found—the first four acts, the first scene of act 5, and the final act of the play. The rest is missing. The play is given to Shakespearean actors who are asked to work out the rest of act 5 for themselves. They immerse themselves in the culture and language of Shakespeare and in the partial script that has been recovered. Then they improvise the unscripted parts of the fifth act, allowing their performance to be shaped by the trajectory, the *thrust,* of Shakespeare's story as they have come to understand it. In this way they bring the play toward the conclusion that its author has provided in the script's final act.

Something like this may help us to understand how biblical authority can guide our own lives now. We have seen the biblical drama of redemption unfolding in most of five acts: (1) creation, (2) the fall into sin, (3) Israel's story, (4) the story of Jesus Christ, and (5) the story of the church, leading to the consummation of God's plan of redemption in the sixth act—an act not yet complete. *We also know the Author of the story.* Now, given the trajectory of the story as it has been told to this point, and especially knowing that we have been entrusted to perform the continuation of act 5—the mission of Jesus and the early church—how are we believers to live our lives today? How can we play our part so as to allow the story to move forward toward the conclusion that God has already written for it?

### Being a Light to the World: Continuing the Mission of Israel

Let's look back to Jesus' words to his disciples near the end of act 4: "As the Father has sent me, I am sending you" (John 20:21). This "you" includes *us* in the kingdom mission of Jesus. *We* continue what Jesus and his first disciples began. But if we are to enter the story at this point, we must look both ways, backward and forward. We look *backward* because the kingdom mission of Jesus is the climactic chapter of Israel's story told in the Old Testament: Jesus fulfills Israel's mission to be a light to the world. We also look *forward* because the New Testament (and especially the narrative of Acts) depicts the early church as it continues the kingdom mission of Jesus. Hence, if we are to understand our own mission today, we must take account of Israel's initial God-given task, of how Jesus fulfilled it, and of how the early church continued the work.

The biblical story is about *what God is doing* in the world, working toward the renewal of the whole creation. God chooses people to join with him and participate in his work—Abraham, Israel, Jesus' disciples, the early church, the daughter churches founded by Paul on his journeys through the Roman Empire. Today, we too are invited to participate in what God is doing. If we are to understand our own calling, we must understand it in relation to those who have heard it before us.

When God promises to make Abraham a great nation and bless all nations through him (Genesis 12:1–3), that promise must be seen against the backdrop of Genesis 1–11, which narrates God's creation of the world and the devastating effects of sin upon it. The nation that would issue from Abraham was to embody God's original intentions for humanity in the creation (Exodus 19:3–6). From the beginning God's redemptive work aims at *recovering and restoring his good creation.* Thus, the people who seek to be obedient to him must seek a redemption as wide as creation itself. Insofar as Israel was obedient to this calling, it would be a light to the world. The attractiveness of its life would draw nations to God.

## Introducing the Kingdom: Continuing the Mission of Jesus

Though Israel largely failed in its calling to be a light to the nations, Jesus did not fail. He fulfilled God's purposes for Israel, then (after the resurrection) gathered a community of his followers and charged them with the task of continuing what he had begun (John 20:21). We are part of that community, and their task to continue in Jesus' mission is also ours.

As we have seen, Jesus' mission centered in the coming of God's kingdom, the restoration of God's rule over all creation and all of human life, the day of God's salvation. Though today some Christians believe that Jesus came to enable us to escape this creation and live eternally in an otherworldly and heavenly dwelling, such an understanding of salvation would have been entirely foreign to Old Testament prophets, to first-century Jews—and to Jesus himself. Salvation is not an *escape from* creational life into "spiritual" existence: it is the *restoration of God's rule* over all of creation and all of human life. Neither is salvation merely the restoration of a personal relationship with God, important as that is. Salvation goes further: it is the restoration of the whole life of humankind and ultimately of the nonhuman creation as well. This is the scope of biblical salvation. It is also the scope of our own calling to be witnesses of that salvation, to continue the mission of Jesus, who prayed for the coming of God's kingdom. In his words Jesus announced the kingdom, and in his actions he demonstrated that the kingdom *had* come. He welcomed the marginalized and formed a kingdom community, taught by precept and example how to live faithfully within that community, and suffered for its sake as he challenged the idolatrous culture of his time.

We follow in Jesus' mission, but our own cultural situation is quite different from that of first-century Palestine. Thus, we need to carry out the mission of Jesus with imagination and creativity. "Jesus did not set up a rigid model for action but, rather, inspired his disciples to prolong the logic of his own action in a creative way amid the new and different historical circumstances in which the community would have to proclaim the gospel of the kingdom in word and deed."[62] Again, Wright's illustration of act 5 in a Shakespearean drama is helpful. He speaks of the work of "improvisation," as actors seek to work out in the fifth act of their play the meaning of the first four acts:

> This "authority" of the first four acts would not consist—could not consist!—in an implicit command that the actors should repeat the earlier parts of the play over and over again. It would consist in the fact of an as yet UNFINISHED drama, containing its own impetus and forward

movement, which demanded to be concluded in an appropriate manner. It would require of the actors a free and responsible entering in to the story as it stood, in order first to understand how the threads could be appropriately drawn together and then to put that understanding into effect by speaking and acting with *both innovation and consistency*.[63]

Innovation and consistency: this captures what it means to follow Jesus in his kingdom mission. If we speak and act with *consistency*, our kingdom mission will be shaped by our understanding of the substance and the trajectory of Jesus' own mission. If we speak and act with *innovation*, we will carry out our task creatively and imaginatively in the new cultural and historical situations to which God leads us.

## Bearing Faithful Witness: Continuing the Mission of the Early Church

The New Testament gives us both Jesus' own example of kingdom mission and that of the early church as it follows Jesus, bearing witness to all that he has been and done and said (Acts 1:8). While Jesus himself concentrates on gathering "the lost sheep of Israel" (Matthew 15:24), he sends his church out to extend that mission among all nations. The disciples must make known the good news of the kingdom everywhere, among all peoples, and then the end will come (24:14).

With the coming of the Spirit, the church has a *foretaste* of the salvation of the kingdom: the kingdom "banquet" has been prepared by the work of Christ, but it waits for a future time, when all the guests have been assembled (Luke 14:15–24). Yet those who follow Christ have already begun to taste the power of salvation that will accomplish the renewal of all things. As the church enjoys this foretaste of the banquet to come, it becomes the prime exhibit of what the future kingdom will look like. Think here of a film preview, a few minutes of actual footage from a film not yet released. This trailer is shown so that the potential audience can catch a glimpse of what the whole film will look like once it is ready to be shown in its entirety. One important function of the church is thus to be a picture, a brief representation, a sample of what the future in God's kingdom will be.

The early church communities in Jerusalem and Antioch establish a healthy pattern of witness to God's kingdom, devoting themselves to Scripture, prayer, fellowship, and the Lord's Supper, to build up their new life in Christ (Acts 2:42–47; 11:19–21; 13:1–3). As a result, these communities do actually become effective previews of the coming kingdom of God, attracting a great many new converts (2:43–47). Because there is ample evidence of God's grace in their lives, these Christians are increasingly sought out by others around them. Within their own towns and cities, their witness to the truth of the gospel is very effective. Beyond this local witness, the Antioch church also sends Paul and Barnabas off to take the gospel further afield, establishing witnessing communities of believers in many new places across the empire (13:1–3). Thus, the church was then (and should be now) characterized by its zeal for witness nearby and missions faraway.

Witness characterizes the meaning of this time period in God's story. Yet this could easily be misinterpreted: one might reduce mission or witness to evangelism or cross-cultural missions. While these dimensions are important to the church's mission, they are too limited. When we grasp that the salvation of the kingdom restores the creation, and all of it, we see that witness to God's kingdom is as wide as creation. Witness will mean embodying God's renewing power in politics and citizenship, economics and business, education and scholarship, family and neighborhood, media and art, leisure and play. It is not just that we carry out evangelism in these areas of life. Again, this is important but not enough. It means that the way we live as citizens, consumers, students, husbands, mothers, and friends witnesses to the restoring power of God. We may suffer as we encounter other equally comprehensive and competing religious stories trying to shape our culture. Nevertheless, a broad mission is central to our being. The contemporary testimony *Our World Belongs to God* captures both the centrality of mission and its comprehensive scope:

> Following the apostles, the church is sent—
> Sent with the gospel of the kingdom
> to make disciples of all nations,
> to feed the hungry,
> to proclaim the assurance that in the name of Christ
> there is forgiveness of sin and new life
> for all who repent and believe—
> To tell the news that our world belongs to God.
> In a world estranged from God,
> where millions face confusing choices,
> this mission is central to our being,
> for we announce the one name that saves. . . .
> We rejoice that the Spirit is waking us to see
> our mission in God's world.
>
> The rule of Jesus Christ covers the whole world.
> To follow this Lord is to serve him everywhere,
> without fitting in,
> as lights in the darkness,
> as salt in a spoiling world.[64]

### Living in God's Story Today

You have traveled thus far with us in this journey through the biblical story. Perhaps by now you have begun to share our vision of how God is at work in his world and his people, shaping both it and them into the great kingdom that has been God's plan from the beginning. But if each of us truly has his or her *own* place in the story, what place might that be? And how does this view of God's vast kingdom help any of us to find our place within it? In the next few pages we illustrate, by means of three stories, how the lives of individuals can become caught up within the biblical story. The first two stories are completely true, naming men and women who have found interesting ways to be involved in God's ongoing work in the world. In the third story, we rejoin our fictional friends Abigail and Percival (from the prologue to this book) to see how a couple of young Christian adults might find their own ideas of life changed by a fresh look at the great story of the Bible.

Our first (true) story comes from the life of Gary Ginter, a man who once thought God wanted him to become a cross-cultural missionary. Instead, God led Gary into a life of service in the world of business.

A founding partner of the Chicago Research and Trading Group (a pioneering futures and options trading firm, "the envy of the industry," according to the *Wall Street Journal*), Gary went on to become chairman and CEO of VAST Power Systems and a principal in three other commercial companies. In the course of his remarkable career, he has established more than twenty *other* businesses—some of them service-industry enterprises in needy communities around the world. By any standard recognized in the business world, Gary Ginter's work has been successful.

And yet Gary himself refuses to define "success" by the traditional measures of profit and power. For him, success in business as in all of life is defined in relation to the coming of God's kingdom. In Gary's own words, anyone called to live out in the world of business the implications of the biblical story will be a "Kingdom Professional":

> Kingdom Professionals do not define success in terms of money, job or status. They do not seek to maximize their income or their security or their status, or to advance their careers. Instead they seek to maximize their impact on the people and places to which God has called them. They measure success by their contribution to what God is up to in their neck of His woods. They see themselves as successful to the extent they are doing what God has called them to do, in the place to which He has led them, in such a manner that their giftedness can be well utilized. Nothing less will suffice; not the shallowness of status, not the ephemeral illusions of wealth, not the corrosive effects of power. What matters to Kingdom

Professionals is that there is congruence between their daily lives and the
further in-breaking of God's Kingdom where they live and work.[65]

To be involved in business and remain faithful to the biblical story, one
must be a "stewardly entrepreneur,"[66] a steward of the opportunities,
talents, time, and money given by God, dedicated to witnessing to his
coming kingdom. Gary says that God has called him to make money, to
live on as little of it as possible, and then to give the rest away. Acting
on these principles, he has been able to establish a number of "kingdom companies," missionary corporations, especially in cross-cultural
settings. These companies are in business not so much for the sake of
generating profit as for the sake of providing employment and producing important goods and services where they are most needed. Many
countries that have closed their borders to traditional mission agencies
and the preaching of the gospel will welcome such Christian entrepre-
neurs or "tentmakers." The business itself becomes a potent witness to
the living reality of God within the lives of his faithful people.

In addition to setting up these "kingdom companies," Gary has also
been involved personally and financially in Circle Urban Ministries,
an organization that meets the needs of low-income families in his
own neighborhood, an economically depressed area of Chicago. But
Gary Ginter's involvements in evangelism and missions, his sacrificial
giving and generosity, his work to promote mercy and justice in his
own neighborhood and in poorer countries of the world—these are not
the *only* way in which Gary offers a faithful witness to God's kingdom.
Central to his witness is his faithfulness to God's creational purposes *in
the world of business.* Gary understands business to be a good part of
God's creation, developed in response to God's first command (Genesis
1:28). Business enterprises can play an important and positive role in
God's world. One loves one's neighbor by providing necessary goods and
services in a stewardly way. Gary witnesses to God's good intention for
business by placing love for neighbor, stewardship of God's resources,
and justice ahead of profit. He strives toward the ideal of a "kingdom
company," a business enterprise shaped by the biblical story that will
bless the lives of its own employees and their families, its suppliers,
and its customers. Such a goal is difficult at a time when the idolatrous
profit motive drives much of the traditional world of business. Faithfulness to God's purposes in business, Gary has discovered, may lead to
suffering, both in financial loss and in reputation. But this is what we
should expect in our witness.

Is there a place in God's kingdom for the gifts of a passionate bird-
watcher? Peter and Miranda Harris have found that there is. A curate
in a church in England, Peter was exploring possible mission work in

Tanzania when God showed him and Miranda a quite different plan for their family. Driven by their love for God's creation, and especially for birds, Peter and Miranda, their three small children, and another English couple moved to Portugal in 1983 to establish *A Rocha* ("the Rock"), a Christian conservation organization.

It was rare then to hear of Christians who were truly concerned about the environment. Nevertheless, the biblical story makes it clear that God deeply loves the nonhuman creation and has made humankind its guardians and stewards. At that time Portugal lacked both committed Christian ecologists and field study centers. Fragile habitats along the country's southern coast needed to be protected. One estuary in particular, a stopping point for large numbers of migrating birds, became the focus of the work. *A Rocha* staff undertook field studies to learn migration patterns, count birds, and survey the species in the area. This data was then compiled in formal reports shared with national conservation lobby groups. The hard work paid off. The government of Portugal has now granted environmental protection to the estuary near *A Rocha*.

The field center at *A Rocha* is unique in its community emphasis. People from widely differing backgrounds and levels of skill, from rookies to PhDs in ornithology, come to help collect data and to learn about the area's ecology. Peter's book *Under the Bright Wings* describes the early years of the organization and some of the struggles faced. It also clearly shows that *A Rocha* has been a wonderful vehicle for pointing people to Christ. People of many different backgrounds have visited the field center at Cruzinha and were welcomed into the community. The everyday activities range from technical fieldwork to conversations about theology. Sometimes people ask about the "Christian" side of *A Rocha*. Harris responds that the community sees "no distinction between the . . . field work and the . . . times when we could talk about Jesus with students who were staying in the house. The former were not secular, and the latter were not spiritual. All were undertaken out of worship and obedience, and all mattered to the Creator and Redeemer of the world."[67] When work in ecology is approached with the goal of serving God by understanding and caring for his creation, it becomes an act of worship and obedience, a way to witness to his inbreaking kingdom. As God works through the gifts and inclinations that he himself has given the staff of *A Rocha*, the fieldwork has thus become an opportunity for witness. Visitors see the glory of God revealed through creation and through the life of a community that lives for Christ. As Harris writes, "As the field studies at Cruzinha developed, we . . . gave time to talking together about the ways in which they were formed by our life in Christ. It was necessary to make this a conscious exercise, because we found the instinct to compartmentalize went very deep in all of us. Only as time went on did it become less studied and more natural."[68] Twenty some years ago, when *A Rocha* was founded, a handful of people came together to plant a seed. God has since caused that seed to grow and to flourish. Today *A Rocha* has become an international organization with work in thirteen countries.[69]

But what of Abigail and Percival, our two young university students eager to know and serve God, beginning to be interested in one another? From their journey with us through the story of the Bible, they have a fresh vision of the breadth of God's purposes in the world. How might such a vision affect their lives, either now or in the future?

Abby, who had always thought of her times of prayer and personal evangelism as her only real "Christian service," has been thinking lately of the many ways in which God may choose to use the gifts he has given her. She wonders about joining the diplomatic corps, or teaching languages in a foreign school, or even setting up her own business as a consultant to people whose work calls them to live overseas. She can see how a Christian might have lots of chances to show God's ways in these different life paths. And since God shows his kingship through his people *wherever* they are, and at whatever stage of their lives, Abby's thinking about her university studies right here and now has also changed. Worship and service are no longer for after-hours. The simple things—going to class, talking with friends, or writing an essay—have new meaning for Abby. She's come to see that these are what she's been given to do *now* with her time and talents, her love for people and for God. God has called her to be a student, to bring the gospel to bear on all her thinking, reading, and writing, and to gain insight into God's world that will enable her to witness to God's rule wherever she is called later.

And Percival? Poor Percy had always, deep down, thought of himself as a kind of second-class Christian. Just going to school during the week and plugging away on the family farm in vacations didn't seem to him like much of a life for God, especially when he compared it with his brother's career as a full-time youth worker in the city.

But Percy now sees that agriculture too can be God's calling. He is taking courses in ecology and farm management, reading up on how clean fuels can be made from corn and other field crops. He has begun to think through some ideas about conserving agricultural lands and water. Percy has been seeking out other Christians who have been talking and writing about these issues for a while. He is finding out what he can learn from their work and how he might find ways to apply it, wherever God may send him. For Percy, as for Abigail, his life as a university student has a whole new significance as he finds ways to seek God's kingdom in the here and now, the place he's been given to learn and work in.

### Living in Hope: Straining toward What Is Ahead

We know from Scripture that one day "every knee should bow . . . and every tongue confess that Jesus Christ is Lord" (Philippians 2:10–11). We know too that one day all of creation will be restored. So we look toward that day with hope, rooting our lives deeply in the gospel so we can begin to make the kingdom known in our own communities even today. We live in hope, eagerly anticipating and straining toward what is ahead (3:13–14).

Hope is important: it is a vital part of the faith that must shape our mission today. "Now these three remain," says Paul, "faith, hope, and love" (1 Corinthians 13:13). *Faith* is the means by which we appropriate the salvation accomplished in Jesus Christ. *Love* is the outward expression of that faith, which marks the life of the believing community. And *hope* is the confident expectation that *God's future kingdom will come.* Hope is a settled conviction about the future, a conviction giving meaning and shape to life in the present.[70] We can see this in many everyday situations. If, for example, you enter university in the *hope* of one day becoming a doctor, that hope will shape your life, directing not only your choice of courses but also dictating what time and effort (and money) you will devote to your studies. Thus, the whole of your life will take on a new look, a new focus, because of your hope for what the future will bring.

The same pattern is evident—but on a much larger scale—where the Christian's ultimate hope of the revelation of God's kingdom is concerned. Lesslie Newbigin puts it like this: "Meaningful action in history is possible only when there is some vision of a future goal."[71] What you and I believe to be the goal of history *will* give particular significance and form to our lives today. If we recognize that we have been called to provide our world with a preview of God's coming kingdom, the hope of that kingdom's coming will shape all that we say and do in the here and now. As we are *pushed* forward in our mission by the impetus and forward movement that we saw in Jesus' own words and works while he lived among us, we are also *pulled* forward by hopeful expectation of the future kingdom to be revealed when Jesus returns.

Thus it matters very much *what in particular* we are hoping for. Yet we often do not give explicit attention to the content of our hope as Christians, our sense of where history is headed. Because our hope is not always carefully examined, there is some danger that its content will not always be thoroughly biblical—and this matters deeply, since (as we have seen) *what we hope for in the future will shape our mission in the present.* What is the *substance* of the Christian's hope? What does the Bible teach about the end of history, the final act of the cosmic drama?[72] To these questions we turn in our last chapter.

# Act 6

# The Return of the King

## Redemption Completed

When God set out to redeem his creation from sin and sin's effects on it, his ultimate purpose was that what he had once created *good* should be utterly restored, that the whole cosmos should once again live and thrive under his beneficent rule. In Jesus Christ that goal of cosmic redemption was first revealed and then *accomplished*: the words of Jesus from the cross, *"It is finished"* (John 19:30), declare redemption to be complete already, even though its final revelation waits in the future. The Bible tells the story of the progressive march of God toward this final cosmic restoration. It also reveals, a little at a time, what that restoration will look like when it is ultimately revealed in its fullness. In this final chapter of our book, we look at history's conclusion in the restoration and renewal of God's good creation.

The last chapters of Revelation give us a clear picture of what lies in store for the creation as God brings history to its conclusion. But throughout the Bible we have already been allowed glimpses of where the story of God's redemption has been headed. The clearest picture of God's kingdom is in the person, words, and actions of his Son, Jesus Christ. Yet many other parts of Scripture have also briefly opened windows on God's ultimate intention for his creation.

## The End of the Story

In the last chapters of Revelation (especially 21:1–5) we see God's final purpose unveiled. John is allowed a vision of a new heaven and a new earth, entirely cleansed of sin and evil.[1] The old heaven and earth (in which sin and death have dominated) give way to a new dominion, over which the Lord again rules.[2] The Holy City, the "new Jerusalem," descends from heaven to earth. This suggests the renewed imposition of God's perfect order for the earth. And we recall that Jesus prayed, "Thy kingdom come. Thy will be done on earth, as it is in heaven" (Matthew 6:10 KJV). The descent of God's heavenly dwelling place, "the new Jerusalem," to earth is the graphic representation that God's kingdom *has* come and his will *is* forevermore to be accomplished on earth—just as it has always been in heaven.

A loud voice from God's throne proclaims,

> Now the dwelling of God is with men, and he will live with them. They will be his people, and God himself will be with them and be their God. He will wipe every tear from their eyes. There will be no more death or mourning or crying or pain, for the old order of things has passed away. (Revelation 21:3–4)

Heaven, the dwelling place of God (which had become separated from the creation because of sin), comes "down" to the earth in a dramatic image of restored unity and harmony between the Creator and what he has created. God himself comes to dwell on the new earth with humankind. Sin and all its effects are removed. There is no more death or sickness or pain, but only peace and harmony, because the relationship between God and humankind has been healed. God is once again as close to us as in the days when he walked with (our ancestors) Adam and Eve in the garden. Relationships among human beings too have been healed: love reigns. The whole of human life is purified, and even the nonhuman creation shares in this liberation of God's people from the former slavery to sin and death. The goal of biblical history is a renewed creation: healed, redeemed, and restored.

Though this vision of the new creation is the climactic conclusion of the last book of the Bible, most of Revelation is not concerned with the future. What it does give us is a glimpse into God's purposes throughout history, purposes leading to this conclusion. Much of the Bible shows us the history of humankind on earth, and especially the experiences of God's people. In this final book, it is as if the curtains of God's heavenly throne room have been pulled back. This allows us at last to see the spiritual battle that has all along been shaping our world's history, a battle we could not see from our own earthbound and historically limited point of view (cf. Ephesians 6:12).

John is writing to a small community of believers in Asia Minor who are suffering terribly under Roman persecution. It must have seemed to them that they were facing the forces of evil all alone. But John sees—and reveals to his readers—that behind the local opposition to the gospel being faced by this first-century church lies Satan's own constant and implacable hatred of Christ and his people. The little church in Asia Minor is fighting a minor skirmish in the ongoing cosmic spiritual battle—but they cannot *see* the vast scope of the war between God and Satan. So to these frightened, faithful Christians comes the message of Revelation: *God will triumph*. Those who are faithful in his service *will* share in the ultimate victory. Even though at present the outcome of their own battle may seem doubtful, Jesus is firmly in control of world events.

John opens the book of Revelation with a startling vision of the exalted Christ. He then explains that he has been ordered to record both what is *now* taking place in history (in his own time in the first century) and what *will* take place in the future (1:19). But the first matter to which the writer gives his attention is to encourage seven representative churches in Asia Minor to remain faithful to the gospel in the midst of their suffering (Revelation 2–3). Then the curtains are pulled back, and John is allowed to see a vision of the throne room in heaven, from which God rules in glory and splendor (Revelation 4). Twenty-four elders (symbolically representing the whole people of God—the Old Testament nation of Israel and the New Testament church) and four living creatures (representing all of creation) bow before God and worship him.

John then sees a scroll with seven seals, representing sovereign control over the direction and goal of the history of the world. When this scroll of God's purposes is at last opened, evil will be vanquished, and God's people (whose names are written in the scroll) will share in his salvation (Revelation 5). An angel asks: "Who is worthy to break the seals and open the scroll? Who is able to direct history to its goal? Who can conquer evil and accomplish salvation?" (paraphrased). At first no one answers the angel's question. John begins to weep bitterly, for he sees that if no one can direct the course of history, humankind is trapped in a meaningless round of evil, suffering, pain, and death. But an elder comforts John, inviting him to look again and see an immensely powerful lion, which has triumphed over its enemies and is able to open the scroll. But when John looks through his tears he sees not the regal lion but a pitiable blood-matted lamb, looking as if it has been slaughtered. The victory of God has been accomplished not on any field of battle, not by a warlike lion, but by the Lamb whose life was given on the cross.

As the Lamb takes the scroll from God, a hymn of praise begins with the twenty-four elders, is taken up by thousands upon thousands of angels, and at last is chanted by every creature in heaven and on earth as they fall down and worship the Lamb, saying,

> You are worthy to take the scroll and to open its seals,
> because you were slain,
> and with your blood you purchased men for God
> from every tribe and language and people and nation.
> You have made them to be a kingdom and priests to serve our God,
> and they will reign on the earth. . . .
> Worthy is the Lamb, who was slain,
> to receive power and wealth and wisdom and strength
> and honor and glory and praise! . . .
> To him who sits on the throne and to the Lamb
> be praise and honor and glory and power,
> forever and ever! (Revelation 5:9–10, 12–13)

The remainder of the book of Revelation shows us Jesus—the exalted Lamb—opening the seals and guiding history to its final purpose: the founding of the kingdom of God. Judgment and salvation fall on the world as the crucified Victor opens the seals and unrolls the scroll of history. John shows that the true motive of history has always been this spiritual battle; though normally hidden from human perception, it is now revealed to him in a series of vivid images. Though the images are intricate and at times both puzzling and frightening, their general import is clear. God himself is the one who, through his beloved Son, is moving history. God's purposes will be accomplished: his kingdom will come. This is the glorious concluding image of the renewed heaven and earth, shared in Revelation 21 and 22.

Imagine the comfort and hope that this book must have given the small, suffering church for which John was writing. It says that, though they may be small in numbers and weak in influence, and though they must for a time continue to suffer under the awful power of Rome, their cause is not hopeless, for they are allied to the winning side. They follow the One who sovereignly rules history, who will crush all opposition to his kingdom. They also will share in Christ's victory.

## Events Preceding the End

The New Testament shows us that three major events will usher in the restoration of creation and the arrival of God's kingdom in its fullness: (1) Jesus returns. (2) The dead are raised bodily (some to share in the life of the new creation and others to final wrath). And (3) the world comes before Christ to be judged.

Unfortunately, these end-time events have often stirred fruitless controversy among Christians. Believers often try to establish a cosmic timetable into which they can slot known historical events. But since there are many such timetables in competition, this sort of curiosity about what God will do, how he will do it, and especially *when* he will do it, too often merely breeds debate and dispute among believers who should know better. There are different understandings among various groups of Christians concerning details of the time of Christ's return, the millennium, the rapture, the final judgment, the antichrist, and the tribulation. Yet David Lawrence reminds us that fixing our attention on such things is a bit like becoming obsessed with the nature, strength, and frequency of the birth pangs when we should be thinking about the baby![3] Though the "labor pains" of end-time events can be fascinating, we must give due attention to the new world to be born out of them. And so our focus here is on the "baby," the new world waiting to be born.

## A New Creation: The Restoration of All Things

Revelation 21 is a vision of a creation completely restored to its original goodness. What we may not notice, however (unless we pay particular attention to the matter), is that this vision of God's ultimate purpose may differ substantially from what we have thought it would be. Revelation does *not* give us a picture of Christians suddenly transported out of this world to live a spiritual existence in heaven forever. Wright comments on this common misunderstanding: "Very often people have come to the New Testament with the presumption that 'going to heaven when you die' is the implicit point of it all. . . . They acquire that viewpoint from somewhere, but not from the New Testament."[4] John's vision in Revelation, indeed, in the whole New Testament, does not depict salvation as an *escape* from earth into a spiritualized heaven where human souls dwell forever.[5] Instead, John is shown (and shows us in turn) that salvation is the *restoration* of God's creation on a new earth. In this restored world, the redeemed of God will live in resurrected bodies within a renewed creation, from which sin and its effects have been expunged. This is the kingdom that Christ's followers have already begun to enjoy in foretaste.

This concept of salvation as restoration (rather than the destruction and remaking) of creation implies significant continuity between the world we know and the world to come. Yet the Bible also suggests some elements of *discontinuity*.[6] For example, Jesus' resurrected body can still be recognized by the disciples, who knew him before his death. Yet it also seems to have the new ability to pass through locked doors and to cover great distances quickly (Luke 24:28–43). When Jesus spoke to the Sadducees concerning whether or not marriage would survive the resurrection, he may have been alluding to a new manner of life that transcends the sexual relationships we know here and now (Matthew 22:30; Luke 20:34–36). So it appears that between our present life and the life to be revealed there may be both continuity and discontinuity, some things familiar and some strange. We do not see as clearly as we would like (1 Corinthians 13:12), but we know that "no eye has seen, no ear has heard, . . . what God has prepared for those who love him" (2:9). However this may be, we do know that our new lives will be lived in resurrected bodies within a restored creation (1 Corinthians 15).

This restoration of the creation will be comprehensive: the *whole* of human life in the context of the *whole* creation will be restored. Too often our view of the future has emphasized solely the salvation of the individual person apart from the full creational and relational context in which human beings live their lives.[7] Often the whole of the biblical story seems to revolve around "me."[8] Yet the vision of Revelation, indeed, the whole story of the Bible, leads us to look forward in hope to a creation restored to wholeness. Every facet of it is to be brought back to what God has intended for it. And within that glorious fullness and perfect wholeness, there is a place for *us*. Redemption is cosmic in its scope.

Human beings were created to enjoy fellowship with God in the full context of creational life.[9] In tempting Adam and Eve to rebel against God, Satan sought to thwart God's plan—and succeeded, at least to the extent that sin and its effects now touch all of creation. But when God set out to deal with sin and its ruinous consequences, his plan was to destroy the *enemy* of his good creation, not to destroy the creation itself. To destroy what he had made would have been to concede a tremendous victory to Satan.[10] J. A. Seiss puts it this way: "If redemption does not go as far as the consequences of sin, it is a misnomer, and fails to be redemption. . . . The salvation of any number of individuals . . . is not the redemption of what fell but the gathering up of a few splinters, . . . [and in such a case] Satan's mischief [would go] further than Christ's restoration."[11] But the story of the Bible moves toward a conclusion in which God's restorative work will utterly undo *all* of Satan's "mischief."

Throughout Scripture, God's kingdom is depicted as a place and time of *cosmic* restoration. In Old Testament prophecies God says, "Behold, I will create new heavens and a new earth" (Isaiah 65:17; cf. 2 Peter 3:13; Revelation 21:1–5). After Jesus conquered sin on the cross and returned from the grave in triumph over death itself, Peter proclaims the good news in Jerusalem, saying "[Jesus] must remain in heaven until the time comes for God to *restore everything*, as he promised long ago through his holy prophets" (Acts 3:21). Paul also emphasizes the universal scope of God's redemptive work: "For God was pleased to have all his fullness dwell in [Jesus], and through him *to reconcile to himself all things*, whether things on earth or things in heaven, by making peace through his blood, shed on the cross" (Colossians 1:19–20). Just as nothing in creation remained untouched by sin after Eden, so nothing in creation can remain untouched by God's redemption after Christ's victory on the cross.

This comprehensive scope of God's redemptive work means, for example, that the nonhuman creation forming the context for human life will be restored to what God has intended for it all along. Thus, the prophets picture a new and fresh harmony and bounty within creation under the reign of God (Isaiah 65:17–25; Joel 2:18–27). Paul says that the nonhuman creation, which for so long has shared in the misery of humankind's fall into sin, is now looking forward to the coming renewal:

> The creation waits in eager expectation for the sons of God to be revealed. For the creation was subjected to frustration, not by its own choice, but by the will of the one who subjected it, in hope that the creation itself will be liberated from its bondage to decay and brought into the glorious freedom of the children of God. (Romans 8:19–21)

A comprehensive redemption also means that human cultural development and work will continue. The cultural achievements of history will be purified and will reappear on the new earth (Revelation 21:24–26).[12] There will be opportunity for humankind to continue to work and develop the creation—but now released from the burden of sin.[13]

### I Am Coming Soon!

The marvelous imagery of Revelation 21 and 22 directs our gaze to the end of history and the restoration of the whole of God's creation. John ends his book with the promise (repeated three times: 22:7, 12, 20): "Behold, I am coming soon!" He exhorts his readers to stand firm in the faith, warns those who remain outside the kingdom, and invites all who find themselves "thirsty" for the salvation of God revealed in John's visions to come and drink freely of the water of life. Jesus is coming soon. All who believe and hope in Jesus, as John the apostle did, will echo his own response: "Amen. Come, Lord Jesus."

# Notes

## Preface

1. Contemporary Testimony Committee of the Christian Reformed Church, *Our World Belongs to God: A Contemporary Testimony* (Grand Rapids: CRC Publications, 1987), paragraph 19.

2. We are aware of the various arguments biblical scholars have raised against the unity of Scripture. We address some of these concerns and various hermeneutical issues in a more scholarly way in "Story and Biblical Theology," in *Out of Egypt: Biblical Theology and Biblical Interpretation* (ed. Craig Bartholomew et al.; Grand Rapids: Zondervan, 2004).

3. N. T. Wright, *Jesus and the Victory of God* (London: SPCK, 1996), 443, 467–72.

4. For two good discussions of an emerging emphasis on the centrality of mission for the biblical story, see Richard Bauckham, *Bible and Mission: Christian Witness in a Postmodern World* (Grand Rapids: Baker, 2003); and Christopher Wright, "Mission as a Matrix for Hermeneutics and Biblical Theology," in Bartholomew, *Out of Egypt*.

5. N. T. Wright, "How Can the Bible Be Authoritative?" *Vox Evangelica*, no. 21 (1991): 7–32; idem, *The New Testament and the People of God* (London: SPCK, 1992), 139–43.

## Prologue: The Bible as a Grand Story

1. N. T. Wright, *The New Testament and the People of God* (London: SPCK, 1992), 40, italics added.

2. Lesslie Newbigin, *The Gospel in a Pluralist Society* (Grand Rapids: Eerdmans, 1989), 15.

3. Alasdair MacIntyre, *After Virtue* (Notre Dame: University of Notre Dame Press, 1981), 216.

4. *Scientia potestas est.* This phrase comes from Francis Bacon (1561–1626).

5. We make a distinction between *having* a story that shapes our lives and *articulating* that story.

6. If a basic story is similar to a worldview, then it is intriguing to note that James Sire suggests that a Christian ministry may be to help people become conscious of their worldview, to foreground what is there but of which they may not be conscious (*The Universe Next Door: A Basic Worldview Catalog* [3d ed.; Downers Grove, IL: InterVarsity, 1997]). Nick Pollard, an English evangelist who works with high school and university

students, tells a delightful story in this respect. Nick's evangelistic approach is to help students become aware of their basic story or worldview so that they can see how this relates to Christianity. Nick tells of a young man going home, delighted to tell his mother that he had discovered he is an Epicurean hedonist!

7. Lesslie Newbigin, *Foolishness to the Greeks: The Gospel and Western Culture* (Grand Rapids: Eerdmans, 1986), 61.

8. "God's Word . . . is a vast, over-reaching, all-encompassing story—a meta-story" (Eugene Peterson, "Living into God's Story"). This article originally appeared on the website "The Ooze: Conversation for a Journey" (www.theooze.com). The article can be accessed at https://secure.electricurrent.com/freshresource/articles/index.cfm?task=deta il&ID=1081&bSHOW=no&navResources=2.

9. N. T. Wright, *New Testament and People of God*, 41–42.

10. Peterson, "Living into God's Story."

11. Wright's analogy of a five-act play is discussed in more detail on pp. 197–98.

12. N. T. Wright, "How Can the Bible Be Authoritative?" *Vox Evangelica*, No. 21 (1991): 7–32; idem, *New Testament and People of God*, 139–43. We have adapted the illustration slightly by suggesting six acts instead of five.

## Act 1: God Establishes His Kingdom

1. Throughout this book the name *Yahweh* will normally be translated LORD, as in many English versions.

2. In a later part of the book, we discuss the meaning of the name *Yahweh*.

3. Paul makes some similar points in Colossians 1:15–20: Christ is "the firstborn over all creation. For by him all things were created. . . . And he is the head of his body, the church."

4. Jean L'Hour, "Yahweh Elohim," *Revue biblique* 81 (1974): 530.

5. Gerhard von Rad, *Genesis: A Commentary* (trans. John H. Marks; Philadelphia: Westminster, 1961), 46.

6. Henri Blocher, *In the Beginning: The Opening Chapters of Genesis* (trans. David G. Preston; Downers Grove, IL: InterVarsity, 1984), 27–38.

7. John Stek, "What Says the Scripture?" in *Portraits of Creation: Biblical and Scientific Perspectives on the World's Formation* (by Howard Van Till et al.; Grand Rapids: Eerdmans, 1990), 230.

8. Von Rad, *Genesis*, 50.

9. Dietrich Bonhoeffer, *Creation and Fall: A Theological Interpretation of Genesis 1–3* (trans. John C. Fletcher; London: SCM Press, 1959), 25.

10. Von Rad, *Genesis*, 51.

11. John Walton, Victor Matthews, and Mark Chavalas, *The IVP Bible Background Commentary: Old Testament* (Downers Grove, IL: InterVarsity, 2000), 28.

12. For the different views on the plural "Let us," see Gordon Wenham, *Genesis 1–15* (Word Biblical Commentary; Waco: Word, 1987), 27–28.

13. See Bruce Milne, *Know the Truth: A Handbook of Christian Belief* (Downers Grove, IL: InterVarsity, 1999).

14. Augustine, *Confessions* 1.1.

15. See below.

16. Von Rad, *Genesis*, 58.

17. Lynn White, "The Historical Roots of Our Ecologic Crisis," *Science* 155 (1967): 1203–7. For an excellent treatment of stewardship, see Peter De Vos et al., *Earthkeeping in the Nineties: Stewardship of Creation* (Grand Rapids: Eerdmans, 1991).

18. The book of Genesis is structured by ten *toledoths*—five before Abraham and five after him. *Toledoth* is a Hebrew word that can be translated "This is the story of . . . ,"

"This is the account of . . . ," or "This is the history of . . ." Genesis 2:4 is the first of these *toledoth* sayings. The narration of history begins here: "This is the story of the heavens and the earth" (2:4–4:26). The remaining nine *toledoths* are "This is the story of Adam's line" (5:1–6:8); "This is the story of Noah" (6:9–9:29); "This is the story of Shem, Ham, and Japheth" (10:1–11:9); "This is the story of Shem" (11:10–26); "This is the story of Terah" (11:27–25:11); "This is the story of Abraham's son Ishmael" (25:12–18); "This is the story of Abraham's son Isaac" (25:19–35:29); "This is the story of Esau" (36:1–37:1); "This is the story of Jacob" (37:2–50:26; our translations).

## Act 2: Rebellion in the Kingdom

1. Eugene Peterson, *Working the Angles: The Shape of Pastoral Integrity* (Grand Rapids: Eerdmans, 1993), 82, 83.

2. Gordon Wenham, *Genesis 1–15* (Word Biblical Commentary; Waco: Word, 1987), 61.

3. As argued by Gordon Hugenberger in *Marriage as a Covenant: A Study of Biblical Law and Ethics Governing Marriage, Developed from the Perspective of Malachi* (Leiden: Brill, 1994).

## Act 3: The King Chooses Israel

1. The Hebrew word for vanity is *hebel*.

2. The word "misdirect" is used here to describe how sin works in misdirecting or twisting God's good creation. Al Wolters describes the biblical worldview in terms of the words "structure" and "direction"—God's originally good creational structure, its misdirection away from God's purpose by sin, and its redirection by redemption. See Al Wolters, *Creation Regained: Biblical Basics for a Reformational Worldview* (Grand Rapids: Eerdmans, 1985).

3. Rookmaker, *Art Needs No Justification* (Downers Grove, IL: InterVarsity, 1978).

4. See Psalm 8:6.

5. On this topic see Nicholas Wolterstorff, chapter 6, "A City of Delight," in *Until Justice and Peace Embrace: The Kuyper Lectures for 1981 Given at the Free University of Amsterdam* (Grand Rapids: Eerdmans, 1983). Wolterstorff speaks of how to develop cities that honor God and are a blessing to those who live in them.

6. Cities in early Mesopotamia were not designed for people to live in. They mostly housed the public sector, consisting mainly of religious and storage buildings. John Walton, Victor Matthews, and Mark Chavalas, *The IVP Bible Background Commentary: Old Testament* (Downers Grove, IL: InterVarsity, 2000), 41.

7. The identity of the sons of God is much disputed. F. B. Huey says, "Most students of Genesis 6:1–4 agree that it is one of the most disputed passages in the Old Testament. It has been described as 'a riddle,' 'strange,' 'difficult,' 'unintelligible,' 'unsolved,' and 'cryptic.' This history of its exegesis has been characterized by bitter controversy that seems no closer to resolution by today's scholars than by their ancient counterparts" (F. B. Huey Jr. and John H. Walton, "Are the 'Sons of God' in Genesis 6 Angels?" in *The Genesis Debate: Persistent Questions about Creation and the Flood* [ed. Ronald Youngblood; 2d ed.; Grand Rapids: Baker, 1990], 184). Who are the sons of God? There are three basic positions: (1) They are some kind of supernatural beings, traditionally fallen angels. The daughters of men were humans. The sin was marriage between two kinds, and God's order is transgressed. (2) The sons of God are the godly line of Seth, and the daughters of men are the ungodly line of Cain. The sin is marriage between the godly and the ungodly. (3) The sons of God are rulers, and the daughters of men are common women. The sin

is oppression and polygamy. For a full discussion see Huey and Walton, "Are the 'Sons of God' in Genesis 6 Angels?" 184–209.

8. See Gordon Wenham, *Genesis 1–15* (Word Biblical Commentary; Waco: Word, 1987), 159–66 for the relationship between the story of Noah and the ancient flood stories.

9. Karl Barth, *Church Dogmatics*, vol. 3/1, *The Doctrine of Creation* (trans. J. W. Edwards et al.; Edinburgh: T&T Clark, 1958), 178.

10. A comparable verse is Jonah 4:11, where God rebukes Jonah for his lack of compassion: "And should I not be concerned about Nineveh, that great city, in which there are more than a hundred and twenty thousand persons who do not know their right hand from their left, *and also many animals?*" (NRSV, italics added).

11. O. Palmer Robertson, *Christ and the Covenants* (Phillipsburg, NJ: Presbyterian and Reformed Publishing House, 1980), 4.

12. See Gordon Hugenberger, *Marriage as a Covenant: A Study of Biblical Law and Ethics Governing Marriage, Developed from the Perspective of Malachi* (Leiden: Brill, 1994).

13. See William Dumbrell's excellent book, *Covenant and Creation: A Theology of Old Testament Covenants* (Nashville: Nelson, 1984).

14. The repetition of this phrase at the start and end of 9:1–7 is what we call an *inclusio*, an envelope that alerts us to the centrality of this issue in this section of Genesis.

15. See D. J. Wiseman, "Babel," *New Bible Dictionary* (ed. J. D. Douglas et al.; 3d ed.; Downers Grove, IL: InterVarsity, 1996), 109–10.

16. Gordon Wenham, *Genesis 1–15* (Word Biblical Commentary; Waco: Word, 1987), 245.

17. The stories of Abraham, Isaac, Jacob, and Joseph are nearly five times as long as Genesis 1–11.

18. See, for example, Genesis 1:22, 28.

19. Genesis 3:14, 17; 4:11; 5:29; 9:25.

20. Dumbrell, *Covenant and Creation*, 71.

21. Cf. also Genesis 22:16–18.

22. Here we encounter the mysterious doctrine of election. Abraham and his descendents are chosen to be God's people from among all the nations (see Deuteronomy 7:7–11). This is a mysterious doctrine, but one thing is quite clear in 12:1–3. God's purpose in calling Abraham is in the long run to secure blessing for all the families of the earth (12:3). Election is election to service and not just to privilege. As Lesslie Newbigin comments, "To be elect . . . means to be incorporated into his [God's] mission to the world, to be the bearer of God's saving purpose for his whole world, to be the sign and the agent and the first fruit of his blessed kingdom which is for all" (*The Gospel in a Pluralist Society* [Grand Rapids: Eerdmans, 1989], 27).

23. Dumbrell, *Covenant and Creation*, 66.

24. Gordon J. Wenham, *Story as Torah: Reading the Old Testament Ethically* (Edinburgh: T&T Clark, 2000), 37.

25. See Genesis 15:18–19 for the promise of the land and its extent.

26. There is much discussion surrounding the meaning of circumcision and how it functions to confirm the covenant. One view finds the cultural background of circumcision in ancient Egypt—which we believe has merit. There is ancient Egyptian artwork in The Tomb of Ankhmahor (the Physician) in Saqqara, near Cairo, showing young men around the age of puberty being circumcised. The tomb is dated to just before the time of Abraham (c. 2200 BC). In ancient Egypt circumcision was a fertility ceremony practiced on adolescents as they reached marriageable age. The foreskin was viewed symbolically as a barrier to fruitfulness. Circumcision "aided" the already developing sexual powers of the young man. Abraham had visited Egypt on at least one occasion prior to this, staying there for some time (Genesis 12:10–20). God thus uses a well-known custom and modifies

it for his covenantal purposes. God's command was to circumcise a ninety-year-old man and an eight-day-old boy—both of whom were unable to father children. This signifies that God will sovereignly remove the barrier to fruitfulness and give Abraham a son. God confirms his earlier covenant with Abraham (Genesis 17:1–2). Note the twofold covenant structure in Genesis 17: "As for me [God] . . ." (17:4); "As for you [Abraham] . . ." (17:9). God would keep the covenant promises he has made to Abraham in Genesis 12 and 15. Abraham is to believe God's promise. This call to faith is given in a sign that will strengthen Abraham's faith. He recognizes God's commitment to removing the barrier so he might be fruitful (Romans 4:11). Incidentally, this also helps us to understand the "circumcision of the heart" (Deuteronomy 30:6; Romans 2:29). Circumcision of the heart is the removal of the barrier (sin) that hinders a fruitful relationship with God.

27. See David J. A. Clines, *The Theme of the Pentateuch* (2d ed.; Sheffield: JSOT Press, 1997).

28. Ibid., 29.

29. Genesis 15:6 is important in the New Testament for Romans 4 and justification.

30. Søren Kierkegaard, *Fear and Trembling: Repetition* (trans. H. V. Hong and E. H. Hong; Princeton, NJ: Princeton University Press, 1983), 22–23.

31. Wenham, *Story as Torah*, 37.

32. For a useful discussion of the Joseph narrative, see Paul C. Borgman, *Genesis: The Story We Haven't Heard* (Downers Grove, IL: InterVarsity, 2001), section IV.

33. Wenham, *Genesis 16–50* (Word Biblical Commentary; Dallas: Word, 1994), 20.

34. See Psalm 105:42–43, where the connection between the exodus and God's promises to Abraham is directly made. Exodus as a whole tells of God's formation of a people in three ways: chapters 1–18, by God's mighty acts of redemption; 19–24, by covenant; and 25–40, by his indwelling presence.

35. It was not uncommon for foreign princes and princesses to be raised in the Egyptian court. See James K. Hoffmeier, *Israel in Egypt: The Evidence for the Authenticity of the Exodus Tradition* (New York: Oxford University Press, 1997), 142–43.

36. Also known as Sinai.

37. See, for example, Brevard S. Childs, *The Book of Exodus* (Philadelphia: Westminster, 1974), 47–89.

38. Terrence Fretheim, "Yahweh," *New International Dictionary of Old Testament Theology and Exegesis* (ed. W. A. VanGemeren; 5 vols.; Grand Rapids: Zondervan, 1997), 4:1296.

39. Cornelis Houtman, *Exodus* (trans. J. Rebel and W. Woudstra; 4 vols.; Kampen: Kok, 1993–2000), 1:9.

40. J. Philip Hyatt, *Commentary on Exodus* (New Century Bible Series; London: Oliphants, 1971).

41. Hoffmeier, *Israel in Egypt*, 147.

42. Colin J. Humphreys, *The Miracles of Exodus: A Scientist's Discovery of the Extraordinary Natural Causes of the Biblical Story* (New York: Harper Collins, 2003), 133.

43. J. Marr and C. Malloy, "An Epidemiologic Analysis of the Ten Plagues of Egypt," *Catalyst*, May 1996.

44. Humphreys, *Miracles of Exodus*, 138.

45. Gordon Spykman, *Reformational Theology: A New Paradigm for Doing Dogmatics* (Grand Rapids: Eerdmans, 1992), 289.

46. Hoffmeier, *Israel in Egypt*, 150. However, less likely are links between the frogs and the god Hekat, the cows and the god Hathor, and the bulls and the god Apir.

47. Ibid., 153.

48. John I. Durham, *Exodus* (Word Biblical Commentary; Waco: Word, 1987), 263.

49. In view is the whole of Israel's life, including the political dimension. As some have observed, "treasured possession" has political implications; the Akkadian word is used

to describe a vassal of a great king. But stronger than this is the use of the word "nation" (*gôy*) rather than the more common "people" ('*am*) in "holy nation." This probably alludes to Genesis 12:2, where Israel as a political entity is in mind. As Dumbrell says of Exodus 19:6, "Probably then we are here, as we noted in connection with Gen[esis] 12:2, thinking of Israel as offering in her constitution a societary model for the world" (*Covenant and Creation*, 87). From this perspective Israel's political particularity as an ancient Near Eastern nation is also of universal, political significance.

50. Dumbrell, *Covenant and Creation*, 90.

51. Ibid., 80.

52. We note these covenantal elements in Exodus 19–24 in what follows. The same elements are found in Deuteronomy: (1) a preamble that identifies the two parties of the covenant (Deuteronomy 1:1–5); (2) a history of the relationship between God and Israel (1:6–4:49); (3) principal stipulations (chapters 5–11); (4) detailed stipulations (chapters 12–26); (5) blessings on obedience and curses on disobedience (27–28); (6) witnesses to the covenant (30:19; 31:19; 32:1–43). See Meredith G. Kline, *Treaty of the Great King: The Covenant Structure of Deuteronomy: Studies and Commentary* (Grand Rapids: Eerdmans, 1963); Peter C. Craigie, *The Book of Deuteronomy* (Grand Rapids: Eerdmans, 1976), 22–24. Craigie gives a bibliography for further study.

53. Terence E. Fretheim, *Exodus* (Interpretation; Louisville: John Knox, 1991), 263. In this section we make substantial use of Fretheim.

54. Ibid., 281.

55. Ibid., 271–72.

56. Ibid., 277.

57. Ibid., 273.

58. Ibid.

59. Gordon J. Wenham, "Clean and Unclean," *New Bible Dictionary*, 210.

60. Just how to understand these numbers is a matter of debate. See Gordon J. Wenham, *Numbers: An Introduction and Commentary* (Tyndale Old Testament Commentaries; Leicester, UK: Apollos; Downers Grove, IL: InterVarsity, 1981), 60–66.

61. J. Gordon McConville, *Deuteronomy* (Apollos Old Testament Commentary; Leicester, UK: Apollos; Downers Grove, IL: InterVarsity, 2002), 36.

62. This is an adaptation of the famous and oft-quoted saying of the Dutch statesman and theologian Abraham Kuyper: "Geen duimbreed is er op heel 't erf van ons menschelijk leven, waarvan de Christus, die àller Souverein is, niet roept: 'Mijn!'" (There is no thumbwidth of the entire domain of our human life of which the Christ, the Sovereign over everything, does not proclaim: "It is Mine!") Cited from Cornelis Veenhof, *In Kuyper's Lijn: Enkele Opmerkingen over den Invloed van Dr. A. Kuyper op de "Wijsbegeerte der wetsidee"* (Goes: Oosterbaan & Le Cointre, 1939), 43.

63. This is reminiscent of the call of the *meuzzin* from the minaret, in the Islamic religion.

64. Cf. Paul's instruction in Romans 12:1–2 to present *the body* as a living sacrifice.

65. McConville, *Deuteronomy*, 34.

66. Some scholars have noted that the order of the detailed laws in Deuteronomy tends to follow the commandments; hence, sections on the detailed laws are an exposition of the Ten Words. Many Christians continue to find these passages very difficult. Indeed, they represent an important divide between the ways in which Christians tell the biblical story. Among proponents of a story approach to the Bible, scholars such as Stanley Hauerwas and Richard Hays insist that we allow the later stage of the story, meaning Jesus' teaching, to be the final judge of these difficult, earlier parts. Hauerwas and Hays take Jesus to be a pacifist and thus find these passages contrary to a Christian ethic.

67. Walter Brueggemann, *The Land: Place as Gift, Promise, and Challenge in Biblical Faith* (Philadelphia: Fortress, 1977), 45–46.

68. See Donald Sinnema, *Reclaiming the Land: A Study in the Book of Joshua* (Toronto: Curriculum Development Centre, 1977).

69. Brueggemann, *Land*, 191.

70. Ibid., 49.

71. An important place where this theology is picked up in the New Testament is in the Beatitudes: "Blessed are the meek, for they will inherit the earth" (Matthew 5:5). See Brueggemann, *Land*, chapter 10.

72. Verses like Joshua 10:40 and 11:16 might suggest that all the Canaanites were destroyed from the land. But it is clear from other passages in Joshua and the Old Testament that this was not the case. Such language is hyperbole, making the point that Joshua gained control over the land.

73. For a useful discussion of this issue, see Wenham, *Goodness of God*, 119–47; C. S. Cowles, E. M. Merrill, D. L. Gard, and T. Longman III, *"Show Them No Mercy": Four Views on Canaanite Genocide* (Grand Rapids: Zondervan, 2003); and Norbert Lohfink, *"ḥāram,"* *Theological Dictionary of the Old Testament* (ed. G. J. Botterweck and H. Ringren; trans. J. T. Willis, G. W. Bromiley, and D. E. Green; rev. ed.; 12 vols.; Grand Rapids: Eerdmans, 1977–), 5:180–99.

74. Lohfink makes an argument that the inhabitants were free to surrender to the Israelites, but if they refused they were to be killed. See Lohfink, *"ḥāram,"* 197.

75. Wenham, *Goodness of God*, 125.

76. Barry Webb, *The Book of the Judges: An Integrated Reading* (Sheffield: JSOT Press, 1987), 209.

77. J. Gordon Harris, Cheryl A. Brown, and Michael S. Moore, *Joshua, Judges, Ruth* (New International Biblical Commentary: Old Testament Series; Carlisle, UK: Paternoster, 2000), 157.

78. The LORD's response is not mechanical. Webb (*Judges*, 209) rightly notes that the "motif of calling upon Yahweh is handled in such a way as to preclude any simple connection between repentance and deliverance. In the face of Israel's persistent apostasy Yahweh does not so much dispense rewards and punishment as oscillate between punishment and mercy."

79. Walton et al., *IVP Bible Background Commentary: Old Testament*, 146.

80. On Nazirite vows, see Numbers 6:1–21.

81. Webb, *Judges*, 172.

82. The book of Judges is not unaware of the dangers of kingship. See Judges 8:22–27.

83. William Dumbrell, *The End of the Beginning: Revelation 21–22 and the Old Testament* (Homebush West, Australia: Lancer Books, 1985), 10.

84. John Goldingay, *Theological Diversity and the Authority of the Old Testament* (Grand Rapids: Eerdmans, 1987), 94. For a similar view see Richard Nelson, *The Historical Books* (Nashville: Abingdon, 1998), 126–27.

85. Nelson, *Historical Books*, 119.

86. William Dumbrell, *The Faith of Israel: A Theological Survey of the Old Testament* (Grand Rapids: Eerdmans, 1998), 275.

87. Dumbrell, *End of the Beginning*, 52–53.

88. For an excellent discussion, see Leila Leah Bronner, *The Stories of Elijah and Elisha as Polemics against Baal Worship* (Leiden: Brill, 1968).

89. Nelson, *Historical Books*, 141.

90. Francis Andersen and David Noel Freedman, *Amos: A New Translation with Notes and Commentary* (Anchor Bible; New York: Doubleday, 1989), 190–91.

91. Jeremiah 11:18–12:6; 15:10–21; 17:12–18; 18:18–23; 20:7–18.

92. J. Herman Bavinck, *An Introduction to the Science of Missions* (Phillipsburg, NJ: Presbyterian and Reformed Publishing Company, 1979), 21.

## Interlude: A Kingdom Story Waiting for an Ending

1. For two excellent treatments of the intertestamental time period, see N. T. Wright, *The New Testament and the People of God* (London: SPCK, 1992), 145–338; and Emil Schürer, *The History of the Jewish People in the Age of Jesus Christ (175 B.C.–A.D. 135)* (rev. and ed. G. Vermes, F. Millar, and M. Black; 2 vols.; Edinburgh: T&T Clark, 1973–79). In volume 1 Schürer deals with the political history of the Jews from 175 BC to AD 135, and in volume 2 he deals with Jewish institutions and theology during the same period.

2. See P. R. Trebilco and C. A. Evans, "Diaspora Judaism," *Dictionary of New Testament Background* (ed. Craig A. Evans and Stanley E. Porter; Downers Grove, IL: InterVarsity, 2000), 281–96.

3. See N. T. Wright, *New Testament and the People of God*, 170–81.

4. Ibid., 272–79.

5. Much debate surrounds the messianic expectations of the Jews of this period. Not all expectations of the coming kingdom of God focused on a messiah. Further, messiahs were pictured in numerous ways: sometimes a royal figure, sometimes a priestly figure; some expected a single messiah, others expected two; sometimes the messiah was a human figure, sometimes divine. See N. T. Wright, *New Testament and the People of God*, 307–20; L. W. Hurtado, "Christ," *Dictionary of Jesus and the Gospels* (ed. Joel B. Green, Scot McKnight, and I. Howard Marshall; Downers Grove, IL: InterVarsity, 1992), 107.

6. Three major pilgrim festivals were celebrated each year in Jerusalem—Passover, Pentecost, and Tabernacles. All carried political connotations and stirred hope for liberation as the Jews celebrated their deliverance from Egypt and their gift of the land. Other festivals were celebrated in the towns and villages: Yom Kippur (Day of Atonement, Leviticus 16), Rosh Hashanah ("Head of the Year," New Year's Day, near the autumnal equinox for some of the calendars, as in 1 Kings 8:2), Hanukkah (1 Maccabees 4:52–59), and Purim (Esther 9:20–32). Cf. David Wenham and Steve Walton, *Exploring the New Testament: A Guide to the Gospels and Acts* (Downers Grove, IL: InterVarsity, 2001), 35–36.

7. At the time of Jesus' birth, the Pharisees numbered only about six thousand, the Essenes about four thousand, the Sadducees and priests about twenty thousand (Wright, *New Testament and the People of God*, 209).

## Act 4: The Coming of the King

1. "Gospel" is Mark's word (Mark 1:1). Matthew uses the word "record" or "book" (Matthew 1:1), Luke "narrative" or "account" (Luke 1:1).

2. Herman Ridderbos rightly says: "The central theme of Jesus' message, as it comes down to us in the synoptic gospels, is the coming of the kingdom of God. . . . It may be rightly said that the whole preaching of Jesus Christ and his apostles is concerned with the kingdom of God" (*The Coming of the Kingdom* [Phillipsburg, NJ: The Presbyterian and Reformed Publishing Company, 1962], xi).

3. Hans Küng, *On Being a Christian* (trans. E. Quinn; Garden City, NY: Doubleday, 1976), 91.

4. "Shepherds appear on nearly every list of despised professions in the rabbinic literature. Despite their numbers and seeming usefulness of their work, they were held in contempt because of their vulgarity and ignorance and especially because of their lack of moral character. . . . [Shepherds] belonged to the lowest stratum, if not among the outcasts" (Walter E. Pilgrim, *Good News to the Poor: Wealth and Poverty in Luke–Acts*

[Minneapolis: Augsburg, 1981], 80). Likely their ceremonial uncleanness and Sabbath breaking necessitated by their profession also added to their outcast status.

5. Robert H. Gundry divides the three-year public ministry of Jesus into three stages, each roughly a year in length: a year of obscurity, of popularity, and of rejection (*A Survey of the New Testament* [rev. ed.; Grand Rapids: Zondervan, 1994], 111–17). This rough chronology is reflected in this introductory paragraph.

6. Gerhard Friedrich, "*Euangelizomai, euangelion*," *Theological Dictionary of the New Testament* (ed. G. Kittel and G. Friedrich; 10 vols.; Grand Rapids: Eerdmans, 1964–76), 2:710–12, 721–25.

7. George E. Ladd captures the dynamically active power of God's kingdom to restore his rule over the world: "Our central thesis is that the Kingdom of God is the redemptive reign of God dynamically active to establish his rule among human beings, and that this Kingdom which will appear as an apocalyptic act at the end of the age, has already come into human history in the person and mission of Jesus to overcome evil, to deliver people from its power, and to bring them into the blessings of God's reign. The Kingdom of God involves two great movements: fulfillment within history, and the consummation at the end of history" (*A Theology of the New Testament* [ed. Donald Hagner; rev. ed.; Grand Rapids: Eerdmans, 1993], 89–90).

8. The notion of king can be easily misunderstood in a world without kings. The biblical notion of a king with absolute authority over the entire lives of his subjects is far from democratically minded people. As Lesslie Newbigin writes: "Kingship is not a particularly popular commodity in our world. The ancient world was full of kings and queens; we have few of them and—highly as we cherish them—we limit their powers rather strictly. The ancient idea of kingship as the exercise of sovereign rule over others by a single individual is not one for which our world has much room." He goes on to say that in the biblical world a "king is the one to whom total obedience is due, and from whom one can expect protection, help, and the righting of wrongs" (*Sign of the Kingdom* [Grand Rapids: Eerdmans, 1981], 21).

9. David Bosch, *Transforming Mission: Paradigm Shifts in the Theology of Mission* (Maryknoll: Orbis, 1991), 36–39.

10. Luke is the Gospel writer who especially pays attention to the prayer life of Jesus. He notes eight occasions when Jesus prays not noted in the other Gospels: Luke 3:21; 5:16; 6:12; 9:18, 28; 22:31; 23:34, 46; cf. also 22:44. Further, he records two parables on prayer not noted by other Gospel writers (11:5–8; 18:1–8). See Stephen Smalley, "Spirit, Kingdom, and Prayer in Luke–Acts," *Novum Testamentum* 15 (January 1973): 59–71.

11. G. W. H. Lampe, "The Holy Spirit in the Writings of St. Luke," in *Studies in the Gospels: Essays in Memory of R. H. Lightfoot* (ed. D. E. Nineham; Oxford: Blackwell, 1955), 170.

12. James Dunn, "Spirit and Kingdom," *Expository Times* 82 (1970–71): 38.

13. N. T. Wright, *Jesus and the Victory of God* (London: SPCK, 1996), 272.

14. Ibid., 435.

15. Ibid., 433.

16. Mark 2:23–28//Matthew 12:1–8//Luke 6:1–5; Mark 3:1–6//Matthew 12:9–14//Luke 6:6–11; Luke 13:10–17; John 5:2–18; 9:1–41. For helpful discussion, see ibid., 390–96.

17. This does not mean that there is no interest in his mission for Gentiles. In fact, Mark 6:45–9:32 shows Jesus moving into areas north and east of Galilee, carrying out his ministry in Gentile areas. Matthew, Mark, Luke, and John all treat Jesus' relation to Gentiles in different ways. For a brief discussion, see Scot McKnight, "Gentiles," *Dictionary of Jesus and the Gospels* (ed. Joel B. Green, Scot McKnight, and I. Howard Marshall; Downers Grove, IL: InterVarsity, 1992), 259–65.

18. Gerhard Lohfink, *Jesus and Community* (trans. J. P. Galvin; Philadelphia: Fortress, 1984), 11.

19. Ibid., 63–70.

20. N. T. Wright, *Jesus and the Victory of God*, 276.

21. Lohfink, *Jesus and Community*, 10.

22. Bosch, *Transforming Mission*, 27–28.

23. Pilgrim, *Good News to the Poor*, 51–54.

24. Ibid., 53.

25. See K. E. Corley, "Prostitute," *Dictionary of Jesus and the Gospels*, 643.

26. S. S. Bartchy, "Table Fellowship," *Dictionary of Jesus and the Gospels*, 797.

27. Ibid., 796.

28. *Rule of the Congregation* (1QSa) II, 3–10, as cited in N. T. Wright, *Jesus: The New Way: Leader's Guide and Program Script* (Worcester, PA: Christian History Institute, 1998), 19. Cf. Leviticus 21:16–23, rules for Levites; Deuteronomy 23:1–8; 2 Samuel 5:6–8; Nehemiah 13:1 versus Matthew 21:14.

29. Lohfink, *Jesus and Community*, 12–14.

30. The Gospels speak of "the daughter of Herodias" (Matthew 14:6; Mark 6:22). Josephus identifies her as "Salome" (*Antiquities* 18.5.4).

31. See L. W. Hurtado, "Christ," *Dictionary of Jesus and the Gospels*, 106–17.

32. In Mark (8:29), Peter confesses, "You are the Christ." In Luke (9:20), "of God" is added. Matthew (16:16) has the fullest account, adding "the Son of the Living God."

33. D. R. Bauer, "Son of God," *Dictionary of Jesus and the Gospels*, 769–75.

34. N. T. Wright, *Jesus and the Victory of God*, 485–86.

35. Interestingly, this phrase "the Son of Man" is used more often to describe Jesus in the Gospels than any other. Further, it almost always is found on Jesus' lips as a self-designation (twice as an indirect report, in Mark 8:31; 9:9; cf. the angels' word in Luke 24:7, the crowd's question in John 12:34, and Stephen's last words in Acts 7:56). It never became part of the later confessions of the church in the way that "Christ" or "Son of God" did. See I. H. Marshall, "Son of Man," *Dictionary of Jesus and the Gospels*, 775–76.

36. See N. T. Wright, *The New Testament and the People of God* (London: SPCK, 1992), 29–97 for exegetical discussion of Daniel 7:13–14.

37. While Mark and Matthew make brief reference to this journey to Jerusalem, Luke makes it a central feature of his book, expanding this section to almost ten chapters (Luke 9:51–19:44). The majority of this lengthy section is taken up with teaching. Jesus instructs his disciples on the costly way of discipleship.

38. Joel B. Green, *The International Commentary on the New Testament: The Gospel of Luke* (Grand Rapids: Eerdmans, 1997), 397.

39. Ibid., 398. The church is referred to as "the Way" in Acts 9:2; 19:9, 23; 22:4; 24:14, 22.

40. Ibid., 396.

41. George Ladd speaks of the demand of the kingdom as resolute, radical, and costly, with eternal consequences (*The Gospel of the Kingdom: Popular Expositions on the Kingdom of God* [Grand Rapids: Eerdmans, 1959; reprinted 1987], 95–106).

42. N. T. Wright, *Jesus and the Victory of God*, 307.

43. See D. R. Catchpole, "The 'Triumphal' Entry," in *Jesus and the Politics of His Day* [ed. E. Bammel and C. F. D. Moule; Cambridge: Cambridge University Press, 1984], 319–21. Catchpole lists twelve triumphal entries that took place in the few centuries before Jesus.

44. L. A. Losie, "Triumphal Entry," *Dictionary of Jesus and the Gospels*, 859.

45. For a discussion of the various interpretations of this key event and for an interpretation we find convincing, see N. T. Wright, *Jesus and the Victory of God*, 406–28, 490–93.

Four interpretations are possible for this event. (1) Religious: cleansing the temple of impurities; (2) messianic: including Gentiles in temple activities; (3) prophetic: announcing destruction of the temple and eschatological restoration; (4) political: disrupting corrupted and exploitive commercial and religious activities. See W. R. Herzog, "Temple Cleansing," *Dictionary of Jesus and the Gospels*, 820.

46. Catchpole summarizes the pattern of "triumphal entries" of kings: (1) achievement of a significant victory; (2) staged and formal entry into the city; (3) celebratory welcome and praise to God/gods; (4) entry into the temple; (5) positive or negative cultic activity ("The 'Triumphal' Entry," 321). Cf. Losie, "Triumphal Entry," 854–55.

47. J. H. Charlesworth, ed. *The Old Testament Pseudepigrapha* (2 vols.; Garden City, NY: Doubleday, 1983–85), 2:667.

48. See N. T. Wright, *Jesus and the Victory of God*, 320–68.

49. The Greek word here is *lēstēs* and most likely refers to revolutionaries who sought to overthrow Rome with violence, as also in Mark 14:48; 15:27; John 18:40. See N. T. Wright, *Jesus and the Victory of God*, 419–20.

50. Lohfink, *Jesus and Community*, 20.

51. For a helpful discussion of the Last Supper, see N. T. Wright, *Jesus and the Victory of God*, 553–63.

52. There is a discrepancy between Matthew, Mark, and Luke saying that Jesus celebrated the Last Supper on the night of the Passover, and John saying it was the night before. There are numerous attempts to reconcile this discrepancy. Cf. Joachim Jeremias, *The Eucharistic Words of Jesus* (New York: Scribner, 1966).

53. N. T. Wright, *Jesus and the Victory of God*, 559.

54. For a helpful summary of the trials of Jesus, see B. Corley, "Trial of Jesus," *Dictionary of Jesus and the Gospels*, 841–54.

55. For a chilling look at the cross in the Roman Empire, see Martin Hengel, *Crucifixion* (London: SCM, 1977). Cf. Joel B. Green, "Death of Jesus," *Dictionary of Jesus and the Gospels*, 147–48.

56. "Among the torturous penalties noted in the literature of antiquity, crucifixion was particularly heinous. The act itself damaged no vital organs, nor did it result in excessive bleeding. Hence, death came slowly, sometimes after several days, through shock or a painful process of asphyxiation as the muscles used in breathing suffered increasing fatigue" (Joel Green, "Death of Jesus," 147).

57. "Crucifixion was quintessentially a public affair. Naked and affixed to a stake, cross or tree, the victim was subjected to savage ridicule by frequent passers-by, while the general populace was given a grim reminder of the fate of those who assert themselves against the authority of the state" (Joel Green, "Death of Jesus," 147).

58. "In a world which longed for personal salvation, and which was full of gods and lords claiming to meet that need, how utterly absurd and indeed revolting to claim that a Jew from a notoriously troublesome province of the Empire who has been condemned as a blasphemer and executed as a traitor was the Saviour of the world! How on earth could anyone believe that" (Lesslie Newbigin, "Context and Conversion," *International Review of Mission* 68 (1978): 301)?

59. A good introduction to the subject is John Driver, *Understanding the Atonement for the Mission of the Church* (Scottdale, PA: Herald Press, 1986).

60. For a good overview, see Joel Green, "Death of Jesus," *Dictionary of Jesus and the Gospels*, 154–63. I follow his interpretation in the next paragraph. See his article for further details.

61. Ibid., 162.

62. Driver, *Understanding the Atonement*, 71–86.

63. For a summary of the sacrificial system in the temple, see N. T. Wright, *Jesus and the Victory of God*, 407–11.

64. There was a spectrum of views in Judaism on the resurrection. Broadly speaking, we can distinguish three views: (1) Some had taken on a Platonic, Hellenistic worldview and interpreted the resurrection spiritually primarily in terms of an ethereal, otherworldly existence (e.g., Philo). (2) Others such as the Sadducees denied the resurrection altogether because of the radical political implications of the resurrection and the kingdom of God. (3) The Pharisees saw the resurrection as part of the renewal of the whole creation. This last view was the dominant view at the time and will be the only one dealt with here. For an extended discussion of resurrection in postbiblical Judaism, see N. T. Wright, *The Resurrection of the Son of God* (Minneapolis: Fortress, 2003), 129–206.

65. N. T. Wright, *New Testament and the People of God*, 332.

66. For an extended discussion on resurrection in Paul, see N. T. Wright, *Resurrection of the Son of God*, 209–398; in the Gospels, 401–49; and in other New Testament writings, 450–79.

67. For a further explication of the four "commissions," see Mortimer Arias and Alan Johnson, *The Great Commission: Biblical Models for Evangelism* (Nashville: Abingdon, 1992).

68. The last commission in Mark comes in 16:15–18. The earliest and most reliable Greek manuscripts do not have Mark 16:9–20. Hence, it is likely that the Gospel of Mark originally ended with 16:8. We therefore will deal with only Matthew, Luke, and John.

## Act 5: Spreading the News of the King

1. For two excellent treatments of the theology of Acts, see I. Howard Marshall and David Peterson, eds., *Witness to the Gospel: The Theology of Acts* (Grand Rapids: Eerdmans, 1998); and Howard Clark Kee, *Good News to the Ends of the Earth: The Theology of Acts* (London: SCM, 1990). In the six main sections of his book, Kee helpfully outlines the structure of Luke's narrative in Acts: Jesus as God's agent for renewal of his people, the Spirit as God's instrument in the present age, reaching out across religious and cultural boundaries, structure and strategy in the new community, and witnesses to the ends of the earth.

2. Joel B. Green says: "For Luke, the real enemy from which deliverance is needed is not Rome but the cosmic power of evil resident and active behind all forms of opposition to God and God's people" ("Salvation to the Ends of the Earth: God as Saviour in the Acts of the Apostles," in *Witness to the Gospel*, 94). Cf. Ephesians 6:12 and see also N. T. Wright, *Jesus and the Victory of God* (London: SPCK, 1996), 446–51.

3. Joel Green, "Salvation," 97.

4. The structure of Acts will form the structure of this chapter. However, there will be reference to other parts of the New Testament since that is part of this story. As Hendrikus Berkhof puts it: "The book of Acts, the Epistles, and Revelation, which together form the bulk of the New Testament, are predominantly about the work of the exalted Jesus in the church and in the world" (*Christian Faith: An Introduction to the Study of the Faith* [trans. S. Woudstra; 2nd ed.; Grand Rapids: Eerdmans, 1986], 321).

5. Kee, *Good News*, 30–31.

6. This description of the Feast of Pentecost comes from Jubilees 22:9, a Jewish document written in the second century BC. See Kee, *Good News*, 30; citing from *The Old Testament Pseudepigrapha* (ed. J. H. Charlesworth; 2 vols.; Garden City, NY: Doubleday, 1983–85), 2:97.

7. R. L. Brawley contends that there are four major actors in the book of Acts: God, Jesus, Peter, and Paul (*Luke–Acts and the Jews: Conflict, Apology, and Conciliation* [Society of Biblical Literature Monograph Series 33; Atlanta: Scholars Press, 1987], 110). Brian

Rosner rightly comments: "Brawley's list of four main characters has one glaring omission: the Holy Spirit. He regards the Spirit as 'nothing more than a convenient designation of God. . . .' H. C. Kee's description of the Spirit as 'God's instrument in the present age' is closer to the mark. To trace the activity of the Spirit is to observe the progress of the word" ("The Progress of the Word," in *Witness to the Gospel*, 224).

8. Kee in his chapter on "The Spirit as God's Instrument in the Present Age" (*Good News*, 28–41) describes the work of the Spirit under four headings: "The Spirit as the Instrument for Launching the Good News to the Ends of the Earth" (30–35), "The Spirit as Agent of Confirmation of Community Membership" (35–36), "The Spirit as the Agent of Empowerment and Guidance" (36–39), "The Spirit as Instrument of Judgment" (39–41).

9. Gerhard Lohfink, *Jesus and Community* (trans. J. P. Galvin; Philadelphia: Fortress, 1984), 19.

10. For a helpful discussion of this gathering theme in Acts, see David Seccombe, "The New People of God," in *Witness to the Gospel*, 349–72.

11. David Peterson argues that Luke places three crucial statements about the word of God growing and multiplying in order to structure the book of Acts in four major sections. In the first section the church in Jerusalem develops under the leadership of the twelve apostles (Acts 1:1–6:7). The second section is *unplanned expansion* of the gospel into Judea, Samaria, and certain Gentile areas through the seven "deacons" and others who are scattered from Jerusalem through persecution (Acts 6:8–12:25). The third section brings a *planned and organized expansion* into Asia Minor and Europe under the leadership of Paul, an expansion originating in Antioch (Acts 12:25–19:20). In the fourth section the word of God grows as Paul testifies to the gospel throughout his arrest and trial (Acts 19:21–28:31). See "Luke's Theological Enterprise: Integration and Intent," in *Witness to the Gospel*, 542–43.

12. Leland Ryken, *Words of Life: A Literary Introduction to the New Testament* (Grand Rapids: Baker, 1987), 87. See also Brian Rapske, "Opposition to the Plan of God and Persecution," in *Witness to the Gospel*, 235–56.

13. See Michael Green's description of the attractive life of the early church in *Evangelism in the Early Church* (London: Hodder & Stoughton, 1970), 178–93. See also Adolf von Harnack, *The Mission and Expansion of Christianity in the First Three Centuries* (New York: Harper & Brothers, 1961); and Roland Allen, *The Spontaneous Expansion of the Church* (Grand Rapids: Eerdmans, 1962), 7.

14. Kee says that the impact of the community's life "was so positive and attractive that daily there were more converts and the number of the community's membership was increasing" (*Good News*, 87).

15. Rosner, "Progress of the Word," 226.

16. Ibid., 216.

17. Heinz-Werner Neudorfer, "The Speech of Stephen," in *Witness to the Gospel*, 275–94.

18. Harnack, *Mission and Expansion*, 368. Cf. M. Green, *Evangelism in the Early Church*, 173.

19. Allen (*Spontaneous Expansion*, 7) articulates three factors at work in the spontaneous expansion of the church: (1) unplanned and spontaneous evangelism; (2) attractive life of the church; (3) planting new churches. "This then is what I mean by spontaneous expansion. I mean the expansion which follows the unexhorted and unorganized activity of individual members of the Church explaining to others the Gospel which they have found for themselves; I mean the expansion which follows the irresistible attraction of the Christian Church for men who see its ordered life, and are drawn to it by desire to discover the secret of a life which they instinctively desire to share; I mean also the expansion of the Church by the addition of new churches."

20. Lesslie Newbigin, "Crosscurrents in Ecumenical and Evangelical Understandings of Mission," *International Bulletin of Missionary Research* 6, no. 4 (1982): 150.

21. Peterson, "Luke's Theological Enterprise: Integration and Intent," 542–43. On the centrality of the growth of the word of God, see Rosner, "Progress of the Word," 215–34. The texts that speak of the increase, spread, and growth of the word of God are Acts 6:7; 9:31; 12:24; 16:5; 19:20; 28:30–31.

22. Roland Allen, *Missionary Methods: St Paul's or Ours?* (Grand Rapids: Eerdmans, 1962), 107, 132.

23. Robert C. Tannehill summarizes: "Acts 13–14 presents a representative picture of Paul's mission and includes many themes that we will encounter again. He preaches first in the Jewish synagogue but turns to Gentiles when the synagogue preaching is no longer possible. He announces the one God to Gentiles who have no contact with Jewish monotheism. He repeatedly encounters persecution and moves on when necessary, but does not abandon the mission. He works signs and wonders. He strengthens new churches. In this mission Paul is fulfilling the Lord's prophecy that he would 'bear my name before Gentiles and kings and sons of Israel' and 'must suffer for my name' [Acts 9:15–16]" (*The Narrative Unity of Luke–Acts: A Literary Interpretation* [2 vols.; Philadelphia: Fortress, 1986–90], 2:182).

24. Allen suggests that Paul's practice was to "establish centres of Christian life in two or three important places from which the knowledge might spread into the country around. This is important . . . because he intended his congregation to become a centre of light." He goes on to say that "all the cities, or towns, in which he planted churches were centres of Roman administration, of Greek civilization, of Jewish influence, or of some commercial importance" (*Missionary Methods*, 12–13).

25. See David Bosch, *Transforming Mission: Paradigm Shifts in the Theology of Mission* (Maryknoll: Orbis, 1991), 123–23; Dean Gilliland, *Pauline Theology and Mission Practice* (Grand Rapids: Baker, 1983).

26. L. J. Kreitzer speaks of the "the contingency" of Paul's letters: "More than ever before scholarship has come to appreciate how the circumstances surrounding the production of a letter help to contribute to our understanding of its contents. In short, the greater our knowledge of precisely how and why the apostle Paul . . . came to write a given letter, the better our chances of understanding not only its original message, but of interpreting the meaning for us today" ("Eschatology," *Dictionary of Paul and His Letters* [ed. Gerald F. Hawthorne, Ralph P. Martin, and Daniel G. Reid; Downers Grove, IL: InterVarsity, 1993], 255).

27. This is not at all to suggest Paul was a theologian who sought to arrange his teaching in a systematic theology. Paul was first a missionary and evangelist. However, he was trained as a rabbi (Acts 22:3; Philippians 3:5–6) and struggled with the meaning of the good news of Jesus Christ, working in the context of a Jewish understanding of redemptive history. There is a discernible structure to his reflection on the gospel.

28. See George E. Ladd, *The Pattern of New Testament Truth* (Grand Rapids: Eerdmans, 1968), 89.

29. Ladd rightly states that "the center of Pauline thought is the realization of the coming of the powers of the new age" (ibid., 89).

30. Herman Ridderbos, *Paul: An Outline of His Theology* (trans. J. R. de Witt; Grand Rapids: Eerdmans, 1975), 44.

31. Ridderbos speaks of Paul's "resurrection-eschatology" (ibid., 57).

32. Ibid., 55.

33. Joel Green, "Death of Christ," in *Dictionary of Paul and His Letters*, 205.

34. Bosch, *Transforming Mission*, 153.

35. Oscar Cullmann says, "In Pauline thought the missionary motive, as the precondition of the coming of salvation, permeates the whole theology of the apostle" ("Eschatology and Missions in the New Testament," in *The Theology of the Christian Mission* [ed. Gerald H. Anderson; London: SCM, 1961], 50). In another place Cullmann writes, "The missionary proclamation of the Church, its preaching of the gospel, gives to the period between Christ's resurrection and the Parousia its meaning for redemptive history" (*Christ and Time* [trans. F. V. Filson; Philadelphia: Westminster, 1950], 157). The eschatological mission of the church "takes place precisely in the intermediate period" and *"gives to this period its meaning"* (idem, 162–63, italics his). Cullmann goes on to discuss the way this motif "runs through the entire theology of the apostle" (idem, 163).

36. When speaking of the upbuilding of the church, Paul primarily employs two Greek words: *charismata* (leading to our English word "charismatic") and *diakonia* (related to *diakonos*, "deacon/minister/servant"). The *charismata* are the full scope of gifts given to the church, as illustrated in 1 Corinthians 12–14, Romans 12, and Ephesians 4 (cf. 1 Peter 4:10). The second refers more to gifts that are rather fixed and require continuing recognition. In English we employ the term "office," which may be somewhat helpful. However, the terms are quite fluid. I employ the terms "gifts" and "ministries" to show this distinction. See Ridderbos, *Paul*, 440–46.

37. Ibid., 159–204.

38. See ibid., 159–81; Ladd, *Pattern of New Testament Truth*, 93–95.

39. See Ladd, *Pattern of New Testament Truth*, 95; Ridderbos, *Paul*, 161–66, where he entitles the section "The Eschatological Character of Justification."

40. Ralph Martin sees reconciliation as the center of Paul's theology. See his "Center of Paul's Theology," in *Dictionary of Paul and His Letters*, 94. See further Stanley Porter, "Peace, Reconciliation," in *Dictionary of Paul and His Letters*, 695–99; Ridderbos, *Paul*, 182–97.

41. See Ridderbos, *Paul*, 197–204; James Scott, "Adoption, Sonship," in *Dictionary of Paul and His Letters*, 15–18.

42. Ridderbos, *Paul*, 278–326.

43. Ibid., 265.

44. Ibid., 303.

45. Of course much of the law has been abrogated especially ceremonial and civil expressions of the law that are part of the Old Covenant. Yet the law can still direct God's people when the creational normativity and cultural expression are recognized. See Al Wolters, *Creation Regained: Biblical Basics for a Reformational Worldview* (Grand Rapids: Eerdmans, 1985).

46. Ridderbos, *Paul*, 293.

47. R. P. Meye, "Spirituality," in *Dictionary of Paul and His Letters*, 913.

48. Meye speaks of gratitude as the "heartbeat of Pauline spirituality," which "marks the dividing line between belief and unbelief, between the obedient and the disobedient heart" (ibid., 915).

49. An excellent summary of Paul's missionary concern in his Epistles can be found in David Bosch's *Transforming Mission*, 123–78. The title of the chapter is "Mission in Paul: Invitation to Join the Eschatological Community."

50. Ibid., 137.

51. Bruce Winter, *Seek the Welfare of the City: Christians as Benefactors and Citizens* (Grand Rapids: Eerdmans, 1994). Winter has an extensive discussion of Peter's treatment of this theme. He sees parallels between the book of 1 Peter and the command of Jeremiah to an exiled people. Jeremiah says: "Seek the peace and prosperity of the city to which I have carried you into exile" (29:7). Peter urges the church to do good, seek peace, and bless the unbelieving world (1 Peter 3:9–11) where they live as exiles (1:1; 2:11; plausibly

exiled from Rome). They are to resist the evil in the culture of their day. But at the same time they are to "live such good lives among the pagans that, though they accuse you of doing wrong, they may see your good deeds and glorify God on the day he visits us" (2:12). Winter follows this by explaining the task of believers in various social realms in the public life of the Roman Empire. They were to be holy in all they did (1:15).

52. Winter, *Seek the Welfare of the City*, 82.

53. Ridderbos, *Paul*, 487. It is possible to stress either the present or future coming of the kingdom at the expense of the other and to distort Paul's teaching. A view of "realized eschatology" stresses the present coming of the kingdom to the neglect of future fulfillment. An "apocalyptic" view stresses the opposite. See Bosch, *Transforming Mission*, 139–43.

54. For an elaboration of Paul's teaching on "The Future of the Lord," see Ridderbos, *Paul*, 487–562.

55. Scholars have puzzled over this abrupt ending to Acts. Why does Luke not tell us what happens to Paul? Why are we left with so many loose ends? David Wenham and Steve Walton summarize four possible reasons for this abrupt ending in the book of Acts: (1) Luke has no more information. This is the contemporary situation when he finishes the book. (2) Luke intends to write a third volume. (3) When Luke mentions Paul's two-year house arrest, he implies that Paul is released because a prisoner's accusers must appear within two years. (4) Paul is tried and executed, but Luke deliberately does not report this. Wenham and Walton point out basic problems with each of these theories. David Wenham and Steve Walton, *Exploring the New Testament: A Guide to the Gospels and Acts* (Downers Grove, IL: InterVarsity, 2001), 285. Rosner rightly argues that the abrupt ending indicates "the ongoing nature of the progress of the word" ("Progress of the Word," 230–32).

56. Luke Johnson, *The Acts of the Apostles* (Collegeville, MN: Liturgical Press, 1992), 476.

57. Kee, *Good News*, 107.

58. Walsh and Middleton, *The Transforming Vision: Shaping a Christian World View* (Downers Grove, IL: InterVarsity, 1984), 35.

59. N. T. Wright, *Jesus and the Victory of God*, 443, 467–72: "Since writing *The New Testament and the People of God* I have realized that 'what time is it?' needs adding to the four questions I started with (though at what point in the order could be discussed further). Without it, the structure collapses into timelessness which characterizes some non-Judaeo-Christian worldviews" (443n1).

60. N. T. Wright, "How Can the Bible Be Authoritative?" *Vox Evangelica*, no. 21 (1991): 7–32; idem, *The New Testament and the People of God* (London: SPCK, 1992), 139–43.

61. We have adapted N. T. Wright's illustration by suggesting six acts instead of five.

62. Hugo Echegaray, *The Practice of Jesus* (trans. M. J. O'Connell; Maryknoll: Orbis, 1984), 94

63. N. T. Wright, *New Testament and the People of God*, 140, italics and capitalization added.

64. Contemporary Testimony Committee of the Christian Reformed Church, *Our World Belongs to God: A Contemporary Testimony* (Grand Rapids: CRC Publications, 1987), paragraphs 44–45. It goes on to spell out that mission in areas of gender and sexuality, singleness, marriage and family, education, work, leisure, science and technology, political authority and citizenship, war and peace (paragraphs 46–55).

65. Gary Ginter, "Kingdom Professionals: An Old Idea in New Wineskins," *Paraclete Perspective* 2, no. 1 (spring 2002): 8. Reprinted on http://www.tentmakernet.com/articles/ginter.htm.

66. John Wierick, "The Profit Prophet," *World Vision Magazine*, December 1988–January 1989, 19–21. Available on the Internet at http://www.generousgiving.org/images/uploaded/WIERICK_Profit_Prophet_Ginter.pdf.

67. Peter Harris, *Under the Bright Wings* (London: Hodder & Stoughton, 1993; reprinted, Vancouver: Regent College Publishing, 2000), 117.

68. Ibid., 108–9.

69. More information about *A Rocha* can be found on their website: http://en.arocha.org/home.

70. See Richard Bauckham and Trevor Hart, *Hope against Hope: Christian Eschatology at the Turn of the Millennium* (Grand Rapids: Eerdmans, 1999), 35–43.

71. Lesslie Newbigin, *The Gospel in a Pluralist Society* (Grand Rapids: Eerdmans, 1989), 114.

72. Hendrikus Berkhof, *Christ, the Meaning of History* (trans. L. Buurman; Richmond: John Knox, 1966), helps us see the importance of the end for the meaning of history. See also Anthony Hoekema's chapter "The Meaning of History" in his book *The Bible and the Future* (Grand Rapids: Eerdmans, 1979), 23–40.

## Act 6: The Return of the King

1. Perhaps the word used to describe "new" here is important. Anthony Hoekema reports that "both in II Peter 3:13 and in Revelation 21:1 the Greek word used to designate the newness of the new cosmos is not *neos* but *kainos*. The word *neos* means new in time or origin, whereas the word *kainos* means new in nature or in quality" (*The Bible and the Future* [Grand Rapids: Eerdmans, 1979], 280). H. Haarbeck, H.-G. Link, and C. Brown also believe that the different Greek words are significant: "In secular usage *kainos* denotes that which is qualitatively new as compared with what has existed until now, that which is better than the old whereas *neos* is used temporally for that which has not yet been, that which has just made its appearance." I am not sure the language can bear the weight of such a fine distinction. The authors do go on to say that "the longer these words were used, the less strictly was the conceptual differentiation maintained" (Colin Brown, ed., *The New International Dictionary of New Testament Theology* [4 vols.; Grand Rapids: Zondervan, 1975–85], 2:670). In any case, it is true that "new" here points to *renewed* rather than *brand new*.

2. Some Christians believe that the Bible speaks of a destruction and annihilation of the present world and the creation of a brand-new one. They appeal to texts such as Matthew 24:29; 2 Peter 3:10–13; and Revelation 21:1. Perhaps the words of 2 Peter raise the most difficulties. The question is whether the fire of judgment will *annihilate* or *purify* the world. Fire can do both. In Scripture the fire of judgment destroys what is evil but purifies what is good. Malachi (3:2–3) speaks of the refiner's fire that destroys impurities but purifies metal. In a similar way Paul speaks of fire of judgment that tests the quality of human work. It will either burn it up in destruction or purify it (1 Corinthians 3:13–15). It is like that with the creation; the creation will be purified, but the evil that pollutes it will be destroyed. The language of 2 Peter can mean both things. See Al Wolters, "Worldview and Textual Criticism in 2 Peter 3:10," *Westminster Theological Journal* 49 (1987): 405–13.

3. Questions about the end times, signs of the times, the antichrist, the millennium, the great tribulation, and the rapture "often appear to be of more interest than the new creation which is to be born!" This is like being more concerned about the "nature, strength, and frequency of labour pains rather than about what is going to be born (Rom[ans] 8:22)," writes David Lawrence, *Heaven: It's Not the End of the World! The Biblical Promise of a New Earth* (London: Scripture Union, 1995), 9–10.

4. N. T. Wright, "New Heavens, New Earth," in *Called to One Hope* (ed. John Colwell; Carlisle, UK: Paternoster, 2000), 33. Wright says "from somewhere" and knows well where that somewhere is! This view of the end is the result of the combination of biblical teaching with pagan Greek philosophy in the early centuries of the church. It is especially in Augustine's early work, harmonizing Scripture with Neoplatonic philosophy.

5. Some have suggested that Jesus is preparing a place in heaven for us and will return to take his people back there. They point to John 14:2–3: "In my Father's house are many rooms; if it were not so, I would have told you. I am going there to prepare a place for you. And if I go and prepare a place for you, I will come back and take you to be with me that you also may be where I am." However, this reading does not fit the context. Lawrence (*Heaven*, 32) has offered a paraphrase of this text that much better fits Jesus' words to his disciples: "In my Father's presence [i.e., house] there is room for all. As I go to the Father via the cross I prepare the means for you to enter his presence wherever you may find yourselves. Having opened the way for you to enjoy the same intimacy with the Father that you have seen me enjoy, I will return to you in the form of the Spirit, so that even whilst you live on earth you will share with me in the heavenly places." The metaphor of preparing a place in the Father's house is not of heaven but living in the presence of God with Jesus. It is here the disciples are to dwell (cf. John 15:1–17).

6. Hendrikus Berkhof recognizes that there is both continuity and discontinuity between our present life and the life to come. But he says that continuity must have the first and last word: "A much-discussed problem is that of the continuity and discontinuity between our earthly life and the life that awaits us. . . . On account of God's faithfulness also in and beyond death, the continuity must have the first and last word in our faith and in our thinking" (*Christian Faith: An Introduction to the Study of the Faith* [trans. S. Woudstra; 2d ed.; Grand Rapids: Eerdmans, 1986], 490).

7. It has been rightly noted that this narrowing of salvation in the West is the result of the powerful force of the Enlightenment worldview. Under its onslaught the gospel narrowed its scope. "The early Christian belief [i.e., biblical] that the Fall and Redemption pertained not just to man, but to the entire cosmos, a doctrine already fading after the Reformation, now [under the power of secularism has] disappeared altogether: the process, if it had any meaning at all, pertained solely to the personal relation between God and man" (Richard Tarnas, *The Passion of the Western Mind* [Toronto & New York: Random House, 1991], 306–7). A. Koeberle writes that "this cosmic aspect of redemption was increasingly lost to Western Christendom since the Age of Enlightenment, and to this day we have been unable to restore it to its strength and clarity" (quoted in G. C. Berkouwer, *The Return of Christ* [trans. J. van Oosterom; Grand Rapids: Eerdmans, 1972], 211).

8. Berkouwer speaks of a "soteriological self-centredness" (*Return of Christ*, 211). Lesslie Newbigin is critical of those who privatize "this mighty work of grace and talk as if the whole cosmic drama of salvation culminates in the words 'For me; for me'" (*The Gospel in a Pluralist Society* [Grand Rapids: Eerdmans, 1989], 179).

9. Lawrence puts it nicely: "It is clear that here at the beginning humans and the created order *belonged together*, and therefore we could only fulfill our potential and reach our destiny if we functioned as part of the rest of creation" (*Heaven*, 19–20).

10. Hoekema comments: "If God would have to annihilate the present cosmos, Satan would have won a great victory. For then Satan would have succeeded in so devastatingly corrupting the present cosmos and the present earth that God could do nothing with it but to blot it totally out of existence. But Satan did not win such a victory. On the contrary, Satan has been decisively defeated" (*Bible and the Future*, 281).

11. J. A. Seiss, *The Apocalypse* (15th ed.; London: Marshall, Morgan & Scott, 1938), 483.

12. According to Berkhof these verses indicate that "the cultural treasures of history" will be brought into the New Jerusalem (*Christian Faith*, 523, 543). See also Berkhof, *Christ, the Meaning of History*, 188–92, where he quotes Abraham Kuyper, who believes the same thing.

13. See Lawrence, *Heaven*, 110–13.

# Scripture Index

# Subject Index